Frits Barend and Henk van Dorp interviewed Johan Cruyff from 1974 to 1986 for *Vrij Nederland* and from 1987 to 1997 for *Nieuwe Revu*. Cruyff also made countless appearances on their popular radio and TV shows in Holland. In *Ajax, Barcelona, Cruyff: The ABC of an Obstinate Maestro*, which was authorised by Cruyff, Barend and Van Dorp have brought together the best of their interviews and features on this phenomenal sportsman.

AJAX, BARCELONA, CRUYFF

AJAX,
BARCELONA, CRUYFF

the ABC of an Obstinate Maestro

FRITS BAREND AND
HENK VAN DORP

Translated by
David Winner and Lex van Dam

BLOOMSBURY

This paperback edition published 1999

Copyright © Uitgeverij Vassalucci, Amsterdam 1997
Copyright © 1997 by Frits Barend and Henk van Dorp
Translation copyright © David Winner

The moral right of the authors has been asserted

Bloomsbury Publishing Plc, 38 Soho Square, London, W1V 5DF

A CIP catalogue record for this book
is available from the British Library

ISBN 0 7475 4305 4

10 9 8 7 6 5 4

All papers used by Bloomsbury Publishing are natural, recyclable
products made from wood grown in well-managed forests.
The manufacturing processes conform to the
environmental regulations of the country of origin.

Typeset by Hewer Text Ltd, Edinburgh
Printed in Great Britain by Clays Ltd, St Ives plc

CONTENTS

TRANSLATOR'S NOTE

Johan Cruyff is perhaps the most original of all football's global superstars, so it is apt that the first book about him published in English should be this one – a quirky and refreshingly cliché-free collection of interviews and articles by Holland's leading sports journalists.

Being Amsterdammers themselves means Frits Barend and Henk van Dorp never even thought of referring to their subject as a 'flying Dutchman' or a 'Dutch master'.

Of the five books about Cruyff published in Holland last year to mark his 50th birthday, this was the only one which had his blessing and co-operation. The flame-haired Barend and bearded Van Dorp, who present Holland's most influential sports programme on the RTL-4 TV channel, have known Cruyff well for some 30 years. The book reflects that intimacy and a lot of background knowledge is taken for granted.

This volume was the first about football ever published by Vassalucci, the respected Amsterdam publishers better known for their East European poetry and highbrow literature. The result is quintessentially Dutch and radically different from most British football biographies.

We have tried to retain as much of the Dutch flavour as possible and added explanatory notes in brackets where it seemed most necessary. To present a fuller picture of Cruyff as a player, we have also included three articles covering the period in the late sixties and early seventies that were not in the Dutch edition.

Nevertheless, there are some key moments of Cruyff's career, well-known in Holland, which are referred to so obliquely that they are worth picking out.

For instance, the wonderful Ajax side of the early seventies, one of the finest club teams ever, tore itself apart in 1973–4, largely because of internal rivalries. Some lesser players, such as Arie Haan, resented Cruyff's dominance and thought they could do as well without him. At the time, Ajax players elected their own captain and when, by a small majority, they chose Piet Keizer over Cruyff, Cruyff decided he'd had enough and headed for Spain.

In his first season with Barcelona, Cruyff inspired the club to win the Spanish league for the first time in 14 years, but, despite being joined later by fellow Dutchman Johan Neeskens, the side never reached the same heights as Ajax. In the nineties, he established himself as Barcelona's greatest ever coach, guiding the club to four successive Spanish championships and winning the European Cup.

For Dutch fans, the most bitter-sweet moment of Cruyff's career was the 1974 World Cup in West Germany. Coached by Rinus Michels and led on the field by Cruyff, Holland dominated the tournament playing their sophisticated trademark 'Total Football' in which defenders, midfielders and forwards switched positions constantly. Their failure to beat their less gifted hosts in the final is generally attributed to underestimation of German fighting spirit and an unprofessional approach. Holland's left winger Rob Resenbrink, for example, was unfit, but played the first half in order to fulfil his boot contract. The defeat is still a source of distress and regret in Holland.

Four years later, Cruyff declined to play in the 1978 World Cup in Argentina. The almost equally mysterious failure of the KNVB (Dutch FA) to invite or agree terms with Cruyff as Dutch national coach in the eighties and nineties is discussed in several chapters.

Finally, a word on Cruyff's distinctive style. On the relatively few occasions he has been interviewed for British television, he comes across as refreshingly forthright and articulate. In Dutch, however, with his thick Amsterdam accent and his curious habit of referring to himself as 'you', Cruyff can be enigmatic and elliptical to the point of incomprehensibility. Occasionally, as he explains in the final chapter, he does this on purpose ('If I wanted you to understand it I would have explained it better.') We've tried to strike a balance between making him easy to understand and retaining his inimitable voice.

David Winner and Lex van Dam
January, 1998

FOREWORD

I realise that around my fiftieth birthday a lot is being written about me. Friends and acquaintances have been approached for anecdotes. Experts are asked to say what they think of me. I don't think we should pay too much attention to all these publications and broadcasts. I am sure people know that I don't like this fuss: I love football – particularly beautiful football.

I said I would co-operate with just one book, especially since it wouldn't take too much of my time to do. I don't mind co-operating, but I usually prefer not to get involved in such things. Really, we should thank my daughter Chantal for this book. At the end of last year she told me she thought it would be nice if something could be published that I approved of. When Frits Barend and Henk van Dorp suggested putting together a book of all the interviews they have done with me down the years, I thought it was a good idea. I understand it took them a month to find all this material and to read or listen to it, a fact I quite enjoyed because it was good to know that they are as chaotic as me when it comes to saving things. Barend and Van Dorp have been following me since my first years with Ajax. They interviewed me whenever it suited them and whenever it suited me. Funnily enough, I preferred it when they came to me when things were going badly because then I had something to explain. Sometimes they wanted to come when things went well. Luckily, as they said themselves, more often than not, things went well rather than badly.

I know they have not been too gentle with me in interviews. And they were right not to be. Giving my permission for publication of this book with all the interviews from 1974 until today, sets the record straight. Other people have spoken about many things. They say a lot of things, but in this book, it is exactly written as I said it. Sometimes the language might seem a little strange, or eccentric. But it's the way I talk, so why not put it in the book?

Hopefully, this book will show that my beliefs about beautiful football and getting results have not changed over time. What I felt 20 years ago, I still feel. I still like wingers and love attacking football. I still love the exceptional. Everything that seems normal today seemed crazy to me twenty years ago – the many conflicts about my contracts, boot contracts and transfers – but it couldn't have been done differently. I'm quite curious myself because I've never looked backwards, because it never changes anything. Just like after a game.

A couple of things are certain. I'm going to celebrate my birthday, as always, with my family, and this book would not exist without my wife, children, and without my daughter Chantal, who had the idea.

Johan Cruyff

Prologue

OUR TEAM IS READY TO TAKE PART IN DECISION-MAKING – CRUYFF IN THE GOLDEN AGE OF AJAX

In the early seventies as Johan Cruyff emerged as a world star and Ajax won the European Cup three years running, Frits Barend wrote four editions of the annual 'Topclub Ajax'. These are his profiles of Cruyff which appeared at the start of each year that Ajax ended as champions of Europe.

1. The Cruyff Question

Many footballers in recent years have taken out extra football insurance. It ensures they will receive 100,000 guilders, for example, if they suddenly have to give up playing professional football. At Ajax, Nico Rijnders, Ruud Krol and Dick van Dijk have such protection. After cases like those of Willy Dullens, Lambert Maassen, Henk Groot and, more recently, Koos Knoef, ever more professional footballers are beginning to weigh the costs against the risks they take. For a number of years, Johan Cruyff has been looking to take out extra insurance. But in Holland there isn't a single insurance company willing to insure footballers. The only company which handles football insurance is Lloyds, in London. Ajax has insured all their players with them, so the club will not be damaged if a player is forced out by injury. However, Lloyds have the right to say no to individual players. The company insures Jumbo Jets for 86 million guilders, which the hijackings last September demonstrated is clearly risky, they have four times refused to insure Johan Cruyff. According to Johan, it's because a company refuses to insure the same person twice over. But Ajax's insurance only covers the club. And Rijnders, Krol and Van Dijk have their individual policies to fall back on. So Cruyff can only guess at the reason. Maybe it's because of his so-called flat feet, the reason he didn't go to the army, or his ankles, which turned out to be weak when he played for the Dutch national team. Maybe they are the reasons he can't get his extra policy. Most likely, the refusal is partly because Cruyff is quite simply the most talented attacker in the Netherlands. That means that when he's fit, on thirty-four sundays of the year he is attacked by crazy defenders who are not just trying to play the ball. And because he is no longer unknown abroad, foreign defenders are also very keen on stopping 'Kroof'.

'Cruyffie' was born Hendrik Johannes Cruyff on April 25th 1947. He joined Ajax as a junior and while he was playing with the B-juniors, signed a contract at the age of sixteen. Wim Suurbier and the current Blauw Wit goalkeeper Ronnie Boomgaard were similarly honoured at the same time. Jany van der Veen was the Ajax youth trainer at the time. When he took Cruyff under his wing, he decided to make his pupil into a two-footed player. Cruyff was a very fast, agile player with a good shot in his right foot. But he lacked body power and his left foot was too weak. Van der Veen made Cruyff train with weights on his ankles. To develop his lower body muscles, he had to lie on his back, and then lift his feet with the weights attached and bring them down without touching the ground. Slowly but surely, Cruyff developed a hard shot in both feet, which was especially useful when he had finished slaloming through the enemy defence.

So at the age of 17, Cruyff made his debut in the Ajax first team, at a time when Ajax were fighting against relegation. Sometimes he was in the starting line-up, as he was in the first match after Rinus Michels took over from Englishman Vic Buckingham. That was against MVV at the beginning of 1965. Ajax won 9-3 and the name 'Cruyff' was read for the first time with attention.

In the 1965-66 season he became a regular in the first team and won a championship at the age of 19. The breakthrough in Europe came the next season via the European Cup and two internationals. His international debut was in Rotterdam on September 7th 1966. Holland's opponents, in the first round of the European Championship, was Hungary, who only a couple of months earlier had played Brazil in the most spectacular game of the World Cup in England. The whole Ajax attack – Swart, Cruyff, Nuninga and Keizer – played and Cruyff scored in a 2-2 draw, a good result at the time. Two months later, against Czechoslovakia, the first 'Cruyff drama' began. Half an hour after the break, East German referee Glockner (the same man who was in charge of the World Championship game between Feyenoord and Estudiantes) sent him off. A situation developed when dozens of spectators invaded the pitch. Complete chaos was avoided because it was clear to many people why Cruyff had been sent off: an angry kick when he was provoked. But there was considerable surprise when Glockner later explained that Cruyff had been sent off for striking him. Nobody had seen that. Even slow motion television replays, although not used as proof, failed to detect a blow or even a movement in that direction. On Friday November 11th, five days after the game, Cruyff went before a disciplinary committee. Ajax asked for a punishment that would not hurt the club. To oblige, the committee decided to suspend him only from international matches – but for a whole year rather than a couple of matches. Cruyff was the first Dutchman sent off during an official international match. One of the consequences of 'the Cruyff question' caused by the pitch invasion was that barbed wire was put up around the pitch at the Olympic Stadium.

Two days later, Cruyff played again for Ajax. Feyenoord, who had refused an Ajax demand to play in the Olympic Stadium, were swept aside 5-0 in an overflowing De Meer stadium.

Exactly a month later, Cruyff played a leading role in Ajax's first real achievement in the European Cup, in a game that made many people respect them: thrashing Liverpool 5-1 in Amsterdam. In the second leg, on December 14 1966, Cruyff made football history by destroying Liverpool defender Yeats and scoring two great goals in front of the Kop. The goals were an Ajax speciality at the time: a deep pass to Keizer on the left, who beat two defenders and gave the ball to Nuninga who played it quickly to the well-positioned Cruyff. In his television commentary, Herman Kuiphof called him 'the impish Cruyff'.

In 1967, he signed a four year contract which will keep him at Ajax until July 1971. Since then, he has been in the news continuously.

He didn't do his army service. An importer of a certain brand of football boot sued him because he wanted to play in a different brand. Cruyff often suffered ankle injuries just before Dutch international matches. He apparently started a sports business. In various opinion polls, he was chosen as footballer of the year. On December 2nd, he was married in the Amsterdam Town Hall by A.A. Verheij, the Alderman for sport and youth. His bride was Danny Coster, daughter of Amsterdam businessman Cor Coster (who instantly became known throughout Holland as 'The Father-in-Law'). It was a marriage from Heaven of the first order. There were reports that a Mexican club was interested in buying Cruyff for four million guilders. Cruyff opened a shoe boutique at 12a Kinkerstraat. On one occasion, after travelling to Italy to buy shoes for the shop, he turned up late for training with the national team. National coach Kessler told him never to come again, but after Cruyff apologised, he was allowed back. In a television interview, he announced that Ajax would let him go at the end of the season. That was on Saturday evening. On Sunday Ajax played as badly as NEC, and on Monday all newspapers reported that the chairman, Van Praag, was denying what Cruyff had said. Later, in Wassenaar, as Bep van Houdt reported in *Het Parool*, the 'agreement of Wassenaar', was reached: if a Spanish buyer emerged who would pay a certain amount (in the region of a million guilders), Cruyff could leave at the end of the season. Vic Buckingham, who had just been hired as coach of Barcelona, came to Amsterdam a couple of times and telephoned a couple of times, but that's as far as he got. There were many press interviews in which Cruyff was described as a person who wanted to be rich within a couple of years.

Looking back at all those dramas, Cruyff is the last one to deny he made mistakes. He also understands that the Amsterdam public doesn't mind all the talk about money as long as he plays good football. And, unfortunately, the good football was subdued last season. His only objective is to make sure he doesn't fall back in earnings from 40,000 to 10,000 guilders. Such a drop in income would be difficult for anyone to cope with psychologically. This season Cruyff wants to show that his greatest pleasure is playing beautiful football. Preferably, he wants to play in midfield in future. From there, it is easier for him to run into the attack, where defenders usually tread on his feet. Wherever he plays, with his radius of action, his ability to run past defenders at speed, his inimitable movement, his hard shot with both feet, his running for every ball, his stamina and his positional sense, Cruyff should be able to make defences despair. That's all he wants to do this season, in the Dutch team as well as for Ajax, but only if his modern financial and social requirements are taken care of.

Topclub Ajax
1970

2. Farce at De Meer

With varying degrees of success, the famous actor Johan Cruyff appeared regularly in the 1970-71 season at Watergrafsmeer in a comic drama entitled 'Cruyffie, the son-in-law from Amsterdam'. The farce was written by the actor himself, his father-in-law Cor Coster, and the director of the theatre, Jaap van Praag (also known as 'Uncle Japie'). It will probably run for the next seven seasons at the Ajax Theatre in the Middenweg in East Amsterdam, though in less dramatic and more predictable episodes. Johan Cruyff was tied by contract to the non-subsidised Amsterdam drama company 'AFC Ajax' by a contract which was due to end in June 1971. When director Rinus Michels unveiled the first performances of his team to the public last August (1970), Johan Cruyff was missing with a so-called groin injury. For a footballer, a groin injury (and how strange a term that is for a part of the body the dictionary defines as 'the border betwen the lower body and upper leg'. Before August 1970 normal people would never say 'I have a problem in the groin' when they could easily say 'I have pain around my genitals') involves an injured muscle and it means he can't sprint or shoot. The maddening thing about the injury is that it is not easy to spot, and, apart from a few moments at night, you'll hardly have a problem. It always seems to be cured, but as soon as you try to do a little bit too much, the pain shoots back into your upper leg. Cruyff suffered such an injury. For the Ajax company it was like trying to perform Punch and Judy without Punch. And Cruyff was an irreplaceable Punch. To put it simply: he was severely missed.

On September 12, he finally reappeared against DWS Amsterdam. But an unlucky challenge by his former colleague Frits Soetekouw, ended Johan's performance after just half an hour.

A new anguish began. Articles in the press led one to believe that Cruyff was both cured and not cured. On Saturday afternoon on

October 10th, Cruyff reappeared for a public rehearsal in a small theatre near the Olympic Stadium to practice against Blauw Wit. But again he had to leave the field prematurely. Because he didn't go to see the Ajax doctor, John Rolink, on Monday, people whispered that Cruyff was faking it and saving himself for next season. Six months earlier, newspapers had been full of stories about Cruyff longing for a transfer to a foreign club; he wanted to leave Ajax or get a better contract. He was a valuable commodity and became so famous last season that he was in Madame Tussaud's waxworks museum in London. Of course Cruyff wasn't faking it. He really was in pain every day.

Finally, after having missed nine league games and three European Cup ties, Cruyff was finally cured and returned for Ajax. On Friday evening, October 30th, he played against PSV, coming back in style.

Once he had recovered from injury, and just before the second-leg European Cup game against FC Basel, Cruyff demanded that he also receive the match bonuses for the three previous European Cup games he had missed. On the Tuesday before Basel-Ajax, there was a pretty fierce argument at the Basel stadium. Ajax refused to meet Cruyff's demands and Johan felt he had been sold short because other players were always paid for European Cup games they missed through injury. He nearly returned to Amsterdam. But a telephone conversation with his pregnant wife in Vinkeveen somehow averted a new drama. Johan played and did more than that: despite all the trouble, he was Ajax's outstanding player as Ajax won 2-1.

Once he was back in Holland, Cruyff asked for a meeting with the Ajax board with all the other players also present. It wasn't the friendliest meeting and seemed a bit strange to a shy guy like Johan Neeskens.

Cruyff remained in the news. He didn't travel with the Dutch team to East Germany because his wife was about to give birth at any moment. A week after the match, Johan became father to a daughter, Chantal.

On November 29th, his name was talked about and he was featured on television thoughout Europe because he scored six goals in a game against AZ 67. His great form had returned. After AZ 67 and the game against Romania, it was clear to insiders and outsiders that Johan Cruyff really was cured. Mario Coluna of Benfica asked Ajax if Johan Cruyff could play in his farewell game. In August Cruyff had been invited to play in a European team against a Benfica team led by Kubala. Because of his injury, Cruyff was later taken off Coluna's list.

On Monday lunchtime on December 7th, Johan Cruyff travelled to Benfica. That day *Het Parool* reported: 'Sombre voices are saying that the Ajax player already has a contract with Benfica in the bag for the famous 1.2 million guilders' – Ajax's price for Cruyff according to the Wassenaar agreement – and that Cruyff would join the Portugese club.

Cruyff decorated the field in Lisbon for precisely 38 minutes, then Kubala took him off. After this big disappointment there was silence for a while. In April, there were new stories and a new period of rumours began. Was Cruyff still for sale at 1.2 million guilders or not? After a lot of yes and no answers, it seemed that Johan was for sale for 3 million guilders in Holland, but for a foreign club 1.2 million would be sufficient. Barcelona were still interested. On April 5th, it was revealed that Johan had paid a quick visit to Spain. He had a free day because, like Rinus Israel, an attack of flu had prevented him travelling with the Dutch team to play in Yugoslavia. At first Johan and his father-in-law denied they had crossed the border. Later, on Veronica's Monday programme, he confirmed that he had been to Spain. When asked why, Johan answered: 'why do you think?' At this time Cruyff also twice visited Brox – or at least he twice parked his car in front of Feyenoord's gates. Father-in-law Cor Coster said later: 'you couldn't always tell the truth because that would be like throwing stones at your own windows'.

Just before the Atletico Madrid-Ajax game, Cruyff gave the Ajax board an ultimatum. He had to have an answer that week or else he would definitely leave to join another club. There were certainly enough offers. By the end of the week, Ajax had failed to deliver. The transfer period began and Cruyff was put on the list. Extremely hard negotiations started. After they began, chairman Van Praag said: 'negotiations are taking place in a good atmosphere. We are not too far apart from each other and I expect things to end well'.

Cor Coster, Johan's negotiator, could not share that view. On June 12th, *Het Parool* reported that an Amsterdam travel agency was willing to pay one million guilders to keep Cruyff at Ajax. Ajax didn't deny there had been an offer, though they did deny the amount. The aim of the travel agency (which had been leaked too early) was to stimulate other businesses in the capital to offer money. In the event, Ajax were only offered 50,000 guilders.

On Saturday June 19th, talks between Ajax and Cruyff definitely seemed to have broken down. There was even a strong chance that Cruyff would head – by an indirect route – to Feyenoord. The plan was that either Belgian club SK Lierse or FC Basel of Switzerland would first buy him for the 'cheap' price of 1.2 million guilders and then Cruyff would switch to Feyenoord in December. Other foreign teams were also interested.

Shocked by all the reports of Johan's impending departure, a certain Mr De Vries telephoned Mr Coster. They had a reasonable conversation during which De Vries offered to negotiate and Coster pointed him in the direction of the Ajax board. The board wanted nothing to do with real negotiations. Nevertheless, Ajax treasurer Timman called Coster and asked who De Vries was. That conversation may have been decisive. Ajax and Cruyff were almost irreparably far apart. Ajax would not have contacted Coster again before the weekend, but because of De Vries's interference this did happen. Timman and Coster even made a new appointment. At 10.30 on Sunday morning, June 20th, Timman visited Coster for a cup of coffee. At one o'clock, they called Majorca, where Johan was on holiday. At five past one, Johan said 'yes' and Cruyff was under contract with Ajax until 1978.

Coster immediately called Mr De Vries to thank him for his small but important help in this complicated process.

The next day, Coster bid farewell to publicity (as he put it) when he appeared on the Monday programme on 'Veronica'. Speaking honestly, he said that the negotiations had been like a poker game. He said he was very happy and had only ever had one aim: to keep Johan at Ajax. He was also happy that everything was now settled and hoped that from now on he wouldn't (for example) receive threatening letters any more.

The farce 'Cruyffie, the son-in-law from Amsterdam' really ended its run that Sunday, June 20th 1971. Feyenoord must have been very disappointed with the final outcome because without Mr De Vries, Johan Cruyff might well have been sold to a non-Amsterdam club.

Topclub Ajax
1971

3. What makes Cruyff so Special

The choice of Johan Cruyff as the European Footballer of the Year in 1971 confirmed what we have known in Holland for a long time and what we thought foreigners would never be willing to believe: that the best football in and around Europe is being played in Holland, especially at Ajax. The election of Cruyff after the disappointing European Cup Final against Panathinaikos was the first recognition of the quality of football on offer.

In 1971, after a lot of to-ing and fro-ing, Cruyff signed a contract that keeps him at Ajax for seven years. From that moment, Cruyff, as he said when he signed, has no longer talked about money or being underpaid. Knowing Cor Coster, I'm sure he has no reason to. Last season, Cruyff, like his colleague on the left wing, Piet Keizer, played as never before. Although the team plays for those two, 'Johan' and 'Pietje' (as they are called), have never behaved like prima donnas on the field. Cruyff had more fun playing technically than ever before. Not only was everything in order financially, the team was also playing the way Cruyff (and the public) likes to see. Cruyff is a proponent of the theory that the three different lines of a team (defence, midfield and attack) should play closely together. He prefers to see one or two people from the midfield or defence appear in the front line. That gives him the opportunity to go to the wing knowing there will not be a gap in the centre. In the Ajax line-up, he is not stranded on an 'island' and expected to chase every lost ball. The way Ajax played last year, it was easy for him to receive passes and play the ball to someone else. It was often visible in his game.

Off the field, Cruyff is more professional than his colleague Keizer. Cruyff makes time to talk to journalists after a game, is prepared to receive them at home for a football interview. However, he asks for money from magazines that never normally write about football but suddenly want to write about Cruyff and his life story. Cruyff reasons that they are not interested in news but are using him to stimulate sales of their magazines. The weekly *Panorama* magazine once wanted to interview him. One way or another they didn't succeed. In the week of the European Cup Final, a sensationally-written story appeared claiming that Cruyff had demanded 5,000 guilders plus a large amount for posing to have his portrait painted. Cruyff says the story is untrue: 'If I ask for money, I obviously wouldn't ask that much for an interview'. In any case, there's always plenty to read about Cruyff. He has realised the importance of the exchange of information in professional football and long ago stopped asking for money for interviews – a fashion which existed for a very short time in Dutch football but disappeared some time ago.

Cruyff's election as European Footballer of the Year was in large part because people have started to take notice of him. And that is largely because of his knowledge about football. Cruyff also made sure he was often in the news at the right time of the year. A player like Keizer, who doesn't like publicity, will be in the news less often. The football connoisseur will understand his qualities, but among those who know less, he will never be as much of an idol as Cruyff.

An important reason for the choice of Cruyff is probably the fact that the poll was organised by French magazine *France Football*, which is widely read abroad. They really started to admire and pay attention to him after Ajax's two matches against Olympique Marseille. (In the same way, for example, Cruyff's qualities were openly acknowledged in England only after Ajax's European Cup quarter final against Arsenal, about two months after he was chosen as Footballer of the Year, though some newspapers paid a lot of attention to him a couple of days before the match). The French sporting press did think that Keizer was an equally great footballer, but 'Kroof' was better known.

What makes Cruyff so special? He does naturally what 99.99 per cent of other players cannot do even after training for a long time. He has the natural gift of tremendous starting speed. He has a way of evading tackles that is unique. Piet Fransen of FC Groningen once said: 'Cruyff beats you every time, though he doesn't seem to mean to do it. Before you can see what he's going to do, he's gone past you. He did that to me once. I thought: "Man, I'm going to get him next time". Soon after, he did it again and at the moment I tried to bring him down, he jumped. He could sense what I wanted to do. You hardly even got a chance to hit him. Luckily. Because Cruyff is a player for the crowd. He's fantastic to watch. What I also admire so much about Cruyff is his self-control. Believe me, I wasn't the only one who wanted to get my own back on him. After a match, Cruyff must be completely black and blue. And you never see him retaliate. He sort of defends himself against attacks. He's very clever. Believe me, he uses his back and his arms. And he's right to do that'.

Holland's national coach Fadrhonc has made Cruyff captain of the Dutch team. Cruyff was appointed only after Rinus Israel lost the captaincy because of disciplinary action when he spoke out of turn; after Wim van Hanegem's troubles at Feyenoord which meant he was captain for only one game; and after Piet Keizer refused to take the captaincy from Wim.

The Dutch players are happy with the appointment. Because of his confidence, Cruyff is capable of helping the group and justifying his demands. As with Ajax last season, together with Keizer, he takes care of a lot of financial and monetary issues for the Dutch team. Many people think Cruyff is a better captain on the field than Keizer because he has more self-control.

During the last transfer period, when he was asked, Cruyff gave his opinion on Van Hanegem's threatened – and finally cancelled – transfer to France. He said the KNVB (the Dutch FA) should not allow anyone who plays for the national team to leave Holland. With reason, Willem thinks such views are unrealistic: 'You didn't hear Johan saying this kind of thing last year. He likes things now so it's easy for him to talk. I can remember that Johan wanted to go abroad, whatever the cost. And he still says he would have gone to Barcelona if the borders were open'.

Cruyff enjoyed the freedom he got in his football last season. He even gave the public good value for money in an unimportant last league game against Vitesse: 'The results show that Kovacs has not been wrong. [Stefan Kovacs took over as Ajax coach after Rinus Michels joined Barcelona in 1971 and gave the players far more freedom than his predecessor]. Our team is ready to take part in making decisions. You can only really judge Kovacs if he had got us out of a low point. Of course I hope that doesn't happen. But you shouldn't lose sight of the fact that we only experienced success in the last year'.

Topclub Ajax
1972

Chapter 1

OF COURSE CRUYFF IS THE BEST: A PERSONAL OPINION POLL

The first story is a very personal look back on our almost thirty-year relationship with Cruyff.

He was a ballet dancer on the field. He was right-footed, but liked to move to the left. He scored and made other people score. As a coach, he chooses attack, wants results with beauty, loses with pure football, loves football, is football. Next year, he is fifty and now he is officially the greatest Dutch player. The greatest of all. In an opinion poll for *Nieuwe Revu* magazine he was chosen as the best Dutch footballer, followed by Marco van Basten in second place. For this insight, we needed no poll. The next four names, Frank Rijkaard, Ruud Gullit, Wim van Hanegem and Ronald Koeman, were no shock either, though perhaps the order and the omission of Piet Keizer was surprising.

I once studied sociology, which is the science of the behaviour of human beings in groups, or something like that. Sociologists discovered, for example, that attackers are more creative than defenders and that goalkeepers are more individualistic than outfield players. Those kind of studies persuaded me to pursue my career in journalism.

For me, Cruyff was always the best Dutch footballer of all time. 'But now it is confirmed by official research', said the chief editor of *Revu* and I heard the voice of my teachers.

Why is Cruyff the unmistakable – and now crowned – number one?

Until the coming of Cruyff, the Netherlands was on the margins of international football. We usually beat Luxembourg, sometimes Denmark and Finland, and we could win or draw against Belgium.

That was about it. When Cruyff was a teenager, the Netherlands did not belong with the traditional top football countries like England, Germany, France, Hungary, Brazil, Uruguay and Argentina. I can't say it enough: Johan Cruyff woke Holland up and took it to a world class level. The Netherlands was at the level of an amateur footballing nation when 17 year old Cruyff began his imposing career. Cruyff was an elegant footballer, a juggling ballplayer of the old school who later became a dribbler who could beat opponents easily, as Ronald de Boer does, and had that very sharp acceleration that Ronald, alas, lacks. He had an incredible distaste for losing, the same as Ronald, who learned it from Cruyff, and a big mouth that he always lived up to. This thin, fragile-looking Cruyff dragged Dutch football along in his wake – which was how he got the image of being greedy. Because what is professional football about? It's about money. Cruyff, for example, in parts of Holland, was said to be asking for money for interviews. This was nonsense: a form of sixties-style demagoguery created from the beginning by a large group of Cruyff-opponent, even sometimes, Cruyff-haters. That group has become so strong with the passage of time that his son Jordi is convinced that people (read: journalists) who don't like his father pre-judge Jordi and don't like him. I think Jordi is right.

When Cruyff started to realise that he was becoming a megastar, making him very interesting to all kinds of magazines outside the sport, interesting for tabloids and women's magazines who never wrote about sport, he decided to ask for money for an interview. Why? Because he didn't want to do them, he didn't have time for it, and most interviewers were no longer interested when they heard the price, which is precisely what Cruyff wanted. If they were prepared to pay, at least he got paid for doing something he didn't want to do.

In the same way, I gladly bet on German teams and the German national team. I always hope they don't win, but if they do, at least I win some money. In Euro '96, I won a lot – but I'll get over it.

To get back to Cruyff: if he agrees to do an interview with a 'real' paper (he can always refuse as anybody can) with a radio or television sport programme or with a sports magazine he never asks or has asked for money.

In fact, I believe it was the amateurism that permeated management and thinking about the game in Holland 30 years ago that prevented the

Netherlands reaching the World Cup finals in 1966. The Netherlands should have been there. Cruyff was 19 and already recognised as a great talent. Of the later stars, Wim van Hanegem was 22, Piet Keizer 23, Rinus Israel 24, Wim Suurbier 21, Wim Jansen and Barry Hulshoff both 19. We also had Coen Moulijn, Sjaak Swart, Henk Groot, Bennie Muller, Klaas Nuninga and Willy van der Kuylen. In other words: enough talent. But who minded when Netherlands was beaten by Switzerland and Northern Ireland in the 1965 qualification games: it was normal wasn't it?

In 1969, Ajax played in their first European Cup final, in 1970 Feyenoord won their first European Cup. Even then there was no managerial climate in the Dutch FA (KNVB) to follow the example of Cruyff, and the Netherlands missed the 1970 World Cup as well. Four years passed after the Ajax and Feyenoord European Cups and the World Cup of 1974 when Holland was recognised as a top country with one world class star: Johan Cruyff.

It wasn't bad if you were a journalist. If you went to Southern Europe, or South America or Asia, and you were from the same country as 'Croof', 'Cruff', 'Agax' or 'Norange', you never had to pay for a drink all night. Cor Coster, Cruyff's father-in-law and business partner, did some research and found that about two billion people knew the name Cruyff. He was more famous than the queen of the Netherlands and as well known as Frank Sinatra, although, in the United States, where football or 'soccer', never was and never will be anything, Cruyff can walk on the streets without being disturbed.

'Do you know Cruyff?', they ask me in real football countries. 'Yes. He's a very modest, maybe even a shy man' is my usual answer.

'Did you play football with him?' they asked after a game of beach football in Spain (very funny).

'No, but I played against him,' I say, always modestly, 'maybe about six times.'

'Against him? Is there more than Ajax in Amsterdam?'

'Yes'

'And?'

'Cruyff was a nasty, annoying little guy on the field because you could never beat him. You could never even touch him,' I tell my listeners. 'Even in my youth team (Neerlandia) you don't like losing 8-0 or 9-1.' That's why I initially disliked Cruyff so much.

I also remember one of my first interviews with Cruyff. I puttered up to the beautiful Ajax stadium on my very old Solex motorbike, with my oldest daughter sitting behind me in her little passenger seat. The beautiful, brightly-coloured sports cars of people like Suurbier, Cruyff, Keizer, Rijnders and Neeskens whizzed past me.

Suurbier said: 'Have you enough money for petrol to get you home?'

Neeskens said: 'You need a bigger engine'.

That kind of thing.

Inside the gates of the stadium, my daughter started to play with a little girl the same age while I waited for Johan Cruyff.

'Is that your daughter?', asked the beautiful blonde mother of the other girl. 'Yes,' I said proudly. 'You're waiting for an interview with Johan, aren't you?' she said. 'If you want, I'll take her with me so you can do your interview in peace and, in the afternoon, I'll bring your daughter back.'

From that moment I loved Danny Cruyff. The affection for Johan came later. Often we had prickly conversations. Like everybody else (journalists and publicists are top of the hitlist) Cruyff has his way of handling criticism:

'You didn't play so well today, Johan.'

'Which game were you watching?'

Stars at Cruyff's level make you feel you want to treat them gently in their most difficult moments, when they lose. Which is funny really because Merckx was never so popular as in that first year that he lost the Tour de France; Spain never warmed to Indurain until this year, when he didn't win. Henk and I could never hear a bad word about Cruyff after his dramatic resignation as Ajax coach in January 1988. Seldom have Henk and I seen a family so hurt as the family of Cruyff was the evening and the week after that resignation (even though he did it to himself). His second greatest love, outside his family, is Ajax. Cruyff loves Ajax. When, in the summer of 1991, Ajax bought John van Loen from Anderlecht and sold Ronald de Boer to FC Twente, he called in despair from Barcelona to ask if it was really true.

'They must have gone mad. Ajax have not chosen for football. How, in God's name, can a club like Ajax swap de Boer for Van Loen?'

At the same time, if he had been coach of the national team in the 1990 World Cup, he would have picked Van Loen and Kieft in attack for Holland's [drawn] opening game against Egypt.

'Egypt don't want to play football. I don't want to risk Van Basten and Gullit, so let Kieft and Van Loen batter their defence. Then, five minutes after the break, I bring on Van Basten and Gullit.'

It never happened because Cruyff was never the national coach and the Dutch FA (KNVB) always knows better than Cruyff.

OK. I'm slightly biased in favour of Cruyff. But the nice thing about our relationship is that, before an interview, we both always say: 'for the next few minutes, we are not friends, you bastard'. Cruyff will never be able to live unnoticed. When he had his heart operation, my family called from Israel. In the middle of the Gulf War, the news had been interrupted, not for a Scud attack on Tel Aviv, no: Cruyff had had a heart operation.

As a player, and as a coach, Cruyff has an instinctive mistrust for board members. That's what makes him so nice. Cruyff divides the football world in two: coaches and players against members of the board. The first two groups should stick together against the board. So in all his years in Barcelona, he regarded his chairman Josep Lluis Nunez with mistrust. He has an instinct that tells him: this man is no good. And as many Catalans have confirmed to me over the past couple of weeks, the man is indeed no good, always with that quasi-religious look of his. A year ago, we were surprised when Cruyff told us that in seven years he had not had a meal with his chairman.

'I am the trainer, he is the chairman, we have a business relationship and I think that's enough. You have dinner or lunch with your friends or with people you like. Is that clear?'

'Clear.'

'Do you know that my chairman has never been to an away game in Spain? Never!'

'So Nunez doesn't like football?'

'Precisely. Now you understand. People like that don't become chairmen because they like football but because they like themselves,' Cruyff said after a big dinner.

Cruyff's successor, Bobby Robson, has had dinner three times now with Nunez. So things are good between Nunez and Robson. After eight years, the chairman who has the same tailor as Napoleon finally has a coach who doesn't put him in the shade and who says in interviews that he and Nunez have been great friends for years.

Barcelona has played badly for the last two years, winning no titles. Cruyff was responsible for that as well. But he did transform Barcelona in eight years from being the laughing stock of Europe to being one of the most envied of top clubs. After eight years with Cruyff on the bench, Barcelona is finally seen as being on the same level as Ajax, AC Milan, Real Madrid, Bayern Munich and Manchester United. The fear for the now-fired Cruyff – according to surveys (opinion polls), more popular in the last two months than during his last two years as coach – made Nunez so nervous that he had to buy Ronaldo at any cost.

I'm not saying my wife is a good trainer, but she looks nice and she does speak Spanish and she said: 'so in the bars of Barcelona this summer I can be a champion as well'.

Cruyff laughed: 'You understand more about football than that redhead' and he poured us a glass of wine, leaving us uncertain about his future.

Nieuwe Revu
August 1996

Chapter 2

SIMPLE FOOTBALL IS THE HARDEST – DEPARTURE FOR BARCELONA

On November 20th 1974, Holland beat Italy 3-1 in Rotterdam. Piet Keizer had just retired from football. The Dutch team was Jongbloed; Suurbier, Haan, Rijsbergen, Krol; Neeskens, Van Der Kuylen, Van Hanegem; Rep, Cruyff, Rensenbrink. Italy scored first through Boninsegna, and Rensenbrink and Cruyff (twice) scored for Holland. Because Cor Coster had told us his son-in-law had already decided after the 1974 World Cup that he would not play in another World Cup, we decided to fly back to Barcelona with Cruyff, his wife and children.

On the night of the Holland-Italy game, after Johan Cruyff has spent an hour talking in his familiar polished manner to print journalists, radio reporters and conducting interviews with Spanish, Dutch and Italian television, he finally gets the chance to visit the coffee room at the Feyenoord stadium, where the other players and their wives have been sitting and chatting for a long time. A KNVB official, Carel Akerman, administrative assistant to George Knobel, the national coach, has just entered the room and wants a word: 'Johan, come with me and present a gift to the referee'. Johan follows him obediently, knowing that referees are as eager to shake his hand as any autograph-hunting children.

Referee Kazakov, who turned out to be a real home referee, is barely looking at his present – a KNVB lighter – but asks Cruyff to sign the back of the box it came in. Ecstatic, he thanks Johan and gives him a Russian bear hug. Beaming with pride, he watches as his linesmen, who are even more humble, also ask the laughing Cruyff for his signature.

Finally, freed from all his obligations, Johan walks past the table where some of the players' wives are sitting when Truus van Hanegem asks him loudly: 'Johan where were you after Feyenoord–Barcelona? I thought you were going to show us your house. We were looking for you and couldn't find you'.

Coughing and laughing shyly, Johan says: 'Well, I was really tired. I just went to bed'. At that moment, faced with the torrent of words from Truus van Hanegem, he just doesn't know what to do. He looks tired after his fantastic game this evening and all these obligations are draining his energy. 'I think I've caught a cold,' he tells her.

My God, we think, as we watch and listen from a distance: Johan is going to be ill when we have to interview him, because, the next morning, Thursday November 21st, we had arranged to fly with him back to Barcelona. We try to make an appointment for the following evening, but nothing's happening now. We have to settle for: 'we'll see what happens in Barcelona'.

On arrival at Barcelona airport, Johan is mobbed by a crowd of older women asking for autographs for every conceivable cousin and niece. Strangely, Johan Neeskens, who is also present, is barely noticed. As agreed, we call Cruyff that evening at 6.30, after buying some standing tickets for Sunday's Espanyol–Barcelona derby game from the Barcelona manager Caraben.

With a cold-drowned voice, Johan says: 'I'm sorry lads, but I'm really ill. Why don't you come to the club at one o'clock'. Fearing we won't have enough time, because Barcelona are due to go to their training camp on Saturday, Johan finally suggests we come to the stadium at 10am, after his treatment and before training.

At first, the atmosphere is uncertain. When he arrives, Johan greets us coolly, then does a little running with Neeskens, who looks injured, and with three of Barcelona's Spanish internationals, who, on the night Holland beat Italy, played in Spain's 2-1 victory over Scotland in Glasgow. After some very light training, a Spanish journalist tells us that at Barcelona, as at Ajax, Cruyff trains less than the other players, but more intensely.

We do the first part of the interview in a press room right across from a little chapel deep in the catacombs underneath the Barcelona stadium. Cruyff relaxes when we tell him we will let him read the interview before we publish it.

– How are you?

'Fine. I think when you leave your own environment, you're normally going to have some problems adapting. But I haven't had any problems.'

– Why was that?

'Maybe I was happy to leave.'

– We saw you during the World Cup and before, during and after your transfer to Barcelona. You're now hardly able to have a private life. Can you be yourself at all?

'Well, I chose this job. I have a couple of good friends, a boy and a girl. A lot of people want to be with me, but I don't let too many get close. I know pretty quickly why a person wants to spend time with me. Of course, I'd like to walk around the Ramblas in Barcelona, but you know you can't. You know you can't go into the city. Maybe my wife and I feel like going out once a month – but you can't do that. Anyway, I don't feel I need people.'

– But aren't you isolated?

'You're only isolated when you notice that you miss people around you, and I don't. When I was 17, I had this life in my head. I always wanted to go abroad and, looking back, I think I've chosen the right moment. If I'd left three years earlier, when I was 23, I would have been too young. I know now for example, how I keep people at a distance, and how I sometimes shouldn't do that.'

As we sit next to Cruyff, we are struck again by how small and frail he really is. As a defender, you'd think you could blow him over. All it would take would be a little push.

'As a defender, you first need the chance to push. I always say that kicking someone to bits is not an art.'

– But why is it that depsite your apparently limited strength you play football so much better than everyone else?

'I don't know why. I don't think that much about myself, at least not when we are talking about football.'

– But how do you explain why a player like, for example, Gerrie Muhren, who, according to the Ajax players, has more technique than you, is not as good a footballer as you are? What's the difference between you two?

'Football consists of different elements: technique, tactics and stamina. Stamina I have, tactics I have and technique I've always had. There are some people who might have better technique than me and some may be fitter than me, but the main thing is tactics. With most players, tactics are missing. You can divide tactics into insight, trust and daring. In the tactical area, I think I just have more than most other players. You probably can't teach personal tactical insight. At most, if a person has some, you can perhaps influence it a little bit. It's very hard.'

– So should we call you a tactical miracle?

'Tactics interest me. Almost no one can explain team tactics easily. I'm interested in that stuff. The more easily you explain it, the better the players will understand it.'

– Do you think you're learning something about tactics in Spain?

'I'm not the kind of person who goes home thinking: "well, what did I learn today?"'

– A player like Arnold Muhren is always said to be too light, and you probably weigh even less. Does that have something to do with tactics?

'A player who loses the ball a lot is easily called "too light", but often losing the ball has to do with personal tactical insight.'

– Everything you do looks easy. At first sight, you don't appear to use a lot of tricks. When you beat a defender on the byline by pretending to cross and then flicking the ball behind you, that's one of your few tricks.

'I never practice tricks. I play very simply. That's what it's all about. Playing simple football is the hardest thing. That's the problem of all trainers. Simple play is also the most beautiful. How often do you see a pass of more than 40 metres when 20 metres is enough? Or a one-two in the penalty area when there are seven people around you when a simple wide pass around the seven would be a solution? The solution that seems the simplest is in fact the most difficult one.'

– After Sweden-Holland, national coach Knobel said he was very impressed by your explanation of Dutch football in West Germany. In five minutes you made clear to him what most other players couldn't explain in much longer conversations, even during the Ajax time about the way Ajax played. Was the Dutch team that played this year in Germany the ideal team?

'Well, I don't talk too much about tactics, because that's my professional secret, but I think everyone should be able to play in all different positions on the field. I'm not just saying this. It has to be based on real knowledge. If, as a forward, in certain situations, I have to play in the left back position, then I have to be able to function as a left back, with all the consequences. So I need to know: should I play for position? Or try to cover people? Is it responsible to try to go past someone? Or should I just kick the ball into the stand? And if Ruud Krol plays in attack, he has to know what my specific tasks are. Should he chase the ball? Or should he come back a little bit? That's why it is so important everyone listens when you have a tactical talk. The left winger can't go to sleep when Michels talks about the right back.

– So was the Dutch team during the World Cup in Germany the ideal team, in your eyes?

'In the circumstances, yes. But some players could have done more. They were the best at that moment in the places where they played, but sometimes they should have done a bit more. At some moments they should have created more, or they should have played more simply. Players should always concentrate on their best points. But it's always like that. That's why I come back to the simple thing: the difference between right and wrong is often not more than five metres. The way we played in the Dutch team, the left winger was absolutely not allowed to lose the ball. That was his strict assignment. But you understand that football can never be played perfectly.'

Time is up. For more than half an hour we have talked solely about technical football matters. Cruyff understands we are nowhere near finished and asks how much time we need. He takes us from the stadium to a restaurant where the players go for lunch, and then asks us to come to his home at 2pm.

When we arrive at his building in a quiet suburb of Barcelona, a doorman is waiting for us. He calls Cruyff to ask if he is expecting visitors and then allows us to enter the lift.

At home with Johan, we ask him about his relationship with his father-in-law, Cor Coster.

'He's done a lot for me. He volunteered to take the blame for all the changes we've brought to Dutch football. Most of the changes were rather revolutionary, which is why we couldn't always be elegant. Looking back, I think we've been right in everything we've done. I've given a lead and I think all other Dutch players have been able to follow. Players have been taken care of financially and have been taken seriously.'

– How do you feel about being a millionaire?

'I've always said money doesn't interest me, and that's really true. I don't earn money for its own sake. People used to call me greedy. I just don't want to be used and this is the time when I can earn money.'

– When do you think you'll stop playing?

'Sometimes I find it hard to think about it, because I don't know what I'll do. I've bruised and insulted so many people that I think a lot of them are waiting to get back at me. That's one of the reasons why, when I'm 31, in April 1978, I'm going to stop.

'I just don't want to give those people the satisfaction of seeing me not playing my best any more. Look what happened to Piet Keizer last month. That was really bad. I felt very sorry for him, but he could have expected it. I'm not being wise after the event, but he should have been quicker than them.'

– Who is 'them'?

'I always call Ajax 'them' because 'him' sounds so personal.'

In recent months Ajax chairman Van Praag has at various times said Cruyff will certainly return to Ajax when his contract with Barcelona expires in 18 months' time [in 1976]. Cruyff loathes such statements because he doesn't think it's right to upset the Barcelona board. Although there is a good chance Cruyff will come back to Ajax, Van Praag and his big mouth can only prevent it, given Cruyff's remarks about the '76–'77 season.

'Ajax finally think I have a moral right to the signing-on fee that was asked for my seven years contract. I'm talking about the two-sevenths part Ajax wanted from me because two of the seven years had gone when I left Ajax. I don't want to say any more about it. I'm being treated correctly here and Barcelona have asked me not to talk about a possible return to Ajax. Nothing is certain. Maybe I'll stay, maybe I'll go.'

– Why did it go wrong with Ajax almost a year and a half ago?

'There is so much behind that, I'd have to open a whole world. I can't answer that.'

– Was it the fact the players took away your captaincy of the team? Or was that just the last straw?

'It was the last straw. The other players said they didn't like that I was changing my lifestyle and was isolating myself. But it wasn't like that. They started to live differently; they started going into town and asked me to go with them. But I never went in to town myself before. When I left, there were problems that could have been solved, looking back at it. The World Cup proved that. But at that moment I just couldn't stay.'

– You often fought with Dr Rolink. What do you think of him?

'Rolink was a good doctor for Ajax.'

– What do you mean?

'For Ajax, I said. I think I've said enough.'

– Is it so bad you can't talk about it?

'I don't know. In a normal society you might say it stinks, but in the world of football, you have different rules.'

– Rolink once said to you, 'Johan, I've seen photos of your joints and they don't look that good.' But you knew you'd been to hospital for nothing and those pictures had never been taken. Was that affair the start of your bad relationship?

'It doesn't make sense to talk about it any more. It's over with . . .'

– Why is it that you've been injured so often at Ajax and almost never at Barcelona?

'At Ajax, I always played on but they blamed me if I didn't train. I always played in important games, even though I was often injured. Of course, if I was really badly hurt, I didn't play. Sometimes a week of rest would have been better for me, but I had to play.'

– Have you had many pain-killing injections in your career?

'Too many. That can't be good.'

– When you left Ajax, almost nobody thought they would play worse without you, because the guys who had been the boys suddenly became the stars. Were you surprised when Ajax did so badly?

'Well maybe I was one of the boys myself. In my time, Arie Haan scored twenty goals from midfield. Since I left, how many has he scored? The other day, Rexach scored three goals against Feyenoord from my passes. So who's the boy? Who does the dirty work? Remember, Piet Keizer used to do a lot of that kind of dirty work. I never said, "I'm better than you." I've always admired everyone's qualities. One player may be technically better; another is a stronger runner. I never picked the team, although people always suggested it.'

– You talk very lucidly about football and tactics. Perhaps the other players always thought your ideas were at the core of the way the team was built. Maybe that's why they said that your suggestions influenced team selection?

'That might be right, but even so the trainer picks the team and makes the changes himself, because every change affects the whole tactical structure of the game. That Ajax miracle team just grew organically. If you had 10 Van Hanegems it wouldn't be a team, but in that Ajax side no two players were the same. But if something went wrong in the team, it was my mistake. Luckily, things also sometimes went right because of me.'

At about five o'clock, we prepare to say goodbye. On Saturday, Barcelona will go back to their training camp, which is no different to a Dutch training camp; in other words lots of card games and discussions about the game.

Early on Sunday afternoon, November 24, we go to the Espanyol stadium, which we've heard is small. At 3:30 we take our places in the stands to wait for the sun to set behind the main stand at 4.45 when the game will start. Before the match the 40,000 crowd is entertained by people running around with huge white flags honouring a local sporting hero.

The game is one of the best and most sensational we've ever seen. Barcelona, the big favourites, lose 5-2 to their tiny neighbours

Espanyol. Johan Neeskens is completely played out of the game by a clever, bald midfield player, the ageing Jose Maria. It's a revelation to see how Jose Maria plays to the gallery to eclipse the Dutchman. When Neeskens comes lunging in with a challenge, he dances away at the last moment, then theatrically gestures to the crowd as if to say: 'What is that guy playing at?'

Cruyff had a good game but, at 0–2 down, he had to move up to play as a conventional centre forward where he badly missed a winger like Piet Keizer alongside him. Espanyol hadn't played brilliantly, but they used the same tactics as Feyenoord. After the game the city is transformed from the bastion of 'Barca, Barca' to an Espanyol stronghold. Cruyff doesn't seem emotional. He is one of the few Barcelona players not singled out for abuse by the thousands of fans at the stadium. As he gets on the team bus he says, 'Well, if you need me just give me a call tonight.'

On Monday morning, we meet for the third time. We ask Johan if he notices the Franco regime's special favours for football.

'I don't know anything about it. I'm not getting involved in politics. That's why I don't make any statements about it, and even if I understood it, it would be difficult to make statements anyway. I would want to play football anywhere in the world, but that doesn't mean I agree with a political system.'

– Back to the Dutch team. You never were openly clear about the problems with Fadrhonc a year or so ago, though you knew that going to the World Cup with Fadrhonc as coach would have been a flop.

'I don't need to be in the foreground. Not everybody has to know what I do. You have to realise that he got us through the qualifying rounds and he's a nice man. Once, against Norway, he left Keizer out of the team and people said that was my decision. Nonsense. But it remains true that I play to win, and if I can't do that with friends, they have to leave. Look. Some people say I never let other people share in my success. Around the time of the World Cup, I did an advertising campaign with Philips. Has anyone ever told you how those video recorders were handed out to the players and officials afterwards?'

– Why did you lose the World Cup final to West Germany?

'Well, I knew that I wasn't going to play amazingly well. I had a self-sacrificing task. It was a tactic I chose myself. Well, maybe I suggested it. It was the same tactic we had used against Bayern Munich, when we beat them 5-0 in a friendly.'

– Michels wasn't the Ajax coach when you played Bayern. Did he agree to these tactics?

'Yes, he suggested it himself. Apart from the fact that Rensenbrink, Jansen and Rijsbergen were unfit, one important element was that the co-operation between me and Arie Haan, who was our last defender, didn't work. Our tactics depended on that. Moreover, I was emotionally exhausted in the final. The relationship between Haan and myself in the first half against Italy last Wednesday also went wrong. Their striker played right up against our sweeper, which forced Arie to play far behind the rest of the defence. Usually, our pattern is best when Arie has the ball and is playing in front of the defence. Then he is the extra midfield player who fills the gap left when one of the original midfield players joins an attack.

'That's why we went wrong against Italy in the first half. We made the field too big. If I had to go back, it meant I had to run 40 metres. It's too much. It should be about ten metres, more or less. If we want to function as the Dutch team as optimally as possible, we have to play wide and keep the field as small as possible.' He demonstrates with his hands. 'After the break against Italy, we kept the field small. So every time the ball was headed out of defence or cleared by the goalkeeper we were able to keep possession; but in the first half we were caught in no man's land.'

– Is there a lot of nonsense written about you in the foreign papers that haven't interviewed you?

'You don't know half of what's written about me. An Italian paper once printed a story that I had a small room at Ajax where I would go before a game with a prostitute. If I start replying to that sort of nonsense, it would be giving the newspapers what they want.'

– Isn't it the same for every top sportsman?

'Yes, that's true, but if you see that a lot of people don't want to work, why put everyone on the same level? I think you have to pay according to the amount of work you do. I think everybody can do everything, maybe with the exception of a couple of things like football. Imagine that I was unemployed, I would be a carpenter, and after a week or a month's practice, I would make a table. I think Dutch people can do more than they think but people just don't try hard enough. I am a football player for Barcelona. That brings responsibility. You have eleven people on the pitch who have to make sure that the 300 people employed by Barcelona continue to have food on their tables. And every 14 days, we have to entertain 90,000 people. It's a responsibility and I don't neglect it. I do believe that I give a little entertainment to people and that I'm fulfilling a need.'

– How hard do you really work?

'In the past four months, August, September, October and November, we've had four different four-day training camps for European Cup games with Barcelona. We played four tournaments in five days, had an eleven-day training camp, and I was away with the Dutch team three times, for five days each time. I also played eight competitive games, which take two days each if you include travelling and training. That's another 16 days. So, in total I've been away from home for 78 days out of 120. That leaves me with 42 days. If you subtract half of those for training, taking care of yourself and friendly games, it's only 21 days. Then there were five days doing commercials and another two days doing interviews. So I have 14 free days in four months.

'A normal worker has 16 weekends in four months: 30 free days. And he has evenings off, which I don't. I don't want to complain, trying to calculate like this, but often people forget how much we are away from home.

'Take last Friday. I've just been away for five days with the Dutch team and on Thursday I'm at home, and you're here. Normally, we would have gone out in the nice weather but now we can't.'

– Despite all that, do you enjoy being popular?

'Well, it is something special. You have to say it's different.'

– Do you still enjoy playing football?

'It's my job. You have to put up with a lot of tension. But I still enjoy football. I have to live so intensively now that I can't participate in the 1978 World Cup in Argentina. It would just be too much for me to spend a couple of months there. Even Knobel can't change my mind about that. I don't want to say I look forward to it, but I do look forward to ending my career.'

– How does it affect your wife?

'My wife makes a lot of sacrifices. She only has me part of the time, when I stop. You can say she lives in a beautiful house, she can buy beautiful clothes. But I don't think that makes up for all the sacrifices.'

– Do you think you'd rather be a bachelor in your position?

'No. Look at George Best. He's proved that you can't go without a woman. You go on your own into town for a drink and people just want to be with you because your famous. That's why you need a wife. You need your wife so you have someone to love. And when you are at home with your children, you forget all your worries. Because of the World Cup, I didn't have a holiday. It affects me. I get irritated more quickly on the pitch. I'm always hearing how nice winter sports are. I'd love to go skiing one day.'

Vrij Nederland,
December 1974

Chapter 3

THANK YOU: LIFE AND FOOTBALL IN BARCELONA

On May 31st 1977, we made the last of our 'FC Avond Rood' programmes for VARA TV. For our last edition, we travelled to Barcelona. Before we spoke to Johan Cruyff on the holy turf of the Nou Camp, he gave us a tour of the catacombs beneath the stadium. During the interview, using three wooden stools placed in the centre circle – or so it seems in hindsight – Rinus Michels was doing something that these days we would call 'fitness'.

On our walk around the catacombs under the Nou Camp, we talked about the incredible significance of an institution like FC Barcelona.

– Does it ever intimidate you?

'It is a challenge. But you know that when people cheer on a Sunday when you do well and you win, it means more to them than simply the pleasure of winning. It's not just a game, football; it's not just about the people on the terraces. You know what struck me most when we won the championship? They didn't say "congratulations", they said "thank you". That was really something. That will always stay with me. It's all they said: "Thank you", everywhere. One time we were shopping on the Costa Brava and an old woman came up to me and said over and again: "thank you, thank you". That made a very deep impression.'

Cruyff has a contract with Puma and in the changing room, he shows us his sponsor's boots.

– In that way, you've changed. You used to be different didn't you?

'I've had to be different. Back then because we had very little advertising in our society, it was all very new. Everybody knows now that I play in Puma. It doesn't make sense to make a fuss about it.'

We walk into a room where the players warm up before the game.

– Why don't the players warm up on the pitch?

'It never happens here. In Holland, you warm up outside to get used to the cold. Here, it's just to warm up the muscles. You also face a problem that before a game there are so many people on the field and before every game they want to take a team photo. There are about 40 photographers here. You never get a moment's peace. So it's best to do it indoors.

'You see this is the heart of the club. It's not only us who use it, but also the volleyball team, the basketball players. Even the Spanish Davis Cup team – they always prepare here. They use this place and all the facilities. That shows this is more than just a football club.'

We approach the impressive little chapel where many of the players pray before a game.

– When you first saw this chapel four years ago, what did you think?

'I'm not a believer. I'd never been to church before that. But it made a powerful impression on me in a way. I knew there was a lot of religion in this country, though I never expected something in the stadium. I found it extraordinary. But thinking about it later, it's logical. Football is not just a game here, and nor is it just about the players or the chairman. It's much bigger than that. It's difficult to explain. I've been told that in 1932 and 1934, the club – and it seems incredible to us – the club asked the government in Madrid for autonomy for Catalonia. So it would be part of Spain, but have its own government. And that came from the club! I obviously don't know exactly what the situation is now, but it shows the importance of the club. And it's like that again now, with the question of the autonomy. Again the club is involved. Catalonia is ruled by Spain, but has its own government. Laws here are different from other parts of Spain. For example, if women in Spain want to do something, they have to get the permission of their husbands. When my wife wants to do something here, I have to sign as well. In Catalonia, it used to be different. Women had rights as we had – they could decide things for themselves, but now they need permission. According to Spanish law, children are the man's property. Until they are eight, they can live with his wife but, after eight, the man has the right to the children. In Catalonia that's not the case, or at least it wasn't. The right to live with a woman here was completely different from the rest of Spain. I don't know other examples, though I'm sure there are many more.'

After the tour, we get three kitchen chairs, put them in the middle of the pitch and start the interview, broadcast on May 21st 1977.

– Johan, welcome. You look very relaxed.

'I'm really enjoy things. There's no reason to be tense, although there are a couple of problems; mainly private things. Last week was a nightmare; my eldest daughter had an operation on a tummy infection, so I haven't been very relaxed but I do feel relaxed now, probably because we're over it.'

– You're not playing so well, with your injuries.

'Well, I've broken part of my leg. Funnily enough, it's a part that shouldn't be there. It's not a normal part of the anatomy. There's a swollen bit that has formed between the shin and calf bone. A bone has formed there and the bone that shouldn't be there is broken. For two weeks I played on it because we had important games, but now that's over I'm not playing anymore.'

– How does part of a bone get there that doesn't belong there?

'I think it's because my legs have been kicked so often down the years. A sort of chalk forms and becomes part of the bone, but it's nothing serious.'

– We've seen you here for two days and your popularity is incredible. Isn't it maddening?

'It's always like this, and while not everyone says good things about me, it's mostly good. You get used to dealing with it, though maybe it's also one of the reasons why I'm going to retire next year.'

– Don't you feel you have to protect yourself mentally? Do you ever think you'd like just to not talk to people or be unpleasant to them purpose?

'Well, I have to because otherwise life becomes impossible. I had a period where I had to ask for money for interviews. Everybody says: "he wants money", but that's not the case. It was just a way to stop 99 per cent of people bothering me. You have to understand, it's not just Spanish journalists I have to deal with. They come from Holland, France, Belgium, everywhere. If you don't set some limits it'll kill you, you just won't be able to cope. And all this attention is nice, pleasant, lovely – but only if I play well. Because if I play badly, you wouldn't be here.'

– You just said that you plan to stop playing at the end of next season, that it's all become too much for you. The most often asked question is about the World Cup next year in Argentina. Can you explain to me why you won't be going?

'I've been thinking about it for three years now and I'm still thinking about it. It's because of a range of factors.'

– Like?

'Let me say something about one thing that's been written about me. When I played against England and Belgium, people said: "oh, he plays so nicely and looks so relaxed, how can he say this is stressful?" Well, it's easy to explain. These games went well, so nobody criticised me, nobody said a word. But if anything had gone wrong, I would have been slaughtered. [Holland beat England 2-0 at Wembley on February

9th 1977 with two goals by Jan Peters]. Okay, that's the risk you take. I like taking risks, so I don't really mind, but it is definitely stressful. And then I played against Belgium [Holland beat Belgium 2–0 in Antwerp with goals by Rep and Cruyff]. People say: Belgium, oh that was so good, he played so well. But how much does it take out of you? Against Belgium, we didn't dare lose, we had to win. They said "you're almost in Argentina", but if we had drawn or lost the game against Belgium, Belgium would been on top. So how can any reasonable thinking person say that it's not a stress situation, it's almost impossible to think of a worse stress situation.'

− Does this also have to do with the fact that you don't want to be away from home again for five or six weeks from your wife and children?

'Yes, of course, I've said that as well. It's not one thing, it's all these things. That's one of the important things, yes.'

− It's often said that your wife doesn't want you to go.

'Pff! I think the whole world thinks differently about my wife, and that's good because if something doesn't interest her, it doesn't interest me. My wife doesn't get involved in these things. She says: "if you think you should do it, then you should do it, and if you think you shouldn't do it you shouldn't do it".'

− You also hear that the KNVB has to do everything to please Johan Cruyff. Is there absolutely no possibility that you'll go?

'Perhaps that's the only maybe. I always have to laugh about people who come up with solutions. They say: just put Danny in a little flat. Well, Danny is not someone who allows herself be put in a flat. That time is long gone! Ha ha. It just doesn't happen. It's something you have to decide for yourself and I don't think there's a solution. At least, I don't know of one.'

− So would you like it if Danny was the only wife of a player . . .

'Well, no I wouldn't like that either. Or if I spent time with her, or that kind of thing. Well I don't like the idea of that.'

– But you're still leaving room for doubt. It's not completely sure if you're going or not going to Argentina.

'I think it's human. Everybody who has to take difficult decisions knows that you are never one hundred percent convinced yourself until the plane leaves. It's not one hundred percent sure. Because it's not only your decision, other people have doubts, and because of their doubts, it looks as if you are uncertain. It's a natural interaction.'

– The closer Argentina gets, the more difficult it is?

'I don't know. Maybe yes, maybe no.'

– George Kessler was going to return as national coach. Everything was fine until he got a phone call which showed him that a number of star players including Johan Cruyff were against him. After that, Kessler refused to work with the KNVB. What did you say?

(laughing) 'I laughed. I've absolutely not spoken about Kessler to anyone on the phone. I don't understand where this comes from. But it's nothing new. It happens every day. Every time anything happens, people say you're involved, they write things, and they don't care if it hurts you.'

– Would you have liked to have returned to Ajax next year for your final season, to finish your career in Amsterdam?

'Yes, there was doubt if we should come back. And, you're right, there was contact. But, as people know, I'm not someone who kicks a person when they're down. I don't like it and I don't like it happening to me, either. The details aren't very interesting. That's how it goes. I've taken a decision to play another year in Barcelona and that's it.'

– Did you ask for a lot of money from Ajax?

'I've never asked about money, never spoke about money. I never talk money right away. You only wait until the end before you talk about money.'

– You would have agreed to the same contract as Suurbier and Krol.

'Here's what I say: the details are not important any more. There were many possibilities, and the club could have paid directly or indirectly.'

– The details have never been looked into properly.

'I don't know. Maybe they said "it's impossible", I don't know.'

– Now you are playing the diplomat who doesn't want to hurt anyone.

'That's right. That's what I said: I don't like kicking someone when they're down. I've had nice times, I've also had problems. It didn't happen, that's it.'

– National coaches we've spoken to, people like Zwartkruis and Knobel who don't work with you every day, tell us that you, more than anyone else, can explain the secret and therefore the power of the Dutch team: the positional details such as playing with an attacking libero, the goalkeeper who operates as an outfielder, the striker like you who drops deep . . .

'The special thing about the Dutch team is movement. Everybody moves. That's the basis of it. If you say at any given moment: Cruyff is playing too deep, he should be in midfield, then you don't understand it. You can only switch positions if one position is free. We don't play normal midfield positions. That gives opposition defenders a problem because one of us will come from the right, another from the left, or all five through the centre, and the defenders have to look out. Plus, if they don't follow me, I'm free. And if I'm free, it makes it easier. If they follow me, they're one man short in the defence. If everybody moves forward, you need an extra defender, so the goalkeeper has to be able to play as well. It's as simple as that. The next thing is that people have to run with the ball, and they should run just as much without the ball, which means that you always have two or three people you can pass to. It makes things easy, but the hard thing is to make sure you are free – to lose your marker.'

– And you compress the play to make the playing area small, so you're playing near the last defender . . .

'Yes, because if you have a midfield player who comes into the attack and then has to run back 80 metres, well he can do that three times and then you may as well forget about him, he has to take a rest. You need to be practical all the time. It's better if the same player only needs to run twenty metres, or you can make it even less by saying: come back slowly because I'm already there and I only have to run five metres to take care of his position, so he only has to run back ten meters. It means you can keep going longer. The only special thing I have is insight; I see things a fraction earlier, and can play the ball a fraction earlier to where it should be.'

– Johan, we've followed you for two days, thank you very much for the tour and the interview.

'Can I ask you something? My kids would like to have your autographs. It's your last programme of the year. And maybe you'll make a decision to come back too. No, three signatures please: for my two daughters and my son. Thanks. Just don't ask for money for an autograph. Even I've never done that.'

FC Avondrood,
May 1977

Chapter 4

I ALWAYS HATED RUNNING IN THE WOODS – JOHAN CRUYFF AND THE THEORY OF BALANCE

In 1979, Cruyff was forced by financial pressures to return to the football field with the Los Angeles Aztecs. After a year, he moved to the Washington Diplomats. At 33 years old it was widely presumed among footballing 'connoisseurs' that he could not handle the pace of the European game, and he was consequently written off as a top player. He returned to De Meer, though only as a 'technical adviser', on November 30th 1980. During the famous game against FC Twente, Cruyff came down from his seat in the stand to join trainer Leo Beenhakker on the bench when Ajax were losing 1-3. Ajax promptly scored four goals and won the game 5-3.

'Name me five trainers in Holland who are suitable for such a demanding club as Ajax. I don't know one. It's unbelievable.' Cruyff has only worked at Ajax as a trainer for three months. 'You wouldn't believe the things I've seen. There's no organisation; there's nothing right here. It's like 15 years ago.'

Cruyff talked about Ajax, about goalkeepers and tactical or positional skills, for four hours. 'I was the boss. It was that simple. I had nothing to do with anyone else. I didn't make it easy for myself. I was very hard on a couple of the established names. I hope, for example, that Tscheu La Ling understands that I put him in such a position because I think he has more potential than he has shown so far.

'I've already had a fantastic time in my three months, but you wouldn't believe what I've seen and experienced. There are players Ajax bought for too much money who think they're the tops, yet I've had to show them the most elementary things. You must ask what the trainers have done with these players for the last couple of years. I've been very tough with them, I've fought with them until they've become crazy.'

– So crazy, we understand, that a couple of the players were happy you didn't go with them to the winter training camp in southern Spain. Because you talked so much to the players, some of them were relieved you weren't there.

'Yes, I know some players felt like that. Really! They'd prefer you to be nice and friendly and show them if they make a couple of mistakes. They don't understand that you'll never stop talking about certain patterns as long as they don't understand the characteristics of a particular tactic. Tactically, some players have almost no idea. It's ridiculous that in those three months I had to tell them about tactics all the time, and then they're relieved that for once I can't see how they're coping with their profession.'

– Goalkeeper Piet Schrijvers played really badly at the start of the season . . . Six months ago the Ajax board bought another goalkeeper, Hans Galje from FC Den Haag, for a relatively large amount of money. Galje was a player that Tomaslav Ivic also wanted when he was trainer of Ajax. Have you ever noticed that the board wants Galje in goal instead of Schrijvers?

'I don't really want to answer that question. I have nothing to do with the board, so that was easy. It doesn't interest me if the board wants Galje in goal or sometimes even wants other players to play.'

– Do you think Schrijvers should return to the national team against France next week?

'That's Rijvers' problem. Let's put it this way. I agree with Rijvers that the best should play against France and as far as I can see Piet is the best goalkeeper in Holland, when he's in good shape. I have to say that I don't know that young guy at Utrecht, Van Breukelen, too well. There's still Jongbloed, but he's really too old now, though I still think Jan is always incredible value for a team. You can never take away a person's vision, and goalkeeping at a high level is largely a question of vision. If Rijvers picked Van Beveren, I would have no problem with him either. I feel no bitterness towards Van Beveren at all. But again it's Rijvers' decision, it's not my problem.'

– What precisely is wrong with Piet Schrijvers' game?

'I've always told Piet: if you continuously blame your defence, then you're just hiding your own failures. And in general I have a problem with players who complain for their own sake, especially goalkeepers who after a goal or a good save start screaming at their defenders in public, you know, players who can't lead, but think they can always start moaning at others when they make mistakes. Real leaders on the field simply calculate when people make mistakes; that's why I thought Jongbloed and Bals were such good keepers.'

– Are you talking about people who actually don't take charge, for example Ruud Krol or Pim Doesburg of PSV, neither of whom have been picked by Rijvers for the international game against France?

'I don't like to name names. You know that. And how often have I seen Krol and Doesburg play? I sometimes see Doesburg on television and then I think: Bals and Jongbloed never complained about a goal. Bals took risks to correct the mistakes of others. And then you hear some people say he was no good.'

– What did you try to change in Piet Schrijvers' game?

'I said to Piet: we play attacking football at Ajax, so you shouldn't stay on your line. You should try to find your position around the edge of the area. Then you have to continuously give directions and six or seven times you'll need to run out fast to make a save. Above all, you have to learn that the great fear of goalkeepers that they will be beaten by a ball lobbed over their head from the half way line is not based in reality. If he plays like that, in the interests of the team, then it doesn't matter – and I told him this – it doesn't matter if once in a while he doesn't save a high ball. As he plays now, he's very important for Ajax. In form and in the right frame of mind, with his experience, he deserves to play ahead of Galje or Storm.'

– What did you find when you started at Ajax in November?

'A very difficult situation: just knocked out of the European Cup, lost a lot of games, lots of injuries, especially of people who can "carry" the team.'

– Among the injured were players who weren't really important for the team, except La Ling.

'I don't agree with you about La Ling. That's my complaint about Ling. I just get irritated by players who have class and don't do anything with it. That he doesn't carry the team isn't because he can't do it, because he does have the class. But to be recognised as a leader, you have to do it on the field and you can't do that by just a couple of actions.'

– In your first game with the team, Ajax–Twente, in the second half you left your seat in the stand, went to sit next to Leo Beenhakker on the bench and started shouting. Ajax came from behind to win. Why did you do it in such a showy way? Couldn't you have saved Beenhakker's face?

'I didn't want to go and sit next to Leo on purpose in my first game. From the stand I could see there were so many essential mistakes that I just couldn't stay there. I meant that with a couple of simple tips we could win the game and it was hard for me to sit there. If those things had gone wrong I'd have looked an idiot. I was also taking a risk. I want to say one thing clearly: I work very well with Leo Beenhakker and with the board. No-one knew what I was going to do. You shouldn't think this was part of my job description.'

– In that game against FC Twente, Piet Hamberg was substituted, not, as we'd expected, La Ling. In our naïve minds, we thought we saw the hand of Cruyff: leave the creative players, don't mess it up, don't change Ling. But it turned out to be Beenhakker's decision to let Ling stay on.

'You're right. I wanted to substitute Ling. There's a bit of a story to that. I already had the board with his number, number nine, in my hand, as you could see on television. Ling also saw me of course and the next day he said: you wanted to screw me. And I said: I didn't want to screw you, but if you play like you did, trying to be a parasite on Schoenaker, who's running around like mad for you and you play like you've got pleurisy in the sunshine and you've only done three things all game, then I am going to screw you. Look, I told him, I was God here and you want to be that. But you don't have half what I had. You did three things all game, trying to beat your man, and I can still do those things, maybe even better. If you want to become God here, you've got to do something to earn it.

'If he'd listened before, with his vision, which he has so much of, he would be much further developed by now. Ling has had too many compliments. That's always wrong. No player ever improved that way. And of course now he has that awful groin injury that he's still not got over. And here we come to the essence. I used to play with very injured ankles or groin injuries. And I played well, but I played within the limits of my handicap. And Ling doesn't do that. If your groin hurts, no, you can't do that one movement he does so well with that big stride inside. But if you're doing your job, you can try to do other things. But no, Ling has nothing except that one movement, "the scissors" as they call it, so his groin injury always comes back. It's logical that he can't get over it. At his age, he should have a bigger range of movements, because then he could play well despite his injuries. When your groin hurts, you can't hit the ball with the inside of your foot, so you do everything with the outside. Ling thought I was trying to get him. I believe he's starting to see I want to do the best for him.

'People say I want to make players into workers. What nonsense! Those people don't understand. I want to make Ajax into a spectacular attacking team and Ling can be a very important part in that. I said to him: if you think you're not playing very well, you can compensate a lot by working. Then you can show your team you're important all the time. Ling once said: I can't run 30 metres after a defender. But I don't want him to. Did you ever see Keizer chase a defender for 30 metres? Never. It's a question of vision. When you lose the ball, with one step you can often avoid having to run 30 metres. As a winger you can stand in such a way that the defender firstly can't run forward and secondly can't get the ball. When you do that you show you're involved in the game, that you're fighting for the team and that one step, which doesn't seem so important at the time, can be so important.

'Ling and I have had tough times, but I believe he's starting to see what I mean. The last games I was there he did everything I wanted him to do. Then maybe he didn't play well, but I hope it's obvious that that's not what it's about.'

'Do you know who's developed incredibly positively? Edo Ophof. He's going to be the best defender in Holland. If Ajax keep him as a defender – right or left, it doesn't matter – you'll see how good he's going to be.

'Balance in a team is so important. In principle I don't like attacking backs, because they fail as attackers and as defenders as well. In the first place, a defender has to know how to defend: he has to make sure he keeps the man he's marking out of the game. Only then, if it's possible, should he think about attacking. That's why Ophof is so good. In the first place, players have to carry out their tasks. Then they can think about other things, at least those players who serve a function. Arie Haan used to work hard at Ajax, playing for other players. He did it enthusiastically and well. Now he's the important player at Anderlecht. That's logical, but I don't think you can expect him to play for others when he plays for Holland. That's what I mean about balance. Those people who wanted to sell Ray Clarke didn't understand that Clarke could take away two or sometimes three defenders on his own because of his vision. The board shouldn't have seen Clarke as a goalscorer or as a playmaker. He made sure that Tahamata and Ling could play well – and he still scored 30 goals in one season.'

– Not only have you got involved with training, you also advise on buying and selling players and in reorganising the youth education system.

'I arrived at Ajax at a certain point where everything seemed to have gone wrong. The board had hardly any experience and in a situation like that the trainer soon gets the blame. Only someone like me who is above all parties can provide a solution. I wasn't a threat to anyone. I didn't want to become an official trainer or manager or board member. No-one had anything to be scared about with me. That's why I could ask for everything. Before I forget, there's one thing I want to say. When I first started working as a trainer at Ajax, trainer Brom was kicked out. Now I've come back for the second time and Leo Beenhakker has disappeared. You could get the impression that was my fault. And that's not very nice. I worked really well with Leo and I wasn't trying to push my way through whatever the cost. I also said that he shouldn't see me as a threat, and I don't think he did. Because Leo went from the youth team to the first team, the youth education at Ajax stopped. And I don't think that, as happens now, education should be the job of the head trainer because he happens to be in charge of the technical staff. Trainers of the A-team change their team all the time. I told the board that I wanted Jany van der Veen, who was youth trainer in my time and is very suited to youth education. He has a wonderful eye for talent and he should come back. And I also said that what happened in the past was nothing to do with me and I wasn't going to talk about it. I think Jany van der Veen should return and that's what's going to happen. Period. Not in a week but immediately. I also said: get Wim Jansen. I've written a report on the players under contract, but I'm not going to talk about that because that's not fair to the players.'

– You've also been involved in youth teams, even with the 10 to 12 year olds.

'I've advised the board to stop signing youth contracts. Don't give boys of 17 a contract. They should be happy they can learn something at Ajax. In principle, you should keep a 17 year old with the A-juniors, and sometimes let him play in the C-team (the second team), and if he does well there, sometimes he'll go on to the first team so he can get a taste of the atmosphere. If he doesn't understand it and plays badly in the C-team – and by that I don't mean that he fails to beat his man or someone passes him – then you put him back, and not to A-1 but to A-2. He still has a chance. I think the young are getting tougher mentally. When he's 18 you can say "he's done it" and you can pay him back for those years.

'Over the last few years in Holland and also at Ajax we selected far too much for physique. Ajax has only two B-junior teams, teams for 15 and 16 year olds. So what have I seen? Players of 14 who came from C to B who were sent away because they weren't physically strong enough. At that age youngsters are still growing and you shouldn't send them away, especially those players who are technically good. You should develop a third B team for small players who can develop further. I was too small myself when I was 14 or 15. Small people also have two advantages: because they are small, they have to watch what's around them on the pitch and they have to be quick because otherwise someone will walk all over them. So their vision is very well developed. Secondly, someone who's technically strong but physically weak is usually two-footed.'

– When you look at the players bought in recent years would you say that Zwamborn, Meutstge, Boeve, Van Geel, Hamberg, Wiggemansen and Galje were bad buys?

'You can't ask me that – it's not nice. They don't like Zwamborn here but I don't think he's a bad buy. I'm not saying the others are either. But you have to look at the balance in your team: if you have all small players, Zwamborn can be very useful. Ajax has many possibilities with their young players and I think they are allowed to make mistakes. I kept Weggelaar in the team despite the mistakes he made. They didn't matter. He wants to play football, he isn't ordinary, he's a good defender and he listens, he likes to learn. I believe in Kieft. That's why I kept him as a centre forward. And Rijkaard has incredible possibilities, really incredible. He plays in midfield, in the hardest position in the team, doing what I used to do but playing a little deeper. He makes lots of mistakes, but he's one of the few in Holland who can play. Do you realise that Ling, Arnesen and Lerby are able to play because of Rijkaard? If you ask why he doesn't play sometimes, it's because you have to protect him sometimes because he's pure gold.'

– You were the first trainer in Holland without a diploma.

'I have been called a tactical genius. I've trained the first team, the C-team and also the youth teams. And practice has convinced me that you don't need a diploma for that. I only talk about technique and tactics. If Ajax has to train for physical condition I just don't join in. When I was young, I also hated running in the woods.'

Vrij Nederland
March 1981

Chapter 5

I ALWAYS FIND IT DIFFICULT
WHEN SOMETHING ENDS
– LEAVING FEYENOORD

On May 1984, just after he turned 37, Cruyff told us by phone on our radio programme 'Between Barend and Van Dorp' why he had announced that morning that he was going to leave Feyenoord and retire from active football.

– Johan Cruyff, we're both really pissed off, Henk and I.

'Well, that makes three of us'

– You too?

'Yes.'

– Why are you pissed off?

'I find it difficult when something ends.'

– And we're pissed off because you are one of the few people who does those things we don't see in football any more.

'Yes, but on the other hand, when you're doing this, you should be able to do it again next year, otherwise you shouldn't do it.'

– So are you scared that you won't be able to do it any more next year?

'This year I noticed – and maybe other people didn't – that it took an incredible effort and so much energy. I think it's just not fair to Feyenoord who have treated me really well this year. Luckily I've given them something in return. At a certain moment it's going to decline and you can't do anything about it. Then they also build the whole team around you and if you can't do it, it hurts the team. And the relationship has been too good for that to happen.'

– Last week Wim Van Hanegem said on our programme that you really could play another couple of years, definitely another season, if only you'd train a little less.

'Well, it's very hard to separate one thing from the other. I think I have to take into account my mentality. I think if you're being well paid, you have to lead. If you're the best paid, you have to be the best. I'm not the type that thinks: well good, maybe I can't do it today, then I'll do it next week and if I do it a couple of times a year I'll be happy. I'm not like that. I think if you start something you have to finish it and then you have to take it to the top. In the beginning, everything's fine, but then you have to go further, and you have to be more on your toes and it's just harder.'

– Can we ask Cruyff the professional if his heart is still at Ajax?

'I don't think you can ever ask as a professional, because he works. But if you ask as a person, then I'd say that if you play somewhere for such a long period, it's logical that you're an Ajax man in a certain way. On the other hand, you mustn't forget that I played here really nicely and they took care of me. Because it was very hard for me last year. They've been very good to me and I'm very happy that I've given some good things back to Feyenoord.'

– Johan, if you can be very honest, don't you think you have a slight feeling that you've taken your revenge? You don't want to say it, but don't you think something like: I've shown Ajax. I won the cup and the league with Feyenoord: that's what happens when you treat me that way.

'Not if you really think about it. But sometimes, in flashes, yes.'

— Maybe PSV's trainer Reker put it best. He said: "Feyenoord are champions because of Johan Cruyff, and not because he played for Feyenoord but because he played against Ajax".

'No, I don't agree with that at all. Because that would mean me not being professional. It makes it look as if I've used Feyenoord in a personal way, and that's not true. I think I've come through the hard part with them and I've done everything in my power and you shouldn't say otherwise.'

— Is it absolutely certain you're not going to play football again?

'That I'd play somewhere else next season?'

— Yes.

'No, or you'd never stop.'

— To finish, Johan; on January 1st the old international will be played against HFC. Will you take part?

'The thing I have against January 1st is that it's always terribly cold at that time. So I'm not sure if I'll play.'

— And if we put Stanley Brard on the left ahead of you?

'Let's get rid of that misunderstanding one day as well.'

— Do it then.

'No, I don't have time for that now because I have a lot of children waiting for me. About 15 little boys and we have to do something about that.'

— Are you talking about the Feyenoord team?

'Yes, everyone's waiting and they're calling me.'

– Are you a little bit relieved?

'I don't know, I don't know.'

Between Barend and Van Dorp
May 1984

Chapter 6

I DON'T LIKE DOING THINGS I DON'T DO ON PURPOSE – ABOUT THE NETHERLANDS TEAM

On February 27th 1985, Holland beat Cyprus 7-1 in a vital World Cup qualifier. The Dutch team was: Van Breukelen; Wijnstekers, Brandts, Boeve; Schoenaker, Willy van de Kerkhoff, Erwin Koeman; Gullit, Van Basten, Kieft, Tahamata.

The composition of the team is important to follow the conversation we had on March 2nd 1985. It's also nice to note that at the time Jan Wouters was an anonymous player with FC Utrecht. We spoke with Cruyff for an hour for the radio programme 'Between Barend and Van Dorp'. For a year we made a programme about the media for VARA Radio, so we also spoke to Cruyff about his relationship with the media.

– Last week, in your column in *De Telegraaf*, you were looking forward to the Holland-Cyprus game. You wrote that, as the first Dutchman who understands football, Holland should overrun Cyprus. When you wrote that Holland should and can win 10-0, was there any specific meaning for the national team? So the first question is not going to be something you might expect, such as 'how do you feel?' or 'what do you think will happen tomorrow?' but: why did you write that?

'In the first place, we have a lot of young players and they're easily influenced. That's logical when you're young. If you constantly hear: "oh we can't do it any more". If you constantly hear: "we can't handle it". If you constantly hear: "those kind of results don't happen any more", and then you look at Germany-Albania or Albania-Belgium, you just want to head for the exit. At that moment, only one thing was required, and that was a high score. And the least you can do is to go on the pitch thinking: we're going to try to do it. If it happens or not, that's a different story. But you have to go onto the pitch with the idea: we're going to do it.'

– Did you then think consciously five days before the game that you were going to stir things up?

'I don't like doing things that I don't do on purpose.'

– Yes, but did you write that column on purpose? By talking about 10-0 you were provoking Beenhakker and provoking the players. Is this what you had in the back of your mind?

'Yes of course, in the back of my mind. As I say, I think at that moment there was a completely depressed atmosphere. And you also have to think about the 1-0 away win in Cyprus. The feeling was, we can't do it. But I think we can do it. I've said it many times. I think the pool of players we have to choose from isn't bad at all.'

– But then you hear at the press conference two days after your column appears that coach Beenhakker says: why the hell does Cruyff talk about 10-0. It's not realistic.

'I have seen a lot of games in the last six months, seen a lot of players. So if I look at the possibilities of those players from my perspective, I think that the possibilities are not bad at all, and I think if the younger players can get to a higher level, they're not bad at all. Then we can play anywhere.'

– Who taught you, or did you teach yourself, never to answer direct questions?

'I don't think I was taught. I think I've learned by falling and failing.'

– And are you planning to do that today?

'No because I do give direct answers.'

– OK, next question then. Everybody says: Cyprus? It's impossible to get a big score against them any more. Those countries have learned. Michels says it too. They've learned to defend so well that a big score is impossible. Then you say in your column that it's going to be 10-0. It has to be. So you do it on purpose.

'I do it on purpose because, in the first place, I think it is possible. Unfortunately, I was right about Malta as well – that Spain could score more than 10 against them. And I'm not a clairvoyant. I only see the possibilities of the players. And if you look at the possibilities of the players, and I'm sure you spotted this if you read the column, I've mentioned several names.'

– You suggest, among other things, that Frans Adelaar, who has been injured for a long time, should be in the Dutch team, or Jan Wouters, who has also been injured for a long time. I mean, I didn't think it was the strongest part of your column.

'It depends on how you look at it. I think I've been one of the few people who've seen Wouters play against Roda, and seen Adelaar play against Roda. And if I then mention a type of player like Wouters for a certain position, it immediately shows the way I think about how the game should be played. Wouters is not the kind of player who hangs around in the penalty area. He's not the type who can beat someone on the wing. He's someone with insight and pretty good technique, someone who has the instinct to be in the right place nine times out of ten. And that's what you need for my team and my tactics. He can function optimally and you need others who can also function well.'

– Wait a minute, a lot of this will be incomprehensible for a lot of listeners who know nothing about football. What in your view was wrong with the selection for the Dutch team against Cyprus? Why could they have won 12-0 or 13-0 if the team you would have picked had played? What was wrong tactically? And explain it in such a way that other people don't say that Cruyff is always dreaming and talking drivel about football.

'The most important thing in football are the lines. Let's start with that. Attack, midfield, defence. We also know that the barometer in football is the midfield. The Dutch team against Cyprus had no midfield. It wasn't there. They were either playing too wide or too far forward. Like that you can never have optimal possession of the pitch, so you can never play at your best. Is that simple enough?'

– So you mean the midfielders Schoenaker and Van de Kerkhoff didn't play as they should have played?

'Yes. One was too wide, the other was too deep, so only one player was left in midfield. That meant you got a sort of umbrella effect where people were no longer in the right places on the pitch. That causes two problems. There is not enough width because you can't get players to the wing – that's the first point. The second is that the midfielder who is too far forward gets in the way of the strikers. I think that's the easiest way to explain it.'

– OK, for example Dick Schoenaker is a midfield player who scores a lot of goals, and a lot of people think: you've got to have this guy in the team. He works hard, he never lets you down, he never fails with Ajax. But you wouldn't have him in your team. Why not?

'Firstly, I have a lot of respect for Dick and I played with him for a long time in a great way. He's also a friend of mine. So this is not a question, as some people might think, of criticising. It's nothing to do with that. Schoenaker's strength lies in working hard, playing deep and getting into the penalty area. If you play with just one centre forward, then you absolutely must have him. There's no doubt about it. You don't even have to think about it. But if you have two central strikers, then it is illogical to think there will be any space. And if there is no space for him, there's no room for Dickie, so he shouldn't be there.'

– Because playing with two central strikers . . ?

'Exactly. If you have two strikers – Kieft and Van Basten – who only operate in the penalty area, then you need another, more defensive kind of midfield player.'

– Can I interrupt you? Peter Ribbens, our technician, knows nothing about football. Do you understand this, Peter?

'No, I don't understand a word.'

– Johan, you heard that.

'Yes, but I'm only suitable for the people at the top. For the people who really understand these things.'

– How would your midfield have looked?

'I would have had four men, with two in the middle, one a little further forward playing near the two strikers. The two wingers shouldn't leave their position because they are so important for the shape of the team. So for the midfield role I would take two more defensive players. On the right, maybe Wouters and, on the left, Koeman, like Adelaar, younger guys who can get the ball out to a winger at the right moment, but still be calm enough to stay back. And the guy close to the strikers, he needs to have a good shot.'

– Why?

'Because with so many people in the penalty area, it's often easier for a striker to play the ball back forward towards the goal. The central midfielder needs a lot of insight, so that he doesn't get too close to the strikers but can always run in to shoot a ball that's been laid back to him.'

– So who would you have picked?

'If I look at all those qualities, I think of Rijkaard. And, because the wingers don't need to defend, I would take someone like Vermeulen.'

– Really? But he fails every time in important games.

'But we're playing amateurs! We're not playing Brazil. I could play against amateurs. I saw them on Wednesday, and they really were no better than amateurs.'

– No, they've shown that.

'Up front, I want two mobile central strikers. I've already said: Kieft and Van Basten. And on the wing, on the right wing, you need Gullit. And if he can't play, I would take Broncken.'

– And that would have worked?

'You never know. That's the fun thing about football. You can fantasise so much.'

– So this team differs on two positions in defence, two in midfield and one in attack: so five differences from the team that played last Wednesday?

'Yes.'

– *Trouw* newspaper and the football magazine *Eleven* said that Rinus Michels wanted Johan Cruyff to succeed him as an interim coach when he became ill. You went to see him in hospital. Did he talk to you about this?

'When you've known a person so well for so many years it's a question of friendship, and you have to totally separate that friendship from a subject like that. That's the first thing.'

– Yes of course.

'I mean, we're not in each other's pockets. You can't do that. They are separate things. Of course we talk a lot about football. That's logical. It's a common interest. And if he ever said something to me on this subject, then it's also logical that I would never talk about it.'

– We don't understand that logic.

'Because, if the two of us have had a conversation, it was a conversation between the two of us. If he wanted to put it in the paper, then that's his decision. I can't take that decision. So let's completely forget about what I know about him. It also means that because, it's written in the papers, maybe it's true, but I'm not going to say that. I'm sure it came out through other channels somehow.'

– Would you have liked the job?

'I think coaching is nice, very nice. It's also the thing I think I can do best. And I would have done it. Despite all the risks involved, I would have done it, I think.'

– But very concretely, is what the newspaper and the magazine said true or untrue?

'I'm not going to tell you.'

– Then who should we ask?

'You must ask Michels . . . or you must ask the KNVB. The person there who has that list of replacements.'

– Did journalism change your life a lot?

'Yes of course, especially with the idea of not revealing what you think. It doesn't mean I don't think, privately anyway. That's why there's a big difference between the people who know me and those who don't. And there's hardly any similarity between those two types of people.'

– For example, what if I asked you what you think of Leo Beenhakker as national coach?

'Then I would answer from the perspective of a footballer. I would answer regarding football. Then I say the choice of Beenhakker is justified. He worked in Spain, for Ajax, for Feyenoord. He's been at the top, he can communicate well. So, you should try him.'

– Good. Now, if we stop the tape, in a manner of speaking, what do you privately think of Leo Beenhakker as national coach?

'Yes, but the only problem is the tape is not off.'

– No, but, you know . . .

'So then you'll get the same answer again.'

– Would it be a completely different answer?

'Well, then you'd go into details and start to talk about all the other things.'

– But would it be a different answer? Yes or no?

'Yes it would be a different answer.'

– OK. Your leaving Feyenoord is widely discussed in the media. You could have sold your story to *TROS* and *De Telegraaf*. According to Lex Muller in *Algemeen Dagblad*, you've made some nasty jokes with Feyenoord chairman Kerkum. You would have been lying because you knew for a long time that you were going to stop playing. But because of the interest of the *Telegraaf* you would have stopped that for a long time, so you would also have lied to Kerkum – that's what Muller says . . .

'In life, you have sympathies and antipathies. That doesn't mean I have sympathies for *De Telegraaf* and antipathy for *Algemeen Dagblad*. That's not so . . .'

– Is it financially attractive to write a weekly column for *De Telegraaf*?

'I think for a lot of people it's attractive.'

– Are you listening to what you're saying?

'Yes, I'm saying, it doesn't interest me at all.'

– We asked: 'is it financially attractive for you to. write a column in *De Telegraaf*?' and you answer: 'I think for a lot of people it's attractive'. But we are asking you!'

'Because it doesn't interest me if I make a lot or I don't. If I don't want to do it any more, I'll stop. Whether there's some money involved or not, it doesn't interest me.'

– But there must be some small relationship between money and the column.

'No not at all.'

– I find that fairly unbelievable. Can you imagine all those people at home thinking: Cruyff is fibbing?

'Well, that's an opinion they've had for years. But it's very simple. Money doesn't interest me at all. I absolutely have no idea what I own and what I don't own. I haven't got a clue.'

– Well, if you own nothing, it must be hard not to know it. Does it really not interest you?

'Not at all.'

– What kind of image do you think have?

'I think a lot people respect me for my capacities. But on the other hand, I think I've often been seen as unpleasant, and you know after all these years that you're a different person on the inside and on the outside. We've talked about interviews. If you find all you're doing is giving interviews, then you have to stop. Because I think – and I've learned this hard way – the only thing that really matters is how you play on Sunday. Because if even a hundred thousand journalists write about you, and you play badly on Sunday, the only thing you're going to be judged on is what you did on Sunday. The the only weapon I have is to be strong and to achieve what I want to achieve.

'The other way is obviously very seductive: you go to parties, you're nice to people, all sorts of things that have no direct relation to football. And that kills you. That's what I'm trying to say. I've always tried to keep the two things strictly separate. I've never gone out on a Friday evening or a Saturday evening because on the Sunday there was the game. And even if you gave me the most beautiful party ever somewhere, whoever was there, I didn't come. And don't think it was a sacrifice. The football was much more important for me. I never even thought about it.'

— Why don't you invite journalists to your home?

'Why should I? They'd want to talk about football. They need to talk to me about football. And I don't like it if they come in and say hypocritically "oh you've got a beautiful phone" or "oh you've got an ugly phone", things that are totally unimportant. Of course, jealousy is always an uncomfortable subject. A lot of people will play that game. This one has a big house. The other has a small house. And we don't live in Holland in a society where people say: "fantastic that you're having success!" '

— We don't live in a society . . . say that again.

'Where people say: "fantastic that you're having success!" That doesn't exist here. That is a fact.'

— That's just the feeling you have.

'No, not a feeling. It doesn't interest me. I'm Dutch myself. But if you're in America, they say "It's great you're doing so well". And they really mean it. And here it's quite different. And that's a fact. Maybe I'm the same.'

— What kind of country is Holland, do you think?

'What kind of country? Now you're asking difficult questions again. Dutch people are very sober and they belittle things when I don't think they should belittle them. I do a lot of PR and I'm often abroad and if you have to tell them something nice about Holland, then half an hour is not enough. We can do so many things. Take that funny skating tour of the eleven cities: no one else in the world has anything like that. We have something so unique, we should be very happy. We are a small country and we can do so many things. It's so wonderful when you can talk about building sea defences in Zeeland . . .'

– Ha ha ha.

'. . . and if you start looking at Holland in a positive way, it's fantastic. Often these people – because they come from a big country – they say: "what is Holland?" And if you say: "Shell, KLM, Philips" they say, "are they really from that little country?" I've travelled a lot in my life and I've never been anywhere in the world where there are no Dutch people. And that's also funny. Those are big, positive and nice things and I think you can really tell people. You can be proud of that. You shouldn't belittle things.'

– But you belittle yourself as well.

'Yes, maybe I have that disease. But I think a lot of other Dutch people, when they talk about sport, say such things about me. Isn't that the greatest thing? I think there should be more of that. People should be proud of that. People shouldn't say: "that's nice, but . . ." There's always that little "but" in the background. So when you travel, when you're abroad, you're Dutch, and if someone asks you about Holland, you should defend your country. You can be really angry. Many things can irritate you. But you're not going to talk about the things that irritate you about your own country. You don't do that.'

– Try it here. What irritates you?

'We had a long discussion a while ago – the papers were full of it – whether the words "God Is With Us" should appear on our coins and bank notes. I think it's so terrible that it should be taken off. Why should it be taken off? Why in God's name would you even think of doing it? Why worry about it? I don't understand.'

– Do you believe in God?

'I believe, yes.'

– In God?

'Yes. But if you take the Bible and all the question marks, then no. I think something or someone exists that you can call God. I'm convinced of that, yes.'

– How do you cope with God in your daily life? A strange question really.

'How do I cope? I have lost a father twice. A lot of things in my life have happened that aren't normal, not logical. Then I think that there is something or someone who is in charge of things in a reasonable way, or however you would express that.'

– Do you go to church? Do you pray?

'No.'

– In your thoughts, do you talk to Him?

'No. Not that either. But I do know that, in my philosophy, your fate is determined in advance, and all you have to do is to show 100 hundred per cent determination to get the most out of it.'

– Do you ever talk about this at home?

'Do we ever talk about that kind of thing? No, but there are moments when something like that happens in your life. I lost my father two years ago. My second father. And then your eight year old son asks: "where is he?" What do you say? In heaven? Then you have to explain. What, in God's name is heaven? "And where's the body then?" Well, the body stays here. It's been buried. and the ghost goes where? I don't know. The soul. You have to make a story of it. Then you make a story you believe yourself. You say: the body can be dead, but he's with me. And that is with you and hangs around you. I don't want to say it controls you, but at least you have feelings or contact with it in some way. And if you call it Christian or Catholic or whatever, it's just a way of thinking.'

– Did your son understand it?

'I don't know. The only thing I know is that they had to play football the day it happened and he played the best game of his life.'

– People always say to us: What do you have to pay for an interview with Johan Cruyff? Our experience is that we have never paid a cent for all the various interviews we have done with you. Why do you have that image?

'I think I've built that image. That you'll get money for things, if you, how do you say it, if you do things.'

– Is that true?

'Well, in general no. But it's always a nice way to scare people, because then I don't need to take 90 per cent of the phone calls.'

– If I was a journalist on a tabloid and I called you, would you give me a price?

'Like I say, I only give interviews.'

– No, but you have to scare them.

'No I don't have to do that, I'll pass them on.'

– Who to?

'To my father-in-law.'

– And what does he ask?

'It depends. If people are very persistent, the prices go up. Until they get scared. And if they insist on doing it anyway, well, at least you get paid for your time. But that's not the objective.'

– What's the most you've been paid for an interview?

'No idea.'

– But you must know.

'I forget those things so quickly. It doesn't interest me.'

– What is it then? 10,000 guilders? 15,000 for an interview? Are we getting close?

'In good times, when they fell for it, maybe it was between 10,000 and 15,000, I think.'

– And did they fall for it?

'No, because I don't want it. If my starting point is: I don't want to do this but I want to earn some money from it, then it's a question of negotiating, seeing how much those crazy men will pay. But my objective is that I don't want to do this. But if I can't get out of it, I'll ask for a large amount.'

– You look bad. Does that mean you are doing well.

'No, but I have a small problem today. It was when one of my daughters had to go to a tournament. I had to drop her off at school at 6 o'clock this morning, which meant I had to get up at five. And that means I don't look good. That's the very simple answer.'

– If we say, 'God, you look awful', then you say 'I feel fantastic'.

'Yes, but circumstances change. Pressure and having to achieve makes you feel well. But I think you often look bad, because the way you live is not good for you.'

– Then you feel good and look good?

'No. I feel good, but I look bad.'

from Between Barend and Van Dorp
March 1985

Chapter 7

NO FLOWERS – CONFLICT WITH THE NATIONAL COACHES

For a month in early 1986 there were articles in the press about the controversy between the Ajax technical staff (Johan Cruyff) and the KNVB's national coaches (Leo Beenhakker and Rinus Michels). But precisely what this conflict is about is a mystery. Equally little is known of the truth behind the so-called 'Success of Zeist'; a meeting to look into the background of the Dutch football world's latest problems.

On Monday December 16, trainers from the top clubs in professional football met in Zeist, at the headquarters of the KNVB, at the request of national coach Rinus Michels. One day later, the newspapers reported that the meeting had been a great success. The official weekly professional football bulletin on December 18 said: 'Zeist and 'top coaches' find each other'. Although the official magazine was the only one to report that the trainers had agreed with the diagnosis of the football patient (though they differed on the required treatment), the December 16 meeting began a life of its own as 'the success of Zeist'.

If we are to believe the news, then national coaches Michels and Beenhakker and the club coaches of PSV, Ajax, Utrecht and Groningen all completely agreed about the future of professional football. Johan Cruyff, as representative of Ajax and one of the people present, said: 'I also read that we'd agreed on everything and I'm surprised too. Do you know what we agreed about? That we can't carry on like this and something has to be done. But that was really the only thing we agreed about. At least it was the only thing Beenhakker and I agreed about.'

Many things happened on December 16th 1985 and the days that followed – a time when Michels and Beenhakker had their contracts extended. Yet hardly anything has been written about it, and that is why we must examine the events of December 16th.

National coach Rinus Michels, seated at the head of the table, greets all those present. Sitting to his right are his assistant Leo Beenhakker, Han Berger and his assistant Sief de Ronde from FC Groningen and Wim van Hanegem and Wim Jansen of Feyenoord with Nol de Ruiter of Utrecht between them. On Michels' left sit Dick Advocaat and the Ajax delegation of Johan Cruyff, Jany van der Veen and Tonnie Bruins Slot. Because of the chauffeurs' strike that morning, PSV's Jan Reker and Hans Kraay didn't arrive until an hour and a half after Michels started to speak. Feyenoord's trainer Ab Fafie hasn't been seen this morning.

The point of the meeting is to discuss Holland's failure to qualify for the World Cup finals in Mexico. In Beenhakker's analysis, the failure was mainly the fault of players' mistakes with some blame attaching to Beenhakker's predecessor, Kees Rijvers. To the surprise of the club trainers, there is no mention of the deciding qualifying match against Belgium.

When asked his own views on this important gathering Cruyff says: 'On the subject of the coaching and the selection of players for Holland–Belgium, you say a couple of mistakes were made. Let's formulate it cautiously: they were mistakes that a novice coach would see. But no word about this. No, the mentality of the players isn't right; the education of the players hasn't been right for a while now. I've been hearing that for years. But then I ask: who has been responsible for youth education over the last couple of years? Who was the youth trainer of Feyenoord, of Mario Been for example, and later of Ajax, of Frank Rijkaard? Exactly: the future national coach (Leo Beenhakker).

'Because Beenhakker hasn't made mistakes this time and has never made mistakes in the past, we don't have to talk about it. We have to look ahead. That's right. If you want to cure the patient, you have to know how and why he became sick and why he remains sick and what's wrong with him. Everyone can see what's wrong with him.

'After the Holland–Belgium result, a lot of time was spent moaning about the four players including Gullit and Wijnstekers who didn't join in the run on the beach. I've read that the national coaches have used that to show the players weren't interested in the game and couldn't think collectively.

'Look, as a coach either you see that and draw conclusions, or you don't say it. Don't just moan about it. If four players say they don't want to run with the team and you think as a coach, for whatever reason, the whole group must run, then it's very easy: "gentlemen, you don't want to do it? OK, then you can leave" '.

– Would you have sent players home on the day of the game?

'Yes, of course. Certainly the Dutch team would have plenty of alternatives. It wouldn't have happened with me, and I don't understand Michels either. At least, I don't understand the influence and role of Michels. He would never have accepted that when he was younger.

'If you don't take action but complain later, if you only see it as the players' mistakes and not your own, the players will not respect you. And I notice that in the group, I feel it in the way players talk about Beenhakker. And many players know him from when he was at Ajax. They know him through and through. From experience, I know players have to respect the trainer. And the Dutch team lacks that atmosphere. That's very bad. I have my faults too. I sometimes concentrate too much on details. But I do see things clearly and of course I know what I'm talking about. Do you know who I think also has the respect of his players? Nol de Ruiter. He knows what he's talking about.'

When we watch Ajax train on Wednesday January 9th, the morning after the cancelled international match with Italy for which four Ajax players were kept home, the atmosphere is happy. 'Johan did well by us keeping us home' they joke. The mood is indeed as Cruyff described. Beenhakker is regarded extremely critically. Especially after his attacks on the players, the group of international players sitting together say: 'Well what has he achieved? Relegated with Volendam, failed with the Dutch team, sacked by Go Ahead and Ajax'.

Gerald Vanenburg: 'The problem is that he's the national coach. You can't get away from him. Whether you want to or not, you have to take him seriously, even if that's an effort. I talked to Beenhakker.

We agreed we wouldn't say anything about each other any more. Then a day later, I read in all kinds of papers what's wrong with my attitude. There's nothing about his mistakes. It makes you sick. I may as well not have made an agreement.'

Cruyff: 'It remains a problem for the players: if they say what they think, they're scared they'll lose their place in the team. What kind of impression do those players have of Zeist? I stopped four players going to Italy for the international on January 8th. On December 16th we sat and talked about all sorts of things, about a rejuvenated Dutch team that will go to Italy. And then two days later I hear that six of our players have been invited. Then I only get permission for Silooy and Koeman and then, just before the Dutch amateur team goes to China, Michels says: 'Silooy and Koeman are also not allowed to go to Italy.' In other words, Benhakker invites and Michels says no. That's the only way I can see it.

'At the December 16th meeting with Michels and Beenhakker, they suggested that all Dutch representative teams should play with two attackers in future. We had to look around us and see that all the successful countries play with two attackers instead of three. Two strikers – the salvation of Dutch football.'

Cruyff continues on the subject: 'Tell me the names of just two Dutch forwards who can play in a two-striker system. They have to be unbeatable in the air. They have to know when to lay the ball back, when to turn. In Holland, only Van Basten could do it. And I know for certain that if Kieft and Van Basten hadn't been suspended for Holland-Belgium, they would both have played in attack. And if the attacker has the ball on the left, which Dutch midfield player will join the attack at speed? So you tell them to do something they can't do, something they haven't been taught. A team like Everton has an ideal system for two strikers. Everton has the players for it.

'In any case, Ajax teams are always stronger. No matter how much you want them to do it, they can never play with two strikers. And I don't want them to. Play with three attackers, make sure you have lots of space, then you can afford to make mistakes. Then you can tell the players what's going on. Because in a football education you shouldn't only be able to learn. You should also be able to unlearn.

That's why I brought Wim Rijsbergen to teach our young players. Players like him know what it's all about.'

This enthusiasm for thinking through tactics and his astute commentary are partly why Cruyff is such a regular visitor to the Ajax youth sides.

'I'm actively involved with the youth and all our players. If the KNVB says we should only play to get a result in all our representative teams, then I say why in the 14–16 year old team are there only four Ajax players though the best players in Holland in this category are with us. They should call me beforehand and I'll tell them who's good, who they should take.'

– But the national coach should know that himself, shouldn't he?

'They don't know my players. We soon stopped talking. And I'm talking about discipline. I've given Regtop a 14 day punishment. Regtop is a talent. He came from the province of Drenthe to Amsterdam, went off the rails a little. It's logical for an 18-year-old player. But it's going to be fine. It happened a lot in my time too. That boy has to realise what it's all about, but he'll go on. But the KNVB shouldn't pick him and ask me if he can come because they need him, even though I've told him he can't play. Because in that case a player feels he's being rewarded for bad behaviour. So then you don't have the right to complain about the mentality of the players. I told the KNVB I would co-operate as much as possible, but if they start doing things with my players which spoils those players, they can't expect me to be happy.

'At Ajax we're moving in the right direction. At all different ages we have a lot of creative players. We had 14,000 people turn up to see Ajax-Excelsior. At Ajax you're not allowed to play defensively. I don't like it myself. I like dominating football. I like a team that decides for itself what happens on the pitch, that says "we're the best". You also have to think about the potential of your players. How in Holland you can think of playing with two attackers is a mystery to me.'

Vrij Nederland
January 1986

Chapter 8

WITH EYES SHUT TIGHT, AND GOD'S BLESSING – ON TAKING A PENALTY

C ruyff discusses the part played by tension, and the star's fear of missing.

'The Penalty is a speciality and it doesn't have any direct connection with football. Look, if we went outside now and I took 100 penalties, they'd all go in; that's not a problem. The thing is that a penalty seems to be very easy, which is why it's very difficult. The second point is that you always have to score – you're not allowed to miss. There's a very big difference. And it's also about the moment, it's to do with when you take it. If it's 2-0, anyone can do it. When it's 0-0 it's a little harder.

'In the European Cup final on Wednesday [Cruyff was at the Steaua Bucharest-Barcelona game which Terry Venables' Barcelona lost on penalties after extra time, missing four penalties while Lacatus and Balint scored for Steaua] you saw that the technical players had more problems. It's harder than 120 minutes of football in which they've been able to rest three times. Resting is probably the worst thing. If you carry straight on then it's just about OK. But if you have to wait four or five minutes after extra time before it's your turn, then you feel the tiredness even more and you can't take penalties on technique any more.

'And then you see that the first four – two from Barcelona and two from Steaua – all missed. They shoot with their instep, not badly at all, especially the last of the four, Julio Salinas, the Barcelona number nine. That was reasonably in the corner, but he was a little unlucky. But then came the Steaua number seven, and he took it the way I think you should at that moment and that is: close your eyes really tight and ask God' blessing.'

– Do you think tiredness and tension affect a technical player more than a workmanlike player?

'The tension is the same for everybody. All I'm saying is that if you want to hit the ball technically with the instep to score, then you have to be very alert, and you're not very alert after 120 minutes of football.'

– We didn't pay that much attention to it. So was it the technical players who missed on Wednesday?

– Not just the technical ones. Also the ones who tried to take penalties technically. The big difference between that and the person who broke that pattern (the third for Steaua) was that he hit the ball incredibly hard. He didn't place it. I think that's the way to take it.

'But hey, you can also miss like that. I had to take a penalty myself in the Amsterdam tournament. I was 35 or 36, I think. I'd played two games in two days plus extra time, and was living on my nerves. You do your little walk back to run up at the ball. You close your eyes and then you see where it ends up.'

– And you missed.

'That one ended up in the second tier seats.'

– Did you notice that during the penalties the goal seemed to get smaller and smaller?

'It was small before they started. The higher the tension, the smaller the goal gets.'

Between Barend and Van Dorp
May 1986

Chapter 9

I LOVE ALL MY PLAYERS –
ZARAGOZA V AJAX

We finished a lovely period with the weekly *Vrij Nederland* magazine in 1987, leaving for a contract with the supposedly downmarket *Nieuwe Revu* – which boosts its sales with nudes. When we told some of our 'business' colleagues about the change, we got a lot of similar reactions: you can't do that, it's not right, it isn't done, it's just not cricket. We could move from *Nieuwe Revu* to *Vrij Nederland*, even from *De Telegraaf* to *Vrij Nederland*. But we were not supposed to go from the top of journalism to something as ordinary as *Nieuwe Revu*. However we felt that over the last 10 years, as *Vrij Nederland* ceased to be essential reading, so *Nieuwe Revu* won a position in the weekly market – and not only for its tits.

Both Johan Cruyff and – especially – his wife thought our move was stupid: 'How can you do that?' Cruyff had nothing to do with *Nieuwe Revu*. If he ever gave an interview to a non-sports magazine, he'd want to talk to a magazine with class. Fortunately, the children took a different view. They opened the way for the first of what would be many interviews.

The first Cruyff piece for *Nieuwe Revu* came at the time of Ajax's Cup Winners' Cup semi-final against Real Zaragoza, in Spain. During the warm-up we stood on the pitch, followed the players back down the tunnel and then took our places in the stands. We were as surprised as the players when they walked back onto the pitch behind the referee: a sudden sub-tropical rainstorm had taken three minutes to transform the pitch into the kind of waterlogged mess you find behind a newly built dike. And Ajax won.

On Tuesday April 7th, the day before the match, Ajax train at their hotel in a little place called Zuera. National Spanish, Catalan, local and

Dutch press are all there, along with hundreds of schoolchildren, in and out of uniforms. They've been given the day off as the head teachers of the schools in Zuera organised an excursion – a little sightseeing trip to see Ajax and take a look at Johan Cruyff.

When the training at Zuera ends, Catalan television wants to interview Johan Cruyff and use him as a translator for a conversation with Marco van Basten. Cruyff doesn't want to: 'We gave the press interviews yesterday. Now it's over. Until after the match, we're giving no more interviews.' 'But we couldn't make it yesterday', says one of the journalists. 'Just one question for Marco van Basten, Johan. Please.' Van Basten and Cruyff agree. One question. The question for Van Basten for which Cruyff will act as translator is: 'What kind of player is Mr Van Basten?' Both the Ajax men walk away instantly. They're not even listening when the second question comes: 'Are you going to AC Milan?'. Together, the coach and his captain walk across the pitch towards the exit where two small boys and two 10 year old girls are waiting. A tape recorder is stuck under Johan's nose. One by one, the children ask the 20 most relevant questions, such as:

'Do your children still speak Spanish?'

'If Zaragoza made you an offer, would you work here?'

'Wouldn't you like to join in the game tomorrow?'

'Why are you preparing here in our village of Zuera?'

Cruyff couldn't talk to Catalan television because he had to catch a bus, but he talks to the children for at least 10 minutes.

On the plane back to Amsterdam, at the beginning of a long interview, when we asked him why he refused to talk to the Barcelona journalists for a minute but spent 10 minutes with the children, Cruyff gave us a typical answer: 'It's very simple. Television is press, children are not press, so for them the fact we weren't giving any more interviews wasn't relevant.'

It's hard to remember, but at the end of last season and the beginning of this one, the anti-Cruyff lobby was thriving. Ajax dragged their way to the end of last season and started this one badly. Everything was PSV Eindhoven. Ronald Koeman had just chosen to leave Ajax for PSV. Marco Van Basten had publicly criticised Cruyff in the *Haagse Post*, complaining that Cruyff talked too much. Frank Rijkaard wanted to go to PSV. Ajax had failed to sign a big name player like Glenn Hoddle and, when they lost their second league game of the season at home to FC Den Haag, even Cruyff had doubts for the first time in his career, though he no longer likes to admit it.

'OK, the way we lost to Den Haag. Yes, I was worried by that. But I don't remember having doubts. Anyway, it's all a long time ago.'

– But you had a very difficult time last September. Were you ever scared you wouldn't be able to get your ideas across?

'No that didn't worry me. We did have problems because things didn't run as I wanted them to, and those problems were exaggerated by the press.'

– What do you mean?

'Well I'll explain what I mean by the influence of the press. At one point last year there was a moment when two people left and Ajax bought different people. Everything was bad; the people we bought were no good; where could we go? Nothing was right. What was needed at that moment was good football. I knew it was going to take longer than all of you hoped – or didn't hope – because players like Jan Wouters, Danny Blind and Arnold Scholten had to get used to training during the day instead of the evening, to being full professionals. Those players had to acclimatise, and I told them so. That's why I wasn't worried. But in the press they kept comparing Wouters to Vanenburg, always favouring Vanenburg. I didn't take that personally either, because comparing Wouters and Vanenburg is like comparing apples and pears; it's not comparing like with like, and it is unfair for that reason.'

– No matter how you explain it, Ajax started the season by losing their first league game at home. And you know from your career so far that Ajax will always be discussed and criticised.

'I don't have a career.'

– No career? Come on.

'As I see it, I have no career. I look at things differently to other people. I work for pleasure. That's the bottom line. The rest is secondary. The moment I think I can't do it, or I have other shortcomings in the way I work with the players, the pleasure will be gone. And I would stop immediately.'

– After the bad pre-season and the home defeat against Den Haag, did you ever think about the way you function at Ajax?

'When I started, I obviously had no experience, so I could hardly go by my experiences as a coach. That's why I relied on my intuition.'

– What did you do after that defeat by Den Haag, which was three days before the match against PSV?

'I'd had experiences like that as a player of course. That's why I knew there was no point in having an argument about it. After the game, I think the players and I had the two most peaceful days of the season because we didn't say anything. I left them alone completely. Anything I could have said would have been adding oil to the fire and that was the last thing they needed.'

– So after the Den Haag defeat you must have been a broken man.

'I didn't say I wasn't broken. Of course I was broken, especially because of the details I went on about for the whole of last year. In the first year I told them repeatedly about lack of concentration. That concentration was exactly the thing that completely disappeared against Den Haag. And if you say I was completely broken after the defeat, I'd have to say you were right because at that moment I asked myself what in the name of Jesus I'd been working on. But as you say a lot of people thought I'd be down after the defeat, because we had to play PSV four days later. But they don't know me. That's not the way I'm made. Last year in the PSV game I put two unknown 19-year-olds into the team. If I was scared I couldn't do that, I couldn't do my job. I'd have to stop. After all I don't need to do it to put bread on the table.'

– Why did you decide to play Aron Winter and Rob Witschge against PSV last September?

'It might have been because I'd lost it completely at that time. I was in another world at that time. I was only concerned with one thing. When someone said something at home, I might have heard what they said. I might have nodded yes. But I didn't really hear it. You're there but you're not there.'

– Then you decided to play Rob Witschge on the left wing against Eric Gerets, the best right back in Europe. What did you say to him?

'. . . All I said was: you're the left winger, just make sure you keep an eye out for the right back and, when you get the ball, you've got to get past him. When you beat him, cross the ball and when you're in front of goal you have to shoot. The rest is your problem but you can't do more than your best.'

– And what did you say to the other boy making his debut, Aron Winter?

'That was a bit harder because Winter was playing against Gullit. I told him: Gullit is your man. I told him he had to get away from Gullit when he had the ball, that he should play naturally, that he shouldn't take any notice of anybody, not PSV or the fact that he's in the first team, not the crowd. The only thing I told him was: play according to your own nature. You can tell Winter this because he has great qualities. You can't say that to Witschge. You have to say to him: do your best, that's all I ask. Winter is involved with the game. He looks to his own intuition and insight for solutions whether he's attacking or defending. During the season Winter had a period where he tried to think about everything: taking a little pass, having a little look. And immediately everything went wrong. That's not Winter. Get the ball and play – that's Winter. He can go far. He has great qualities.'

– Will Winter and Witschge become regular first team players at Ajax?

'With Witschge it depends on him, but he's going the right way. With Winter it's certain.'

– You've always always said you liked the tough line of Rinus Michels.

'Yes.'

– We think you're the opposite of Michels.

'I don't know, but that's not my problem.'

– Michels thought of the Ajax players as numbers. We think you love your players.

'I don't know. I love my wife and kids.'

– Take Rijkaard a year ago. He played poorly for a while, but you wouldn't accept any criticism of him because his wife had had a miscarriage. You even asked us to go easy on him because of it.

'It was true.'

– So you're different from Michels?

'But the same thing happened to me. My wife has also had a miscarriage and I know what it's like. I wasn't the type who shows this kind of thing in football. And later I got the reputation that when I had problems I played well. But that doesn't mean I don't know what Rijkaard has gone through.'

– So, for you, Rijkaard is not a number but a person.

'But that doesn't mean I'm nice.'

– You're very unpleasant. But we still think you love your players.

'OK, OK, I love my players, but it's all my players. Though at home they think I have favourites. That's absolutely not true. It's purely about football.'

– Do you see Van't Schip at home?

'Among others. Especially during that period when, despite all the criticism, I kept him in the team. But this has nothing to do with preferences. I protect my players, especially from outsiders, but inside I'm hard as nails.'

– How come Rijkaard doesn't have the same image as Ruud Gullit?

'Rijkaard is an introvert, Gullit is extrovert, but I really hope he can go far because he has qualities. He's at least at the same level. I think Rijkaard can be even better than Gullit. Rijkaard is tactically more advanced and more disciplined. Technically they're the same. They're both reasonable.'

– Not good?

'No. Reasonable to good. Look, when I say reasonable, I mean compared to the highest level. Because Gullit is an extrovert, instinct is a large part of his game whereas Frankie, how shall I put it, always wants to play thoughtfully. I think Rijkaard can do much more. Because he's still not convinced about his potential, he's easily satisfied. Frankie is now becoming professional. Everyone sees him as an experienced professional because he's played for four years, but he's only 24.

'Take that first game against Zaragoza. Frankie wanted to play football in spite of the bad pitch. You can't do that. It's a weakness on his part that he can't kick the ball without thinking. If the circumstances make it impossible to play football, you're not allowed to play football. In his position, as against Zaragoza, Frankie should restrict himself. That's the class of Ronald Spelbos. He knows exactly when to do what and what not to do when. Do you remember last season when all the trainers' tactics were for Spelbos to win the ball. Bullshit. Spelbos is one of those players with the best technique and one of the few players who can deliver a pass over 50 metres. As a trainer I should use that, make sure other players benefit from it. If you're someone who plays long, high balls 10 times a game and lets opposing defenders get into position are you a so-called good player with good technique? I say: you should go on the stage.'

Nieuwe Revu
April 1987

Chapter 10

CRUYFF'S RECIPE – THE AJAX SYSTEM

For as long as anyone can remember, Ajax have played the 'Ajax system'. With 'the system' Ajax won four European cups with Cruyff and two without him. Cruyff has believed in attacking football all his life, as both player and coach. Read on and you'll realise that 'the system' hasn't changed much in 25 years.

Cruyff did as a coach what he had done on the field. As a former player, he added a new dimension to the old game. At the beginning of the seventies, without fully realising it, Johan Cruyff introduced the concept of 'total football'. He and no-one else made the Dutch team world famous. After the 1974 World Cup, 'La Maquina Narana' (the Orange Machine) was an institution, especially in South America and Southern Europe. At the beginning of the seventies, Cruyff unquestionably halted the growing trend towards defensive football. As a player, Cruyff knew no fear and didn't understand that teams were built to defend.

Now, as if it were the most natural thing in the world, he has added a new dimension to football. When he started as technical director of football at Ajax two years ago, attacking football was regarded as naive and foolish. In 1985, the counter-attack and the veiled attack seemed the only guarantees of success. That's what the experts said, the trainers with diplomas, the journalists who followed them, the *crème de la crème* of grey Holland. But from the start, Cruyff didn't care about the old-fashioned ideas of the cliché-thinkers in and around football.

When success didn't come immediately, they were waiting, those inventors of nothing. When, as journalists, we continued to believe in Cruyff's ideas we were labelled 'blind Cruyff supporters', and that wasn't allowed – we were supposed to remain objective. As a music critic, you are allowed to look forward to a Bernard Haitink concert; as a film writer it's assumed you think everything Woody Allen does is terrific. But as football writers you're not supposed to appreciate the greatest artist Holland has ever had. Despite that, Johan Cruyff has proved his superb abilities. Mediocre coaches will always say 'never change a winning team.' As of a couple of months ago, Cruyff can say 'never change a winning system.'

If you point out to him that he has revolutionised football thinking, he shakes his head and quickly changes the subject. That's because Johan Cruyff, even when he's at a Sunday morning match with his son, is a shy, modest personality who watches without fuss, without being the centre of attention.

Frank Rijkaard says: 'That's the nice thing about Cruyff. He's not arrogant. I played with him and now he's my trainer. If he says something to you, he always does it very modestly. When you used to see Ruud Krol or Soren Lerby, they had, how can I say it, an attitude, I don't know. But Johan never had that.'

Cruyff's system begins with the goalkeeper, with Stanley Menzo. The heart of the system is the so-called central axis. The contact between the centre forward Marco van Basten and the free central defender Frank Rijkaard has to be almost telepathic. As Van Basten puts it, they have to be connected by an invisible cord. Other parts of the central axis are the goalkeeper, the two central defenders, the centre forward and the central midfielder.

The system covers the four corners the field. That means two defenders watching the flanks and two wide attackers – outside left and outside right, as they were once known and are called again at Ajax – as close as possible to the touchline. Watching Ajax play for the first time you would think that two midfield players seem to be in supporting roles. They are the 'controllers', players who not only must do their tactical work without making mistakes but must also help to correct the mistakes of others. If Jan Wouters and/or Arnold Muhren fail in their task, the system effectively breaks down.

Cruyff not only picks his players on the basis of their footballing capacities but also pays attention to their characters. Of course it's no coincidence that modest players like Wouters and Muhren are given the self-sacrificing job.

A few weeks ago we talked quite intensely with Cruyff about his team and his ideas. Now that Ajax have won a European trophy – the Cup Winners' Cup – for the first time since 1973 we spoke to him about his actors and the roles their supposed to play.

The role of goalkeeper Stanley Menzo is well-known. Menzo is a footballing keeper who plays as part of the team. He is not allowed to wait statically on his goal line but has to play a long way from his goal. The thinking behind this is as logical as one-plus-one-is-two. If Menzo was stuck on his line, he would be much less active than when he plays with the whole team. Performing as a partial outfielder, Menzo gives Ajax half an extra player on the field against their opponents. In effect, Ajax are playing with 11 outfield players – the opposition with ten and a half. The philosophy behind this and the need for it is part of Ajax's attacking football. When Ajax defend in their own half, the keeper can stay in his goal. But Ajax attack and a keeper like Menzo is not a luxury but a necessity.

When Cruyff decided in January to extend his contract and learned that Van Basten was going to leave at the end of the season he concentrated his efforts on keeping Frank Rijkaard. Cruyff regards Rijkaard as a great player, indispensable on the way to the top. Rijkaard's strength is that people can always play the ball to him. Even when he doesn't play well, other players can pass to him.

Rijkaard: 'When Johan started as Ajax coach he had a vision in which he continued to believe, even when things didn't go so well. Last year I played in midfield and had to create space for Ronald Koeman so that Koeman could move forward and we would have an extra player in midfield. This year we have the same concept but with different players. That's what I mean by vision. I play Koeman's role. Bosman or Winter plays my role. I know what Cruyff thinks of me. There will come a time when I play above myself. I don't want to compare myself to Platini, but I do hope my career will be like his. In France he was a really good player, but in Italy he became really dominating, really able to decide games. I hope that I will develop the same way at Ajax as Platini has in Italy. Johan is Ajax. He decides the tactics from the first minute to the last.'

Until he was injured, Ronald Spelbos formed, with Rijkaard, the heart of the defence. Spelbos especially developed in a way most people did not expect. Ronald Spelbos (together with Arnold Muhren and

Peter Boeve, the only players with a lot of experience) says: 'Firstly, Cruyff tells me, I play in defence. It sounds so simple. And secondly, I must move the ball as quickly as possible to the place where we can score goals. In particular I have to make sure there is cover. It doesn't make much difference which of us plays. Until my injury, Blind, Silooy and I cut off all attacks. If we played against two wingers, then I would cover them. But I was not allowed to play immediately behind them, I was just in the area.

'We play space-covering. So you cover the space, which means the opposition comes into your space. If the attacker who's normally on Blind's side moves to the centre, then I cover him and Blind covers the space behind "in the area".'

'One of the defensive tasks Johan is very keen on is that we always have an extra man. If we have possession and unexpectedly lose the ball, we have to tackle immediately, or − it depends on where and how it happens − we have to move into our covering positions. Our tasks as defenders start when we attack. That's mainly a question of concentration. You always underestimate how difficult it is to stop someone for 90 minutes. You know the hardest time to concentrate? When we have the ball.

'We also have to make sure Stanley Menzo can get the ball into play as quickly as possible. That's why you hardly never see Menzo taking his time in possession. When he has the ball, he throws it out to the man furthest away from him. Sometimes you can cut out four opponents that way.

'I used to be just a defender. Now I'm part of the team. Until I got injured, I had more self confidence than I've ever had before. You can't be young to do my job. When you're young, you're keen, you want to do more than simply do your job, you want to score goals. Maybe Johan didn't do it on purpose, but Muhren, Wouters and I are the oldest. My priorities in the team are defending and organising.'

This season, Danny Blind, bought from Sparta Rotterdam, plays on the right side of defence, with Sonny Silooy on the left and Peter Boeve as the reserve defender in case of injuries and suspensions. Their job is to cover the space in which they play. They're not allowed to go into attack together.

Sonny Silooy on his position: 'I must also make sure Arnold Muhren plays well. I have to give him cover. On the left, I can't go forward as often as on the right because Arnold can't run around as much as Jan Wouters.'

Peter Boeve, left back until last year and now reserve, about the changes under Johan Cruyff: 'The left back used to have to go forward as much as possible. It was called modern football. That's how we kept the field wide. Now the backs have to be more 'pinched', as Johan calls it, to pay more attention to the centre. That's also because Ajax plays a lot through the centre of the field.'

Two players are certain starters in midfield: Arnold Muhren on the left and Jan Wouters on the right.

Wouters: 'In principle, Muhren and I should stay behind the ball. When Muhren has the ball on the left and Rijkaard comes into midfield, then I move from the right to the middle. If I stayed in my "zone", there would be a dangerous hole behind Rijkaard. When I have the ball, Muhren goes into the middle. When a cross comes from the wing, Johan wants Arnold and I to keep the pressure on the opposition by waiting at the edge of the penalty area to collect the balls that are cleared.'

For that one position of central midfielder, Johan Cruyff has three candidates. In order of appearance, they are: John Bosman, Aron Winter and Arnold Scholten. Bosman is also Marco van Basten's cover as striker and Winter is the shadow for Ronald Spelbos.

John Bosman on the central midfielder's position: 'Cruyff is always very keen that the distance between the centre forward – in this case Marco – and myself should never be more than five to ten metres so that when an attack is stopped you don't give the opposition more space for a counter attack. When we attack, I also have to stay near Marco so that he can play short balls back to me. What I find difficult is that I have to watch where the ball is, know what's going on behind me and also follow whatever Marco does. I have to anticipate Marco's movements, which requires a lot of concentration. Because I'm originally a striker myself, I often want to play too far forward. But I'm not someone they have to play the ball to. I don't have to ask for the ball, I have to create space. In the last couple of games for the national team, that was a problem with Gullit, who also plays in central midfield but who wants the ball a lot for himself.'

Bosman on his defensive tasks: 'You have your own man and you have to keep your eye on him. But at a certain moment, there's a signal from behind, usually from Rijkaard, and then I shift to the man playing just in front of the opponents' defence. Marco takes their last defender and Rijkaard takes his man in midfield. That's how we try to make sure the other side can't do anything.'

When he plays in central midfield, Winter, because of his mobility, has to play more by intuition than Bosman: 'I have to try to win the ball. When I have the ball, I have to make a move and create panic in the opposition.'

When Winter plays as a central defender, he and Rijkaard sort out between themselves which of them will take responsibility for the opponents' central striker and which will join the attack. In that position, he is freer than Spelbos. In the first Dutch Cup game against FC Groningen, things went badly wrong, demonstrating what Cruyff has always said – that if one or two players don't concentrate 100 per cent and fail to do their jobs properly, the system doesn't work well.

In attack, the key characteristic under Cruyff is that Ajax play with two real wingers: Johnny van't Schip or Dennis Bergkamp on the right and, since the departure of De Wit and Allister Dick, Rob Witschge or Van't Schip on the left. After the game, the chalk of the touchline has to be visible on their boots. For 17-year-old Dennis Bergkamp, May was such an important month: 'I have some problems with physics, but I think I'll pass the final exams for college.'

John van't Schip: 'The outside right has to beat his man, keep his eyes on him, keep the field wide, with a cross from left to inside, "closing in" as Johan says. He asks me to also coach the players I play with: Marco or Blind. I've learned that you shouldn't play for yourself but for the team. That's what Johan taught us. Everyone thinks first about their own job. The difference with the outside left is that on the right you play more in combination with Blind, Wouters and me, if I'm there. On the left, you have to deal with Arnold, who almost never goes wide. So, on the left I always have to make a move first, and, if I can't, I play it back to Arnold. If something's wrong with Arnold, Johan sees me as the left midfielder.'

The centre forward, until the end of the season, is Marco van Basten: 'When Rijkaard has the ball, one of the main tasks – apart from negotiating with the groundsman – is to make the pitch as long as possible so that the players behind me have some space. If I'm one-on-one with a defender, if there's only one defender in front of me, then I have to be in a position where they can play it long to me. If there are still two defenders in front of me, someone else has to be available. We have to make use of them.

'When their keeper or defender has the ball, I have to make sure along with the left and right wingers that they can't build anything. We either have to intercept the ball or put them under such pressure that they just kick the ball upfield in panic.'

Everyone involved in tactics at Ajax talks about the 'third man.' Instead of the normal one-two combination, Johan Cruyff wants the possibility of a second player pass to. When Bosman drops off Van Basten and offers himself immediately to the left, Wouters should run free on the right. Wouters is the third man, and that third man is, in practice, hard to defend against. The third man confuses people.

Van Basten has a nice explanation for Cruyff's tactical insight: 'Johan is so technically perfect that even as a boy he stopped being interested in that aspect of the game. He could do everything when he was 20. That's why he's been very interested in tactics since he was very young. He sees football situations so clearly that he was always the one to decide how the game would be played.'

Nieuwe Revu
May 1987

Chapter 11

THE CUP OR I'LL DESTROY YOU! MARCO VAN BASTEN ON JOHAN CRUYFF

The name of the greatest Dutch footballer after Johan Cruyff is Marco van Basten. Unfortunately, they only worked for a very short time together – but did so very intensively. Hence this interview which Van Basten had promised a number of times, because something happened at Ajax. And just before he left for Milan, Marco van Basten came to us with the story himself: a story about him and Johan Cruyff.

The Dutch Milanese have left. For the first time in years, since Gianni Rivera, they're bringing AC Milan back to the top in Italy together. Ruud Gullit, at 24, is near the peak of his potential. In the last couple of years he has proved that on his own he can make a team into champions. Marco van Basten isn't at that level yet, but when everything comes together he'll get there. Van Basten is only 22 and has just lost a season, in spite of winning top prizes. In the next couple of years Van Basten's talents will be judged on their true value. Van Basten, Gullit and, realistically, Frank Rijkaard should play every week in front of 50,000 fans and not for an audience of 7,000 complainers and a handful of real football lovers. The departure of Gullit and Van Basten for Italy will be a loss for Dutch fans and for Dutch football.

Nonsense. You can hardly say that for the last couple of months Holland has gone en masse to see its two top footballers. Secondly, in the years to come, Gullit and Van Basten, if they want to, can do and are allowed to play for the Dutch national team, and will be far more valuable than they have been so far.

Where in France did Platini play when France became European champions in 1984? Where was Maradona playing when Argentina won the 1986 World Cup? And what's the name of the winners of the 1982 World Cup?

We'll miss Marco van Basten. But what happened to him before the crucial PSV-Ajax league game on Sunday April 5th? Didn't Ajax want to win the game? Were they saving themselves for their European game in Zaragoza four days later?

'Something happened, but I'll only tell you after Athens if we get to the final,' said Van Basten in Zaragoza. And after Athens, after Ajax had won the Cup Winner's Cup, he said: 'I'll try to tell you after the Dutch Cup final.'

Those finals have been played, so Van Basten can talk.

'Against PSV I really played very badly. Just beforehand I went to the Amsterdam physiotherapist Richard Smith for my injury. The cure wasn't quick enough, in my opinion. In the press, Richard Smith came across in such a way that I thought: he might be a miracle doctor. He treated me so intensively that afterwards I was shattered. That's what he told me. He said: 'I knew what I was doing'. I was totally shattered on the Sunday of the PSV-Ajax game. From the Thursday until the day before the game they were treating me. After the treatment, I felt like you could kick me around like a little ball and unfortunately that was the week of the PSV-Ajax game. I told Johan about it and all he said was that I shouldn't be treated on the day of the game.'

– Because Cruyff never liked hours of treatment on his body?

'That's true, but I was also thinking myself that it was just taking too long to get better. And I also didn't know I was going to be so tired from those treatments. But unfortunately I was.'

– Why didn't Cruyff substitute you in the game against PSV?

'I don't know. Maybe he hoped that at one moment the ball might bounce in off my boot by mistake.'

– Because of that game against PSV, Cruyff's style of not interfering and Ajax's whole way of playing in that game, we got the impression Ajax used it as a practice match.

'That's how it came across to me, though I didn't live it that way. But you're right. We weren't sharp in that game, we didn't play to anything like our maximum potential. At that time, I had discussions with Johan about my ankle, my behaviour and my attitude on the pitch. He demanded that I justify my star status on the pitch. He said I should be tougher and not complain so much about my ankle. Johan said I should play through the pain for once – that was the best medicine. But the pain remained. After Malmo, I played for a month with painkillers because I couldn't function otherwise. I hardly trained. I just couldn't do it. And Johan didn't like my attitude. He said I was taking it too easy. I didn't want to do it, in his eyes. I don't think Johan understood how I experienced that pain. Until about four weeks ago, I stayed under the care of Smith and I made progress, but then it was such an important period with so many important matches that I said I didn't have time for it. I said let's postpone it for a while.'

– When did Cruyff get involved?

'At the beginning of April, after PSV. The problems with my ankle just continued. At one point I said I really couldn't play and Johan called me in to see him. Pim Van Dord, the Ajax physiotherapist, was also there. Johan said: "I'll tell you what. From now on you only have to play six games. The Cup Winners' Cup semi-final, home and away against Zaragoza and the final. That's three games. And the semi-final and final of the Dutch Cup. That's five, or six if we have to replay the semi-final. You have to make sure we win these two cups. That's what I demand from you." He said very clearly: "I give you a lot of freedom with your injury and in return I demand that you bring us the European and Dutch cups. Your attitude is also my concern". It was very, very hard: bang, bang!'

– So the league didn't count any more?

'No, that went out of his head in April. He was explicitly demanding, especially for the European cup. Later, when things became more exciting in the league, I offered to play again in the league. I wanted to play against FC Utrecht four days before the Cup Winners Cup Final because we were equal on points with PSV and we hadn't won anything yet. I asked Johan on the Thursday if I could play against Utrecht. He said: no, you'll play on Wednesday. The league didn't really count for him. That was clear from everything.'

– And if Ajax hadn't won the Cup Winners' Cup, what would have happened to you?

'When we made that agreement at the beginning of April, he said: "If you don't bring us those cups, then I'll destroy you! Be sure of that: I'll demolish you!" I think he would have started with lots of criticism of me in the press: he's a weak guy, weak attitude, he let's you down. Of course, I didn't think about that when I scored that goal in the European final in Athens, but later I was extra happy because Johan can demolish you, you can count on that.'

Nieuwe Revu
June 1987

Chapter 12

I JUST WANT TO BE INVOLVED – HOW TON HARMSEN GOT RID OF JOHAN CRUYFF

After his tumultuous departure from Ajax to Barcelona in 1973, after his dramatic farewell as a player in 1983, on January 4th 1988, Cruyff, again unwillingly, even though it was his choice, was forced to say goodbye to his great love.

On Saturday January 9th, we talked to Johan Cruyff at his home in Vinkeveen. We had an agreement. We would convey and confront him with the Ajax board's grievances against him.

– Chairman Ton Harmsen, in particular, blames you for trying to get involved in everything and for not listening to him.

'That was my mistake, he's right. That's why I asked for a job description. What happened? Three transfers went wrong because they took too long. Then I'm the victim when I get involved. Trying to get Cyrille Regis from Coventry City took more than a month.'

– In a manner of speaking, you are someone who's always got an answer even if they ask you about Spain's membership of the EEC.

(deadly serious) 'I like to think about things. But again, I know I'm a busybody. That's why I was so happy that in Hamburg the board said they would draw up a job description, which would mean that I wouldn't have to stick my nose into anything other than football.'

– The board accuses you of not being businesslike. And again they talk about mistakes you made in business about 10 years ago.

'That's really below the belt when they refer to those things. They forget one thing, that I'm not a businessman. Ten years ago I got involved in things I didn't understand. Now I get involved in things I do understand.. Was it businesslike that they allowed a talent as great as Van Basten to leave for only 1.7 million guilders, that every young player before I arrived was given a limited transfer fee if he demanded it? Now it's different, with Menzo, with Wouters, with Winter. That's what I took care of.'

– You put your nose in so many things that in training once you told your assistant Tonnie Bruins Slot: make sure there's no roast beef today, only ham and cheese.

'Do we have to talk on that level? Is that how they talk about me in the members' meeting? Please. Those are the things I absolutely never get involved with, the hotels, the food. I stick my nose into so many things that the food in the Hotel Duinoord, where we always prepare for our European games, is exactly the same as it was 20 years ago.'

– You wanted to get rid of trainer Spitz Kohn on December 1st?

'That's right, but of course it wasn't for no reason. He wasn't functioning, he didn't work in the team. No matter how difficult, I then had to make a decision. And it was very hard. But isn't it below the belt to tell you about it? Because when the treasurer said he was looking for another solution, I said OK, go ahead. I didn't fight that did I? What's happening now is that the board only tells you half the truth. That's a pity.'

– The De Boer brothers were going to sign a boot contract with Lotto. You would have been involved with that.

'Another half truth, because it's being suggested I have my own sportswear brand and I want them to play wearing mine. Point one – they've had no offer from my company. Point two – I told those boys: at the moment still money isn't important to you. Why don't you test all the brands and wear the boots you like best? Adidas, Puma, whatever. And when you know which suits you best, take a decision then. I had this myself. I know what it's like to be messed around as a young player.

'Point three– I think you have to poke your nose into these things because boots are the only material thing a footballer has to worry about. They're the instruments he has to use to achieve things. If the boots don't fit well and the player has problems with his ankles or his feet, then I get involved in the consequences.

'But I don't think the board told you that those boys were not allowed to take the contract home. They had to sign it there immediately. I told the boys they should always take a contract home and get it looked at by a lawyer. Nine times out of ten, those young guys will sign a two year contract, with an option for half a year to cancel it. And at that point I only advised them to change that clause in the contract so that, although the firm has to, the player doesn't have to stay for half a year before he wants to walk away from it. I don't know a single player who remembers a contract with terms like that.'

– You're supposed to give too many stories to *De Telegraaf* because you write a column for them, so you have a commercial bond . . .

'I have a good relationship with *De Telegraaf*, at least with a couple of the guys in the sports department. But they shouldn't moan about that because the club used to have a very bad relationship with the paper and because of me the relationship has improved. The board was very happy. They shouldn't start moaning. By the way, when the ticket sales for Ajax-Porto weren't going well, they asked me and Jaap de Groot, who always writes the column, if we wanted to market the game. And I've never said anything negative about Ajax in that column. Now that I've left, the column's being used against me.'

– Still, it's strange that Ajax should negotiate with Racing Paris about Sonny Silooy and that because of those negotiations Arie van Eijden has to make up a lie about a friendly game while you casually give the story away to *De Telegraaf*.

'I didn't tell them. No really I didn't.'

– You wanted to buy Madjer from FC Porto. Harmsen says you must have been out of your mind if you thought you could get him.

'I don't think so. I spoke to Madjer in August during the Barcelona tournament. I was sort of an idol to him and he was very charmed by our football. In Barcelona I didn't talk about a transfer. On the day of the Dutch cup game between Ajax 2 and Sparta, I told the board about the possibility. I worked on it for a week. I spoke to the chairman of Porto. I just told them that after the loss of Van Basten and Rijkaard we wanted to buy someone who would excite the crowd. It should have remained a secret, but the next day it was in the paper.'

– In which paper?

'The *Algemeen Dagblad* and *Het Parool*. The result was that Bayern Munich went with a delegation and bought Madjer for next season. I still think he could have come to Ajax if our interest hadn't been leaked. We had a limited fund for transfers of $800,000. I don't know about his salary – that would have been a matter for negotiation between Madjer and the board. I'm not saying we definitely could have done it, but at least we should have tried.'

– Who leaked Ajax's interest in the Swede Peter Larsson?

'I did. I admit that. I tried to call the treasurer Klaas Bakker on Monday and I tried very intensively to call the chairman, but I couldn't reach him. I left messages everywhere with my number where he could reach me, but he didn't call me. That's why I had to read it in the paper on Tuesday. I can well imagine that the chairman was angry. His anger was justified.'

– Because you were impatient, you increased the offer for Larsson to IFK Gothenburg too quickly from $500,000 to $750,000. That wasn't businesslike.

'First of all, $750,000 is not $2 million, as *de Volkskrant* wrote. It's not even 1.4 million guilders. And is that a lot for such a good player, especially when you got 2.5 million guilders for Silooy?'

– Your business partner Hans Muller said last year that you might be able to get a percentage of the extra money you could get for players, but you really didn't want to do that.

'Yes, you can't do that, it brings nothing but misery. Think about it! Maybe that's one of the reasons why a lot of people don't like me. Because, look back with me. I came to Ajax three times. Each time I came the club had no money, and each time I left the club was full of money. Because even now there's lots of money. That's how bad I've been.'

Nieuwe Revu
January 1988

Chapter 13

I'VE ALWAYS HAD AN EYE FOR THE LOWER RANKS – TWO MONTHS UNEMPLOYED

On March 19th 1988, we made our last 'Between Barend and Van Dorp' programme on Saturday afternoon for VARA Radio. Johan Cruyff, who had been unemployed for two months, was our final guest.

– Johan Cruyff, a hearty welcome. We're a little bit nervous.

'I can see that, but you haven't invited me for nothing, so I'll try to help you.'

– It's our last broadcast. Were you nervous when you trained for the last time?

'As a player you mean?'

– No, your last time as a trainer with Ajax, two months ago.

'Yes, but I'm not going to retire. I'll just take a rest for six months.'

– We're not going to take our pensions just yet either. Were you nervous? Did you know at the time that you were leading your last training session that morning?

'I don't want to get into that. I've been a little cleverer by not getting involved in that situation.'

– You don't like saying goodbye do you? There's always something about your goodbyes.

'Yes, they're just moments, something always happens that hasn't been planned. And by the way, goodbyes are often unplanned. And then you get into strange situations.'

– What do you do all day now that you have nothing to do?

'I don't have nothing to do. I've just spent a long period where all I've done is football. That means everything else has been left behind, so I just do a bit more of that.'

– Are you going out for nice dinners in the evening? Or do you go to the beach with your wife Danny? Do you give yourself an extra hour in bed? Or read Mills and Boon novels?

'I do all those things, though maybe Mills and Boon is exaggerating a little. You're right about the other things, but you've forgetting something: the children play a lot of sport and I've had to give up a lot of things in that respect over the last couple of years, so the weekends are full.'

– So what do you do at the weekend?

'Well, this morning, I drove my daughter's horse somewhere. And then I had to drive back here like a crazy man and later I'll pick up the horsebox again.'

– And you sit behind the wheel?

'Behind the wheel, yes.'

– Do you need a permit to drive a vehicle like that?

'No, it's not a big thing, I'm allowed to drive.'

– Is it a small horse?

'Yes'

– So you do a lot in the horse world now?

'Yes, and that's a sport in itself. And that's nice too.'

– There was a time, when we were young, when that was a posh world we looked up to. Do you find that now?

'Yes, but from the outside a lot of things look like that. And maybe in certain way it is. But they start at the bottom as well. They start in the stables and the horses from those stables and whatever. It's a world in itself, like in football or any sport.'

– And then you understand it so you say to your daughter, or to someone else: no you should take that jump like this, or like that. That's how you are, eh?

'What I did was spend the first couple of months standing next to the trainer to listen to what he was saying. And then you see a whole lot of parallels, because every sport consists of similarities. So then you notice a few little things.'

– Because we called on Thursday night and you were at the Indoor Horse Show in Brabant . . .

'I was at the Brabant Indoor, yes.'

– Then you're really watching who's doing what wrong. Before it happens you see . . .

'No, that's an exaggeration. At that level, it's only for pleasure, as it is with the riders. But of course you have your favourites.'

– Who's your favourite?

'There's a couple of boys I know well. And in the meantime I meet a lot of them. One I see a lot is Sven Harmsen.'

– The son of your ex-chairman?

'Yes.'

– And you get on with him?

'Does one thing have anything to do with the other? And there are others: Albert Voorn, Emile Hendrix, just name them. Wout Jan van der Schans, they're nice guys, nice people who achieve at a high level.'

– But you say: I'm standing next to my daughter's trainer. So first you stand there for a couple of months, and then you'll really get involved?

'Well, not getting involved, but at least you know what they're talking about.'

– So what's showjumping about?

'What's it about? Jumping over the fences.'

– But if we asked you what football's about, you wouldn't say 'to put the ball in the net'.

'Yes, but in this case there are a lot of details you have to deal with. And I'm not going to go into that. But one of the most important things is that you come out well – so just before the jump you have to be in the right place and from there you can get over.'

– Does it worry you when your daughter has to jump one of those 1.2 metre high fences?

'No.'

– And are you tense? Are you very nervous or very calm when your daughter's riding?

'Very calm'

– Really?

'Yes.'

– And your wife?

'Very tense.'

– And if she hits the fence?

'Yes, that's a pity because you wait the whole day for just a couple of minutes. One round only takes a minute and a half. And then it's a pity if you hit the fence. But that's part of the sport.'

– When you leave Vught on a Sunday, on a misty evening, with a horse behind you in the car, what do you think about?

'At that moment I'm my daughter's father. That's how it should be.'

– Is it nicer than being a trainer? If you could choose, wouldn't you prefer to do that in the coming years?

'Well one is a job, the other is another situation. It's private, a hobby. Let's put it that way.'

– This morning you took the horsebox and drove your daughter. And then straight after the broadcast, you'll go back. And this evening at six, you'll get the car out again. And tomorrow morning?

'Tomorrow morning, I'll get up early with Jordi, my son, because he has to play football. Then I'll watch him.'

– And what will you do tomorrow afternoon?

'That depends on the weather. If it's raining, we won't feel like going anywhere. But mostly you meet all kinds of friends and acquaintances at the game and make plans from there.'

– Then perhaps you'll go and watch another game? Maybe an amateur or youth game?

'Yes, I could.'

– Not Ajax?

'No, I won't go and watch Ajax.'

– Why not?

'It's too painful. The way people normally play and the way they've been functioning lately. For whatever reason. I just think it's a shame.'

– How do you come to that conclusion? Because of what you read in the papers or what you see on television?

'You see it soon enough.'

– So what hurts you precisely?

'What precisely? That people play at a certain level, that it's not going too well anymore, and the reason is obvious.'

– And that is?

'Nine out of ten times it's sort of the way they stand on the pitch.'

– 'Sort of'!

'Well, otherwise you have to pick out individuals, so it's better just to say it's sort of the way they stand on the pitch.'

– No it's not. It's sort of being allowed to talk, sort of being allowed to think, sort of the way they stand on the pitch.'

'Yes, but then everyone will know what I'm talking about. That they should at least have some automatic parts to the way they play.

Someone receives the ball from somewhere and automatically plays it to someone else. At that point someone has to be there. And if that doesn't happen automatically, if you don't run forward, if you have to stop and watch, then you're often too late.'

– Last Monday there was a piece in *De Telegraaf* in which Peter Post (the great cycling coach) said: 'I'd like to go to Feyenoord, but only with Johan Cruyff, because he has to stay in Holland'. Do you want to do that?

'Well that's a very nice compliment. We haven't had any contact before so I just read it too. It's just that the person who said that has really done something himself – even though it was in cycling – but then maybe it's all the same anyway.'

– But what did you think when you read it? Or did you get a call telling you that you were going to be in there?

'No. He spoke about a certain way of organising things. That's also the basis from which he works.'

– Would you be able to function in the kind of framework Post envisages –- lots of sponsors, some sort of council to control things on which Post will eventually sit too. Would you like to work at Feyenoord?

'In the first place, Peter Post and I are good friends. We both know what we're talking about. Over the years, we've had a lot respect for each other and you can see that here. We're mainly talking about changing an organisation and that means a board to ensure that the quality is high enough and makes sure everything goes well, or whatever you call that. And for the rest it should be professionals who work there.'

– But, doctor, can you tell us if you want to go there?

'I don't know. I think maybe we should talk. And then we can see what it's all about. And by the way, we might want to, but of course there are lots of other people who would also have to want it.'

– We can remember we were very emotional during that broadcast years ago. It was definite that you were going to leave Ajax as a player, you were going to play at Feyenoord. Your son was eight years old. It was very difficult for him because he's an Ajax boy through and through.

'You don't know. In the first place, he's a bit older.'

– Yes, but maybe he's become even more of an Ajax player.

'We'll have to wait to see how he reacts. On the other hand, because he's a bit older, he's seen what's happened over the last couple of months, the last six months. Also, he doesn't keep his ears closed. Sometimes when we talk about it at home, he catches a little bit. So if you look at it that way, he must have grown up a little. But there is always going to be a question mark on how he reacts.'

– But you must have a sense of how he feels about it.

'I think the biggest emotional problem lies in the fact that he has a father who used to decide what happened at Ajax technically, and he has a hard time from others because of that. So let's say it nicely like that.'

– You wanted to say: 'who was pushed out'.

'No. Well, yes. There are people in the amateurs' section where he goes every day, and that's a problem for him too.'

– I think for you and the whole Cruyff family the biggest problem is that you've been so attached to Ajax and that part of the family has been forced out. That's very difficult emotionally, not just for you.

'Yes, clearly. There's no question mark about that.'

– So how are you at home? Do you talk about it, do you explain? Can you accept it and forget it all?

'Yes, of course you try to explain it in a reasonable manner, not emotionally, especially with the children. On the other hand, it's such that you have to perform at Ajax. So I'll always be nice in that respect. There's always a "but": will they get back at my son? I think I would find that very hard. I don't know what would happen then.'

– Do you think that's a danger?

'I have no idea, but I know of course that anything can happen.'

– You were an exceptional coach at Ajax but you left at quarter to three every afternoon. Why?

'Since they were at school, I've always made a habit of picking up the children at all times. And that means that my day ended at quarter to three when I went to get them. And if I worked in the evening, then I left at six.'

– And that's sacred for you?

'Yes. If you make one exception, there'll be more. So I never made exceptions.'

– Lately, you've often been asked if you're going to Barcelona. And you usually answer: well, I don't know. But you have to be a little clearer. When are you going to Barcelona? And what do you think about it?

'The question is such that the only answer you can give is "I don't know". Namely, the point is that if, at a certain moment, you go to Barcelona . . .'

– What has been discussed between you and Barcelona so far?

'A couple of things. On one hand there have been a couple of problems about a financial matter. That's been dealt with. So that leaves a question about whether both of us are in. They think it's just me. And that all has to be solved first.'

– So that hasn't been solved between you and Barcelona?

'At the moment, no.'

– Good. That's one problem.

'That's one, and before you start thinking about the second, if you follow the way I think, then you have to solve number one.'

– Do you think they want to solve number one?

'Yes, it's all words, but I think they do.'

– Good, then number two: because you've been at Barcelona once before?

'Yes, that was one case. Football automatically comes into the conversation. And then you see that those people have a lot of problems. It's functioning very badly.'

– Because no one comes to watch them.

'That's an automatic consequence.'

– How many people watched you when you played at Barcelona?

'Always between 90,000 and 100,000.'

– It's now between 20,000 and 25,000. Have you discussed the role of the coach at Barcelona?

'Obviously at a certain moment, they asked how I felt about it.'

– The chairman?

'No, the vice-chairman. And then I told them how I thought I could function well. Because it's obviously hopeless if you end up in the same situation that they're in now.'

– And how do you want to function there?

'To be in charge of the technical and footballing side.'

– And buying players?

'Yes, that's automatically part of it; I have to be the one who picks the team.'

– Selling?

'That means that you have to look at the team at the moment. There are too many who don't function, who have to leave.'

– And the vice chairman: do you have a father-son relationship with him?

'No. I'll never get there with him.'

– You'll take care there.

'Yes.'

– Once but never again?

'Let's say it's self-protection.'

– Have you learned from the father-son relationship, the cult that Harmsen built, that he considered you as his son?

'Yes. In hindsight, it's a problem when you've been through so many things, that somehow you're still doubting. You can't say that someone's been acting for two and a half years. It's very difficult. Or I have to be so stupid that I don't understand anything.'

– He was your 'father' when it suited him.

'Well, that might be true but my character is such that I can't accept it easily.'

– You've had difficulties with that. Have you solved it for yourself: the kind of role you played in the father–son relationship?

'You'll never find out. What's been very clear is that he's always been very badly informed.'

– But he could have talked to you.

'That's what you would normally think.'

– But it's nice that you get on very well with his son.

'Yes, always.'

– What is the next conversation with Barcelona?

'Well, we call once in a while and ask what the situation is and we never get further than point one.'

– You love to make things mysterious. You don't want to say you're going to Barcelona?

'No, if it was going to happen, I'd say so, yes. One reason I'd like to do that is for clarity. We're always in a ridiculous panic situation because it's always "sign today – it should have been yesterday." We have to think about schools, moving, everything. It's a gigantic mess. It means you want to know what the situation is soon.'

– When do you want to know for yourself that you definitely want to go there?

'Let's say you take April 1 as the date.'

— That's very soon.

'Yes, well it has to be.'

— Point one is still not solved. If point one isn't solved, the financial question.

'Then automatically point two won't start.'

— Then it won't happen and you won't go. And they don't want to sort out point one?

'Yes, but there are all sorts of complications on their side. I don't know precisely what but I don't get too involved in that because where there's a will, there's a way. So they have to really want me badly.'

— You once said about the chairman, Nunez: 'I never want to work with him again'.

'I never said it like that. It's been taken out of context. I always condemned the situation itself. And I still don't like it. A chairman who has so much influence over buying and selling is directly involved in the technical side. Any trainer who has to work there will always be in trouble. So I said in that situation I never want to work there.'

— Have you talked to him, to Nunez?

'No.'

— But you'd have to talk about this wouldn't you?

'Yes, well, I think the man does understand that.'

— And how high do you think the chances are that you'll go to Barcelona?

'I have no idea. It's like this nine out of 10 times. It's either 100 per cent or not even one per cent.'

– But you want to?

'Yes, but there is also doubt over the longer term. What is "want to"? Of course you know you're going to get involved in a hornets' nest. The longer it takes, the more you think. And then you want to make sure that so many things are arranged that you say, well I'll have a pretty good chance.'

– And at home – because for you that's very important – do they want to go to Barcelona?

'In the first instance, they'd prefer to stay here. But the situation is not as it was, so then at a certain moment you have to choose. There's a couple of negative factors normally: school, children, to name some. But because they go to an international school, those sorts of problems don't exist.'

– Friends? Girlfriends?

'Yes, but it's not too bad for the children. Five minutes after they arrive, they'll have new friends, without forgetting the old ones. I don't believe that's a real problem. Apart from being too far from home, of course.'

– Wouldn't you rather go to Feyenoord than Barcelona? You can stay here.

'That depends on a piece of construction.'

– No, not 'a piece of construction'! Why don't you listen to us for once, it's good for your career. We might accept it if you were a player talking about the shape of your team on the field. But not 'a piece of construction'. Just a right winger, a left winger, a right back and a solution'.

'No, no. Organisation.'

– But in your heart – even though you might find it difficult at Feyenoord as an Ajax man – you know you could go to Feyenoord, because then you could stay here?

'Yes, I don't know. I think in this situation, you have to make an instinctive choice. I can never judge things beforehand.'

– When you're in bed at night do you think what you'll be doing next year?

'At home I'm an optimist. That means that when I'm lying in bed I see all beautiful things. But when I get up . . .'

– But what kind of beautiful things do you see?

'Like Peter Post said: there's a big stadium, it's full again, you see all kinds of nice things happening. But then you get up and you look at reality and you immediately see all the negative things.'

– What would you prefer to do next year?

'I don't want to talk about preferences because that can only disappoint. Also, the next club that takes you says: yes, but we're second choice. Then you get those stories again. So I don't want to start that.'

– Johan, we've spoken about a lot things this year. There's been a lot of criticism of you and it would be cowardly not to talk about it. For example, you have to learn that you have to deal with people who play football much worse than you and are not able to think about football as well as you.

'Yes, that's looking for something. If someone comes with a criticism, then I'll be the first to listen because you recognise it quickly. That's something that at a given moment takes on a life of its own. When you play football for 20 years and the outside world says – and I think so myself – that you've been one of the best, then it means you've played for 20 years with people who are less good. How can you not pay attention to those who play less well?'

– So you've always paid attention to those who play less well?

'I've always paid attention to them. And the nicest thing about that is that they're the ones you can take to the top. Look at Spelbos in the last couple of years. He had a lot of quality anyway in my opinion. But in the last two years, he showed qualities that no-one expected.'

– So what did you teach him?

'I didn't teach him anything. He already had those qualities. When he gets the ball, he has good judgement, good functional technique and he can pass the ball over 40 metres. You only have to make sure there's someone there to receive it. So it appears that he has many more qualities than people thought. I think that's the nicest example.'

– Spelbos in particular is having a bad time at the moment. He's not playing well, he doesn't know what to do.

'Yes, but it might not necessarily be true about him playing badly. The passes don't get there any more. That means, for whatever reason, there's no-one in the space where he's trying to play them. That means he has to take an extra stride and that means he gets into a situation that he doesn't control.'

– And that's why you don't want to watch any more. You don't want to see how difficult it is now for Spelbos at Ajax?

'That's one of the reasons, yes. The problem with Ajax was that there were too many players with big transfer fees. If you won the European Cup with a team like that, four or five would leave at one go. So it's better to lose one or two a year, because they're going to leave anyway. That's one of the reasons why I had problems with the board. I said: I'm not going to keep building a completely new team every two or three years. You've got to get rid of those fixed contracts. If someone's contract finishes at the end of the year, he can sell himself for a fixed transfer sum, and he's busy with that from September. Are you going to work well with that the whole year? It leads to confrontations with Vanenburg, Van Basten or whoever. Also Rijkaard. He started to think in August about how he was going to get away at the end of the year. That's all well and good as long as he achieves.'

– Can you be yourself?

'I think in all those years – those 20 years – I've had two personalities: one for home and one for the outside world.'

– Is that terrible? That you're completely different for the outside?

'It's automatic. I don't even think about it much.'

– When you're interviewed, do you often think you're going to say a lot and then you don't say so much?

'When I'm interviewed I'm often serious or, really, always serious. If you're not like that, you're going to get all sorts of things confused and then you're going to have them rebound on you. Privately I can laugh a lot, I have a sense of humour, I tell jokes. But that's the way it has to be.'

Between Barend & Van Dorp
March 1988

Chapter 14

YOU HAVE TO DIE BY YOUR OWN IDEAS – COACH IN BARCELONA

I n January 1989 we visited Johan Cruyff for the first time as coach and trainer of Barcelona. An interview about Ronald Koeman, Marco van Basten, emotions, Ton Harmsen and God.

'I can't help it if all the papers wrote that from next season I'm going to earn eight million guilders a year. Of course it's not true. I don't even get four million a year. I've learned that you can't be upset about that kind of reporting. We can communicate with the moon, but a simple news item about my contract extension at Barcelona is apparently too difficult. I've no idea how that figure got out. Chairman Nunez can't have said it either because it's just not true. I didn't want my contract extension to be used in the coming president's elections at Barcelona. And I was in a very strong position in the negotiations. Last season it was all miserable and now it's heaven. Last year there were only 25,000 fans and members were giving their tickets to others because they didn't want to go themselves. Yes, that really happened. This year we have 90,000 for every home game. That's why I was in a powerful position. But I don't think you should abuse that. I told the Barcelona board that I was happy with my work, with my working climate and I wanted to earn the same as this year, and that's a lot already. Because I thought it was fashionable, I've asked for another four per cent, being the rise in the cost of living. At one o'clock there's a story about what I earn in a Spanish newspaper and by five past one, ten correspondents have sold it to other papers, because an item like that apparently costs money. And the journalists call me greedy! When I told my father-in-law that I'd extended my contract for the same amount I earn now, he said: "If I was your business agent I'd be ashamed." He's the one who says if someone wants to pay you four million you have to get four million.'

– So you could earn much more?

'Much more, also because AC Milan made me an offer in the region of what they're writing about now. My father-in-law went to Milan about two weeks ago, but I didn't want to go.'

'Look around you,' he says as we sit on a wonderful terrace with the sun on our faces on a January weekday as we look out across Barcelona. 'What's missing here now? We're eating outdoors. My wife and children are happy here. We live near the stadium; when Jordi has to train, he can walk. The stables for my middle daughter are around the corner. We love the area, we're 15 minutes from the beach. I'm happy with the club and the club is happy with me. I would be mad to choose somewhere else just for the money. Why should I twist the chairman's arm in negotiations? At the moment, he needs me because everyone in Barcelona wants me to stay. But there will come a time when there will be less of that and then maybe I'll need him. Because every chairman has a black book.'

– What's a black book?

'Everything's in there. The chairmen of clubs like Barcelona are special people. They're used to everyone doing what they say. In that black book they write down all the things you do to them. For example, it might say that the board isn't allowed into the dressing room, though that may have been taken out because that decision has been reversed.

'You should never put a gun to someone's head. If I asked for three or four million guilders a year, I would have paid the bill myself later. More than that, you'll fall one day and I say it's better to die by your own ideas. Let's say you did earn three million a year and the board tells you to do something. With an income like that you're more likely to think: I'd better do it.'

– You haven't signed. Are you going to wait until April 1st, until after the elections for chairman are over?

'No, that has nothing to do with it. We have a verbal agreement.'

– But you had that a year ago with Ajax.

'But for me an oral agreement is binding.'

– So if Michael van Praag, the new chairman of Ajax who is not unknown to you, called you, you'd say . . . ?

'Sorry Michael, for the next two years I'm staying in Barcelona. But I can give him some advice if he wants it because I know Michael and Ajax very well.'

When we drive through Barcelona after our meal, the name of Marco van Basten comes up.

– He still wants to come to Barcelona.

'But will Berlusconi ever want to let him go? I can make an offer but with AC Milan there's no point talking about money because money means nothing to them.'

– We understand that in a manner of speaking, he wants to come to Barcelona to earn less money.

'If he comes here, he'll certainly earn less than at Milan. There's no way they'll pay as much as Milan. But Marco is like me. He's an intuitive footballer. When anyone asks me if there's any current player in whom I recognise myself, I always say Marco. With Marco you never know what he's going to do. He goes left when you expect him to go right, comes inside when it seems he can only go outside. That's what I like. But Marco is also an intuitive, sensitive player. He wants to smell the dressing room. You can't do that with Milan. I think Milanello, the training centre an hour and a half outside Milan, is wonderful, but I wouldn't want to train there. AC Milan always plays away. Players want to sit every day in the same dressing room as where they play their home games. That makes the home game special. Footballers want to see their shirts each day hanging on the same peg as they're going to be for the home game on Sunday. On Friday here they're putting the first post in the ground for a new training centre, something like

Milanello only much closer to the stadium. I told chairman Nunez I don't mind training there occasionally, but in principle I don't like to leave the stadium and your own dressing room. It gives you an emotional bond to the stadium. For me football is emotion. Van Basten is also very sensitive to that.'

— Isn't that a little exaggerated?

'I'm talking about top clubs and in this case I'm not exaggerating. Koeman has been here twice and has tasted the atmosphere. That's been partly decisive in his decision to come here. Because Koeman also cares about things that aren't written about. Footballers care about more than money. Koeman likes the football that I preach about. He's the ideal man at the back, a defender who is good for 15 goals a season in Spain. He can live in that position because I want players like Koeman who can make decisive moves in tiny spaces. I want them to do as little work as possible to save their energy for that one action. There is a development in football currently in which the most creative players – and that's mainly forwards – are the ones who have to run the most. In a team that plays defensively, the distance to goal for an attacker quickly becomes 50 metres. Defenders have to work less because of that and attackers have to run more. Because I play attacking football, my attackers only have to run 15 metres, unless they're stupid or sleeping. That's why I'd like to have Van Basten. I think I'm not your average trainer. Every trainer talks about movement, about running a lot. I say don't run so much. Football is a game you play with your brains. You have to be in the right place at the right moment, not too early, not too late. When my attacker is one-against-one, I always say: "let him do it by himself". Then the players say: "aren't we going to help him?". And I answer: "In the first place, there's a large chance you'll get in his way, and secondly, as a second attacker you'll take a second defender with you and two-against-two is harder than one against one".'

— At the beginning of May 1988 you signed a one year contract with FC Barcelona. You turned down offers from West Germany and France immediately after your emotional leaving of Ajax in January 1988.

'I only signed in May. But at the beginning of March, I asked Tonnie Bruins Slot, my assistant at Ajax, if he wanted to come with me to Barcelona. Tonnie is good at the things I'm bad at. He always writes everything down punctually. I have an office at Barcelona but I'm never there because I don't like paper. Since March, Tonnie has watched about 30 videos because I would never have had the patience. If I need a right-midfielder he looks at three or four possibilities and then I choose between them. He can see in two seconds if someone can play football.'

– You can't?

'Yes, but I don't have the patience to watch those tapes.'

– At Barcelona you also work with the club's long-serving former player Carles Rexach.

'He's known everyone at the club, we know each other well, he's fantastic to work with. The last problems between the board and the players who were staying were solved the night before I started. I always said I don't want to have to deal with anything from the past. The past was filled with hate and envy between almost everyone at the club. On the day I started, there were a number of players who wanted to have fights about the past. I had to tell them that the trainer is the boss in the dressing room, not the players and, however strange it may sound, that was news to them. But at the same time you couldn't blame them because they weren't used to anything else. The conflicts might have been solved but the wounds had not healed. The tension between the players and the board was obvious. On both sides there was a lack of discipline so bad that the board had a sort of meeting room in the dressing room. And I said the words "dressing room" means it's a dressing room. If you want to talk, do it in the office. I said to the board: "if you want to talk to me, I'll come to your office, you don't come to my dressing room". To an outsider it seems explosive, but it's something normal. Maybe in one way Chairman Nunez didn't like it. But in another way, maybe he was happy someone else did the hard work.'

– When you introduced your players to the public, the crowd whistled at your captain Alexanco. Then you defended him in public.

'Yes. Last season the situation had escalated so much that at a certain moment, the players wrote a letter demanding the resignation of the board. Alexanco did nothing except what he had to do as captain. He was the spokesman and that's how he appeared to the outside world. He didn't let his players down; it was his duty. And I can only admire that. That's character. And you know all too well that the messenger gets killed. Not with me: I kept Alexanco as captain and defended the way he behaved. Although he's not a regular first team player any more, he's still a leader, and there's a unity. In principle, everybody does what I want them to do. That's because there are no Dutchmen who, as you start breathing, say: "yes, but . . .".'

– You appear relaxed. You seem to be less suspicious than you normally are, but you still smoke like every great footballer: by scrounging.

'I don't beg. I just want to smoke less and you can only do that if you don't ask for cigarettes. That's why I asked a waiter for a cigarette. If he doesn't have one, that's it. I don't know if I'm more relaxed. Maybe it's because I'm quietly talking to you. It has to do with circumstances. If my son Jordi had to play at Ajax at seven, we'd have to be there at six-thirty and I'd have to leave at six, so I'd have to eat before or after and I was never home before nine. We don't have to do that at Barcelona because he trains five minutes from home.

'More than that, training is as much a pleasure as it was at Ajax. The nicest thing is joining in. When you join in, you can usually see mistakes. And I can show things better than the players can do it, and I see everything better. That makes them respect me. That sounds like arrogant talk, but it's a fact. I'm the boss but, at the same time, I'm a player. I'm more a player than board member. The days I look forward to are Monday, Thursday and Saturday, the days I can join in the little six-a-side games.'

The next day we'll meet again for training at 10.30. 'Since November, we've trained at 10.30. They used to train all year at 10. Incomprehensible. In the winter months you can only feel the sun after 10.

From 10.30 it's nice on the training field. So why not wait until it's 10.30?'

– The press has access to the training field.

Yes. Before the league season started, I had a conversation with the journalists who hang around the first team all day. I gave them a choice: either we can co-operate or we can work against each other. Coaches here normally keep their distance from the press. They train behind closed doors and once a week have an official press conference. That's not my style. I don't have too many secrets. Your paper has to be full every day, I'm there every day for you. But then do right by what I and the players say: don't use those big inaccurate headlines. Write honest stories. Because if there's a sensational headline about a player, for example criticising another player, I'll have to ask the player and the journalist if he said it, I have to listen to tapes and find out who's right. And I don't want to do that.'

– But if a player thinks you're an arsehole and says that, do you want a journalist to write that?

'That's not what I'm talking about. I'm talking about headlines and things that haven't been said. If a player says it, the journalist does his job, does his duty, and then it's a problem between the player and me. Until now it's been fine. I'm not complaining.'

At the Saturday press conference before the game against Espanyol, Cruyff doesn't forget to give the Catalan journalists stories for their Sunday papers. For example, he blames the Catalan clubs for the difficulty he has in finding Catalan players. 'Why do you say that,' asks a journalist. 'Because I want to explain why there are so few Catalan players in our team.' On Nunez's statement that there will be an explosive big signing ('una bomba') before the club elections, Cruyff says: 'I don't want to get involved in any way with the elections. If this has been said because of the elections it's not my problem. I just don't like making announcements about buying. News will be announced when it happens, and at the moment there is no news.'

– About a year ago you resigned from Ajax. Have you ever regretted it?

'Never the decision itself. They said something, they didn't do it and there you go again: you have to die by your own ideas. No matter how much I wanted to stay in Holland and stay at Ajax, if I hadn't done it I would have been slaughtered. Aad de Mos – when he was coach at Ajax – didn't want Schrijvers, Lerby and I to leave at once. It happened. He accepted it and was slaughtered. Within a year he left. I have never kicked from behind, as Harmsen kept on doing. I have only told the truth. I've said before: there is a God. You can't do things you're not allowed to do to people without being punished. They felt the need to hurt me. I've never hit back. There is a God that doesn't allow you to hurt people continuously. Because Harmsen hurt me, so between him and me it can never be right again. Really he's hurt me twice. My son used to play with pleasure for Ajax: he's hurt him twice. If you go too far, as I've said, there is a God, and I'm convinced of it. That's why I don't need to hit back myself. I think Harmsen regrets it now. I think in March he regretted it.

'Looking back, I'm no worse for it. I'm stronger. It's all gone really well and I've been all right, even if I do have a couple of extra grey hairs. Because the first couple of months after being sacked by Ajax weren't nice, especially because we endured it as a family.

'At Ajax they thought they could destroy my reputation. But you can't break something built over 20 years. I have much more prestige than that. They beat me at just one moment. But in the long run the more civilised feelings always win.'

– Apart from the conflict with ex-chairman Harmsen, your misery at Ajax started with the conflict with Rijkaard. Was that conflict necessary?

'After the departure of Van Basten, all the players looked up to Rijkaard. A top team needs a player the others look up to. But the person concerned, for whatever reasons, kept his head down and the other players kept their heads down. I wanted to change that with Frank. And there you go again: die by your own ideas. When Rijkaard couldn't or wouldn't do it, Wouters did it. You need a leader like that who won't accept coming second, not in training, not in the dressing room, not during the match. If number one doesn't do it, then number two has to. At Barcelona it's Alexanco. He doesn't even play but when he says "let's go" everybody goes. No one stays in their seats. That's what you call charisma.'

– It's not unthinkable that next season Van Basten as well as Koeman will play for Barcelona.

'Oh, that would be fantastic. I'd enjoy sitting on the bench so much. If you go by football emotions, Van Basten belongs here. Because of the emotional way I live my football there's only very few clubs I can work for. I can only be a trainer for clubs who want to play football: Barcelona, Ajax, maybe AC Milan, only there I'd have a problem with working outside the stadium. And I never want to work for a club which has a running track in the stadium. For me football is emotion. Without emotion, I can't do it. What if your team played the way many teams play against us – trying to avoid playing football? I'm not tense when I sit on the bench. Sitting on the bench is for me what playing is for the players. It's the highlight of the week. I want to enjoy it there. Imagine being bored on the bench for 38 weeks? I don't even want to think about it. So it's clear I'm not suited to a lot of clubs.'

– To Ajax, to Barcelona, to AC Milan, to AS Roma.

'You didn't understand me. I could never work for AS Roma. They have a running track around their pitch. That's the worst thing there is.'

Nieuwe Revu
February 1989

Chapter 15

BARCELONA'S BIGGEST ENEMY IS THE CLUB ITSELF – CRUYFF, KOEMAN AND THE CRISIS

Only later did we realise that, just before the Legia Warsaw – Barcelona game, we had seen the first signs of the social revolution in Eastern Europe. We not only visited the hard-to-find monument commemorating the Warsaw Ghetto, but also found ourselves caught in a pitched battle as Legia fans demonstrated against every symbol of the Polish authorities.

'Gentlemen, there is no crisis. I'm sorry,' says Carles Rexach, Johan Cruyff's assistant at FC Barcelona at 10.05pm on Wednesday, September 27th. Barcelona have just secured the necessary 1-0 win in the second leg of their first round European Cup Winners' Cup tie in the packed Legia Warsaw Stadium and reached the second round. Five minutes later, an obviously relieved Cruyff tells the ladies and gentlemen of the press that he's been right all along.

In other words, the week started well. But four days later, after a defeat on Mallorca's awful pitch, Warsaw feels like an exception and Cruyff again has to respond to the Spanish journalist's question: 'Three games, three defeats, no goals. Is there still no crisis?'

In Warsaw it seemed that what the Spanish press referred to as a crisis and what Cruyff called 'a logical process', was over. The Tuesday before the Warsaw game, in a modern western hotel, we saw Cruyff with every muscle strained with tension. Not nervous, not insecure, not panicking: just incredibly tense. The evening before the game, with Rexach and two minders, he played dominoes for an hour without speaking. In normal circumstances, Cruyff would freely discuss team tactics and the misery in Poland simultaneously. After two defeats in four league games, weak performances by Ronald Koeman and the Dane Michael Laudrup, who were bought to strengthen the team, and the possibility of being knocked out of Europe after the 1-1 draw in the home game, we saw the toll it was taking on him or so we thought.

– Looking at the results, are you afraid of being fired?

'No. I assume I will finish the two years of my contract. Maybe I'll stay longer. Last week I had a very good talk with the board. But as a coach you never know for sure. It can always happen.'

When, an hour and a half before the Legia-Barcelona game in the Polish capital, we cautiously suggest that he can sometimes appear tense before a match, a classic Cruyff conversation follows:

'I'm not nervous at all.'

– Not nervous. Tense, tenser than usual before a game.

'Why do you say that? I'm not tense either.'

– How about yesterday?

'I wasn't tense yesterday either. Hey, Charlie,' he says to Rexach, 'these Dutchmen keep saying I'm tense. OK. If you say I'm tense, I'm tense. I'm tense. But believe me, a lot of people will have a bad night tonight because we are going to win. Absolutely for sure. Our team is so much better, we can't lose here.'

Second assistant Tonny Bruins Slot: 'Johan and I have never lost a European cup game together. As a coach, Johan only ever lost his first European cup game, with Ajax against Porto. And I wasn't with him then.'

Poland is grey and gripped by change. An ugly, badly-maintained statue is the sole, feeble memorial to the Warsaw Ghetto. Black market money changing is no longer the preserve of taxi drivers, tour guides, waiters and doormen. Next door to the official *bureau de change* where one dollar is worth 1.461 zlotys, the big hotels will give you 8.000 zlotys, the black market rate. With six Polish internationals in their team, Legia–Barcelona, especially after the 1-1 draw in the first leg, is a welcome distraction from a future without hope. The stadium is full about two hours before the game and thousands of people are begging for tickets outside the gates. Two priests accompany Legia, the Polish army team, as they enter the stadium, inspect the pitch and go to the changing room.

The referee Heinz Holzmann from Austria steps onto the well-kept pitch at 7.15. He pretends he hasn't noticed Cruyff, so Cruyff walks over to him. A hearty greeting follows.

Referee: 'We'd like to check the studs 35 minutes before the game'.

'That's when we'll be busy warming up' says Cruyff.

'Shall we make it 40 minutes before the game then?'

'That's fine' says Cruyff 'I'll come and tell you just before we start our warm-up.' The trio of officials walk away from the Spanish technical staff and talk to each other for a moment. Then linesman Wieser runs back to Cruyff. 'After the warm-up, you won't change your boots again, will you?' says the man with the flag.

Barcelona want to fly home immediately after the game so the players can sleep in their own beds. Another hour after the fairly simple victory, at 11.30, everyone is at Warsaw Airport. Unfortunately, only one check-in is open for 150 passengers, and only one person is on the customs desk. At one o'clock, we've all got through except for a blonde woman, who is stopped by a customs officer on account of her large mink coat for which she has no receipt. The customs official says the coat was bought on the trip, but the rich blonde says she got it last year when Barcelona played in Poznan and 'just brought it along' this time. 'Because we knew it would be 25 degrees here as well', laughs one of the players. She has a choice: pay 1.5 million zlotys at the official exchange rate (about $1,000), or leave the coat behind. So at 1.30 we're still waiting to leave.

Ronald Koeman: 'This is the worst thing. Hanging around. I really fancy a cold beer and a hamburger.' Amid loud cheering, a bus finally arrives. The people who have been waiting for an hour and a half for the one border guard sprint for the door. No-one is allowed to get on though. The bus drives away. To our surprise, some people in the waiting room are reading books. Zubizarreta, the fantastic goalkeeper, reads *El Pendulo de Foucault*, Umberto Eco's 'Foucault's Pendulum', no less. He's already read 'The Name Of The Rose'.

We finally land in Barcelona at 4.45 on Thursday morning and get to bed by 5.30. Flying back straight after the game was a good idea . . .

On Thursday, everyone sleeps in. On Friday, after the draw for the second round of the Cup Winners' Cup is announced, two television cameras and about 15 tape recorders ask 16 players and three trainers: 'Anderlecht – what do you think?' Two hundred times we hear the surprising answer: 'They're a strong team – it's a pity we have to meet them so early in the competition'.

'*Gracias*.'

Cruyff is simply not willing to play the game with the press. Stupid questions are stupid questions and he hardly ever gets good ones. When a Spanish television reporter, just before his interview with 'Johan' (as they always call him), asks us for the names of Anderlecht players, Cruyff says: 'please pretend you don't know any, otherwise the interview will last even longer'.

Although Cruyff would deny it if you confronted him, after a year in which he has managed to keep most people in Barcelona happy, he has done it again. Many people support him, but more are against him. What is it that makes Cruyff still controversial after more than 20 years? A Spanish TV journalist, supported by a number of colleagues standing nearby, offered an instant analysis with the heartfelt conclusion: 'Cruyff is crazy! He is always right, always! In other words, he is crazy!' He was certain about it.

We think the answer is simple. Cruyff doesn't annoy journalists on purpose, he just doesn't do anything to make them like him. He doesn't need them and would much prefer it if they didn't need him. He knows where he's going and doesn't want to be followed. He is controversial by definition because he sets trends, unlike 99 per cent of coaches, who follow them. He doesn't know how to kowtow and compromise does not exist in his way of thinking. But when all is said, Cruyff denies the discussions and negative opinions about himself. He just doesn't want to do the daily press conferences any more.

'I don't do them any more, they cost me too much time. At the beginning of the season, I stopped doing press conferences like the one I had on Friday. They cost me two and a half hours every day. Talking to the press is dangerous. You must have super concentration or you make mistakes. And if you make one little slip here, a minute later it's telexed to Holland and every other country. I get a lot of requests for interviews from abroad. Last year I didn't have time for that and now maybe I can. That's why I only do interviews before and after a game and on special occasions like this. Since we often play twice a week, I often have four of those meetings a week. I think that's more than enough.'

– *De Volkskrant*, a newspaper you didn't expect it from, involved your wife and your private life to show you were a bad coach and you wanted to leave this year.

'They just wrote what was in *El Pais*, didn't they? I'm sure they did. I don't care anyway. *El Pais* is a Madrid paper and I had problems with them last year. They feel I don't take them seriously. And I now know how these things work. People who are against me in Holland can always write what *El Pais* says and then say: 'it was in a Spanish paper'. There's one Dutch correspondent – Stolz, I believe – who sits in Madrid and reads one newspaper and then in Holland people think all sorts of things are going on, that I'm for the chop. Because – be honest – why did you come to Warsaw?'

– Last year you had a reasonable relationship with the press

'Better than this year. The relationship is a little troubled, but not with all journalists. I have an interest and that's football. But a lot of people in and around the club have their own interests. I realise that Barcelona's biggest enemy is the club itself.'

– What do you mean?

'That's too deep to go into. At this club so many things are important. For example, there are always people who want to get rid of the chairman. It can be good for them if we have bad results, so they can attack me and the team, which means attacking the chairman indirectly.

– As at Ajax, Barcelona started the season badly after winning the Cup Winners' Cup. You always said you saw that coming. So couldn't you or shouldn't you have avoided it? Isn't that the beauty of coaching?

'Last year we won the European Cup Winners' Cup. That means players who were not used to winning things won something. It wasn't like that at Ajax two years ago. Experience told me that after success, unconsciously, there's a lack of concentration. You want to blame the players, but at the same time you can't really blame them because it's a human reaction. And the problem is worse when you get hit because most people expected success, especially with the arrival of new players Ronald Koeman and Michael Laudrup.'

– As a coach you have to do something to avoid that.

'What? How?'

– That's your problem.

'Tell me what. If it happened on purpose, you could do something, but that's just the problem. It wasn't deliberate. During training, you point out the dangers. You change the way you play, you point it out during a game, you warn, you sit someone next to the players to tell them. And it happens anyway. Julio Salinas, my top scorer, hasn't scored a goal: I couldn't have predicted that. After the first humiliation, people started moaning about my system again. Rubbish. In Poland,

Serna missed one chance. In the first game, he missed five. Is that because of his capacities or the system? Come on. I've had periods like that myself as a player. But I was lucky to have players around me like Henk Groot, Piet Keizer and Sjaak Swart who pointed things out to me. If I kept the ball too much in training, if I played selfishly, they let me know. The two players who could have done that for Barcelona – Alexanco and Bakero – were injured for the first five or six weeks.'

– Koeman isn't playing well. He says that himself. Why did he have to play in midfield in Poland and Majorca?

'Everything at the moment is being done to get results. When results come, peace will return and we'll get our confidence back. Journalists can complain all they want about us buying Laudrup and Koeman, but of the eight goals we've scored, they've made seven of them. Koeman is playing in a team that's not playing well. You can't get a team that's not playing well to eat out of your hand. But it's good for him: it's a good, hard way to learn.'

– But he didn't play well in Poland and Majorca.

'You've seen two games and you have an opinion. You know his qualities and expect things from him. Ronald has a beautiful long pass, but if the other players are not running to get into space, it makes no sense to pass to them. He can only use his qualities if the team gives him a chance. But I'm not worried about that. It will come. And you know what's also happening? The other players are nervous and they give Ronald difficult balls, balls he should never get.'

– We'll try again. If the Queen of Holland had sat next to you on Thursday evening in Poland . . .

'Then that would have been her bad luck. Of course I was more tense than last year. After seven weeks we had to show something. But I was never nervous that we wouldn't win. Players must see that I trust them completely. At a moment like that in Warsaw they have to concentrate 100 per cent and make sure they do what I say. I was attacked in the press and after a victory like that, you prove again that you're right. But that's all.'

On Saturday evening, Barcelona land in Majorca. On arrival at the hotel, Cruyff gives a press conference for 15 local journalists. He is relaxed, we think.

A day later it's gone wrong again. The Barcelona attack fails, Koeman runs around even more lost than in Warsaw. In Warsaw Koeman was sacrificed because Barcelona were playing poorly and Alexanco played in his position. After Majorca-Barcelona, we fear Cruyff's solution merely changes the problems. Koeman wasn't bought to be a victim of the malaise. Against Real Madrid on Sunday he should play as libero again. Cruyff always says his work gives him pleasure and if it didn't he would stop immediately. Consequently he shouldn't stop Koeman playing the kind of pleasurable football he bought him for.

That's why we ask Johan Cruyff: 'is there never a moment in your life – at night for example – when you think "Damn it, I was wrong"?'

'If there was, I would never talk about it, never. I would put it away. That's part of my character.'

Nieuwe Revu
October 1989

Chapter 16

ORANGE IS A CONCEPT AND SO, BY ACCIDENT, IS CRUYFF – GOOD TIMES, BAD TIMES

During the Gulf War, my family telephoned from Israel. 'What's the matter with Johan Cruyff?' asked a worried niece. The news in Israel had been interrupted with reports of Johan Cruyff's heart attack. Israel kept in touch with the story between the Scuds and Patriots. We interviewed him immediately before his heart operation.

It is Friday evening at one minute to seven. On the couch in front of the television, Johan Cruyff is talking about Barcelona and the Dutch national team. As usual, he avoids discussing the coming game against Real Madrid, as if it were an irrelevance. Then his wife comes in and asks if we want to sit at the table. The Dutch soap 'Good Times, Bad Times' begins, but we are in Barcelona. We all watch together. What misery in Holland! At 7.30 we watch the news. The anxiety over the 15th of January [the UN deadline for Saddam Hussein to withdraw from Kuwait] was also affecting the stars of Barcelona.

In the afternoon, as we sat around a table with the Koemans, we talked about the possible consequences of a war, the influence of the ETA [the Basque terrorist organisation], and the Olympic games. 'If I were Israel', Cruyff says, 'on January 15th I would put the clock forward by 15 minutes. And then later you can say to Iraq: "Oh wasn't it twelve o'clock at your place?" '

In the car we begin to talk about Real Madrid.

'It's very clear at the moment that Real have too many players who don't give everything. And there are very few players who

On June 2nd 1971, Ajax won the European Cup for the first time, beating Panathinaikos of Greece 2-0 at Wembley. Two players are missing from the team photo: defender Ruud Krol (these days a coach seeking work and a diploma), who had broken his leg, and substitute Arie Haan (ex-coach at Feyenoord).

Standing, from left to right (with what they are doing now in brackets): Barry Hulshoff (itinerant coach in Belgium); Heinz Stuy (restauranteur and goalkeeping coach at Telstar), Wim Suurbier (telecommunications salesman), Dick van Dijk (dead) and Gerrie Muhren (footballing vicar and brother of Arnold).

Sitting, from left to right: Piet Keizer (columnist and - sadly - resting Einstein), Sjaak Swart (still a right winger - for FC Zeeburgia), Nico Rijnders (dead), Velibor Vasovic (lawyer in Belgrade), Johan Cruyff (the coach this book is about), Johan Neeskens (assistant coach of the Dutch national team).

Recovering from an operation in 1977 on a bone which anatomically speaking should not have existed, Cruyff is fed by his three-year-old son, Jordi.

Can he still do it or not? The prodigal son proves he can with the astounding lobbed goal in the first game of his Ajax comeback on Sunday December 6th 1981 against Haarlem goalkeeper Edward Metgod.

Back in his Ajax shirt as champions (May 1982).

Entering the Nou Camp: Barcelona player.

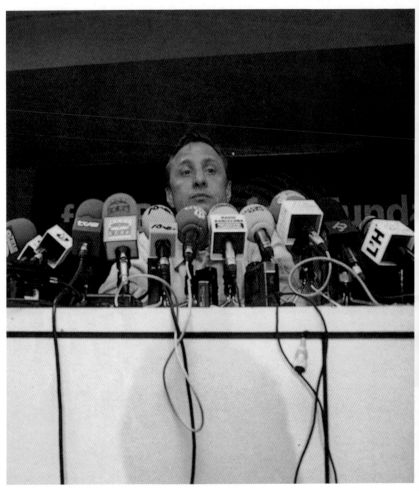

Barcelona routine: the weekly cliché-conference before a game.

Back to his roots: with an Ajax junior team in 1992.

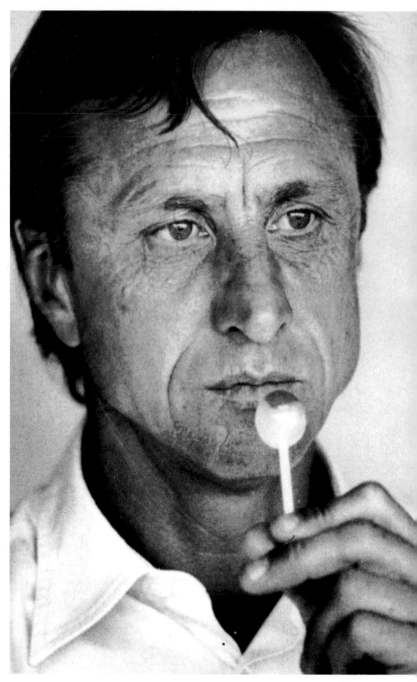

After his bypass in 1991, he swapped cigarettes for lollipops.

can play well each week if they give less than 100 per cent. Very few.'

In the car we have the following, typical Cruyff-journalist conversation:

– The Bulgarian, Stoichkov is a good striker, isn't he?

'He has a lot to learn.'

– Isn't Stoichkov useful?

'Oh, he's very good.'

Suddenly we have a sense of deja vu. We drive past the place where, in April 1989, Cruyff and Barcelona chairman Nunez stuck a pole in the ground to launch the building of a major new sports complex. Guests and journalists were taken on special buses to watch the ground-breaking ceremony.

'Damn it,' says Cruyff 'You were there weren't you? That one pole is as far as they ever got. There's a farmer who wouldn't leave. They didn't think of that at the time.'

Cruyff has only coached two teams – Ajax and Barcelona.

– If you had to make an ideal team from all those players, how would it look?

'If I say that and you write it, then it gets translated and a day later I'm in trouble again. With these kind of things, in countries like Spain and Italy you have to be very careful. You can do it in Holland, but here there's always a journalist who sees you as a meal ticket and I don't want to give them their chance.'

– You've worked with all the good Dutch players we have at the moment.

'Absolutely. Who haven't I worked with? There's Menzo, Koeman, Witschge, Wouters, Blind, Winter, Van't Schip . . . You'd do better to ask who I hadn't worked with. And there's very few I haven't worked well with. The nice thing is that I've had big battles with some of them and later you look back and see they really developed, and that's nice.

'One of the nicest developments has been Frank Rijkaard. You could say I had a tough confrontation with him. But when you see how he's now playing with AC Milan: the intuition, the professional attitude, I think it's beautiful. How he got this far doesn't matter. He has reached the level he was capable of reaching. Everyone knew Rijkaard could play football. Everyone at Ajax can play. They're all beautiful footballers. My task as coach at Ajax was to teach them a professional approach. I shaped them, as a manner of speaking, from junior level to professional. In that process, I owed a lot to Wouters. Wouters, Spelbos and Ophof, to mention a couple of names, who helped turn those talents into professionals. I was able to let Van Basten play against Spelbos, which was very helpful. Van Basten had to go all out in training to get a single chance against Spelbos. It's a question of mentality: learning to play professionally, punishing the weaknesses of your opponents.

'Mentality is the problem for good players. By definition, less technical players have a good mentality, otherwise they wouldn't be playing.

'Again, Rijkaard is the best example. At one time we had to use Wim Jansen to keep him awake, to make sure he was always working. Some people need to be hit once to understand. That's all. Then they're there, because that little bit of extra quality they have immediately takes them to the top. But some of them won't make it to the top. That's a pity. You analyse and analyse. You go through all the details and then you look at where someone's potential really does lie. Take Gerald Vanenburg, because you should understand that he can be indispensable for a team. He has a voice that means he can never be a leader: but he has wonderful technique. If you analyse Vanenburg, you realise he can't be the leader, but he can be the man who holds things together. His big strength during the 1988 European Championship was that he kept the Dutch team together. He played on the right of midfield and he instinctively knew when to hold the ball and when to give it to someone else. If you give it too quickly, the midfield can't keep up. Give it too late and the speed goes out of the game. That's why, in the European Championship, he wasn't allowed to lose the ball or do crazy things. The same with Arnold Muhren on the left side. And they did that really well.

'That was also the great strength of Bernd Schuster at Real Madrid, and the great problem for Anderlecht when Jankovic stopped playing. Schuster and Jankovic are also players who can control a team, bind it together, tie together the lines (of defence, midfield and attack). When Schuster started at Real Madrid he played too far forward. If he hit a 40 metre pass, the rest of the team wasn't quick enough to stay close enough. When he moved further back, they only needed to cover 30 or 20 metres. Frans Thijssen was also very good at that. None of these men are players who decide a game, though a lot of people see them that way. Again, they bind a team together and are not allowed to lose the ball. The man who can decide a game is allowed to take risks. He can try to beat his man, he is allowed to lose the ball.'

– What are the limits for Richard Witschge?

'He can go very far, but he still has to prove himself. He can be as good as Van Basten. In each case, we are talking about extreme qualities, as with Roy, Bergkamp and Van't Schip. Witschge has the advantage that Van Basten has and that I also had. How do you say it? In Spanish they call it "fibra".'

– Temperament?

'Yes, that's what I mean'

– You mean that Van Basten and you are always fighting with everyone, getting yellow and red cards?

'Yes, Witschge does it too.'

– Gullit and Van't Schip don't, but we still like watching them.

'Hang on. We're only talking about players with extra quality. Bergkamp has something extra as well, but he lacks a little in temperament.'

– Is Witschge a future decider of games or will he be a 'binder'?

'We'll see how it turns out. We'll try both qualities. If he can do both, he'll be an exception.'

In a conversation with Johan Cruyff, talking about the Dutch national team is unavoidable. During the World Cup (in Italy), we spoke to him a lot by phone. Before Holland's opening game against Egypt, (which they drew 1-1) he gave us his vision of how Holland should play.

'I've been thinking. If Holland had played well against Egypt, you would have been able to write about it. But because it went badly, I didn't want to talk. It would only have caused more trouble. I would have been doing Beenhakker's job for him and I didn't want to. That's why I didn't go to Italy, because when you get there, you know what will happen.

'To begin with, I do think there are small, weak teams you have to play against. I know it's fashionable to say countries like Luxembourg and Cyprus aren't small any more, but that's nonsense. You saw Malta-Holland. Believe me, Egypt is a little country. You know what the mistake is? People think countries like Egypt can play football. Of course, if you give them space, they can do everything with the ball. Anyone can play football if you have five metres of space. You have time to think, you don't have to act quickly, you don't have to make quick decisions, you're not going to panic easily. That way, Egypt is also not a bad team. So don't give them any space. The same footballer who can do everything if he has five metres, will lose the ball and panic if you only give him two metres. Take Malta, that's an example of how to play against small countries.

'The big mistake in the first game was that Egypt were allowed to have possession for 40 or 50 per cent of the game. So we'd already lost half the game – we couldn't do anything. What we should have done was put Egypt under pressure from the first minute, to undermine them, especially in the first half hour. We should have run riot in the first half hour. I would at least have had two wingers in the team so you can get the ball in front of goal. Next to Van Basten in attack, I would have put a demolition man, someone who runs and runs like Kieft or Van Loen. You decide which in training, on form, how everyone's doing. I'd have had Gullit start on the bench. He wasn't fit yet, so you save him for the demolition. After putting 20 balls in the first half hour in the Egyptian penalty area, we'd have 10 shots on goal and the other ten would end up on the edge of the penalty area. So Ronald Koeman, with that wonderful shot of his, shouldn't have been the last man in defence but instead should have played just behind the strikers. Around the penalty area you should have had a ring of very disciplined players who would have got hold of every ball that was headed or kicked away, so you couldn't be surprised by a counter attack. Again, it's a question of forcing because technically, and I'm talking about the technical level under pressure in a small space at the top level in a World Cup, well, Egypt didn't have that much to offer.

'If I'm right, Egypt only has one striker, so you only needed one man covering him, or maybe two. I'm not sure about that. And the midfield players, whoever they were, would have kept the rhythm of the ball high. And then, after 40 minutes, when you feel they have been damaged and they're ready to crash, you bring on Gullit.'

– As a lover of football, weren't you annoyed that you were at home during the World Cup instead of sitting on the bench?

'No, I don't think so. I only thought it was a pity given the qualities this Dutch team had. This team could have gone so much further, no, should have gone. We talked about Madrid. It's about being sharp. That's why I didn't go to the World Cup in Argentina in 1978. I knew I wouldn't have been sharp. I could only have failed. You know that about yourself. Maybe I would have had that sharpness two years later. It's something you have to feel. I always said before the 1978 World Cup that as soon as the Dutch team qualified I would stop. I'd lived for that farewell.

'The situation of the Dutch team before the World Cup last year seemed so familiar to me. We all saw it coming. It immediately went wrong when they went back to the concept of the European

Championship. You can't do that. What do they say at the fairground? "New chances, new prizes." That's what they say. And I'm only talking about one thing.'

– And if Michels had asked you last April, when he was the board member responsible, to become coach of the national team, would you have said yes?

'Maybe yes. I wouldn't have said immediately that I would do it. I would certainly not have said yes immediately on the phone. I would have had to talk to the players first. I did know what was wrong, I recognised it, so I knew what I was looking for. In that conversation with the players, I would have found out whether they could have got the sharpness back. I do have some experience with that of course.

'I would have said: Gentlemen, we can only go one way. I can only come back if you if you think we can win the competition. So then it is now: back against the wall, knife against the breast. If I hadn't gone through that, they wouldn't have done it. It was about whether the players wanted to go through the wall.

'I wasn't so worried about that, but I did want to speak to them personally. Apparently the players acknowledged this was the only way out: a straight road with no concessions to anybody. Of the ten players who wanted me, I've had fights with nine of them.

'It's obvious the players understood what the Dutch team needed for the World Cup. It's no coincidence that the big players really wanted me. If I had found a solution with those players, the rest would have been fine. The rest, from board to press, is an artificial problem. If you need a row, you create a row, in a manner of speaking. But it wasn't to be. I'm not the type to suffer over it. I would have liked it, but I'm not the kind of person who's dying for that phone call.'

– Do you think you'll be on the bench for the European Championship finals in 1992?

'I'd be happy to do it. But other people must want me to do it. Orange is a concept, but so, accidentally, is Cruyff.' After a short silence, he says: 'But the players are enriched by an experience. It was an expensive one. But they do understand now.' His eyes gleam. Suddenly we are sitting opposite the street kid from the Watergraafsmeer.

– As things stand, it's clear the players will talk about you again if Holland qualify for the finals of Euro '92 in Sweden. Do you think Michels will give you the final responsibility?

'I'm not sure, I'm not sure.'

– Are you trying to be clever?

'No, I don't know. So I don't have to answer. A tournament is a short situation. You always know exactly what's happening. It all happens in two weeks. If half of it is just to be invited, I don't think I want it. We go to become champions. Everyone will have to adapt to that. Because if I'm killed, I'll die by my own ideas.'

– Something's strange here. Michels and you used to be very close when you were a player. Since you've become a coach, something seems to have broken. When Michels fell ill in 1985 and had to have an operation, we thought he would ask you to take over the Dutch team temporarily, especially given the way you talked about each other. But again, like last year, he chose Leo Beenhakker instead of you.

'I can only give you one answer to that, but I won't.'

– But it must have surprised you?

'Again, I'm not saying anything about it. I don't want to touch reputations. Actually, last year I knew for sure I wasn't going to be asked. You can feel it. You know it.'

– As assistant trainer Dick Advocaat keeps saying that because of your shadow there's unrest in the Dutch team.

'That's only because one part of them thinks: he is the best, let him be the coach of the Dutch team. The other half also wants me to be coach, but they think: we can finally see him fail.'

– Are you surprised you weren't asked last year?

'I've said that already: to be honest, no. I know that everyone in football talks for his own advantage. Nobody speaks for someone else's advantage. That's why I think I haven't been asked. Why else wasn't I asked?'

– How should we regard that conversation between you and Michels in Odoorn last year, when you were there pre-season with Barcelona and Michels was looking for a new national coach?

'You must decide for yourself. It was a normal conversation. Michels asked if I could become national coach immediately, but he already knew that I couldn't. I had a contract until 1991 with Barcelona and I couldn't leave for a week six times during the season. That's the advantage of the finals of a tournament: you don't have to think abut anything else, so you can do it.'

If the world stays healthy, Barcelona will play Real Madrid on January 19. Next week we will talk about his team and that game. Whatever the result, Cruyff will stay with Barcelona until summer 1993.

'Just before New Year's Eve, we had dinner for the team and the board. Suddenly the chairman stands up and says: "if the gentleman trainers want to stay, they can sign again". When we came back after the Christmas break, he asked if we'd thought about it. I said yes, we've thought about it and we want to stay and in 20 seconds it was done.'

– Twenty seconds?

'Well maybe it took five minutes. No longer. The salaries of the other trainers? At that level you don't need to talk about it. Anyway, I don't discuss it.'

– And what's your objective now? AC Milan's throne in the European Cup?

'Yes, if we become champions, that's what we want. First we need to make sure we stay normal after the possible euphoria, and then we'll move on to the next big target. That's the challenge that attracts me.'

Nieuwe Revu
January 1991

Chapter 17

THIS TEAM SHINES –
CHAMPIONS OF SPAIN?

B arcelona beat Real Madrid 2-1, putting them ten points clear of Real in the Spanish league and four ahead of Athletico Madrid. For the first time as coach, Johan Cruyff can win a league championship. This interview with him is about the way he works at Barcelona.

Never has a team coached by Cruyff become national champions. With Ajax and Barcelona he won the national cup and the European Cup Winners' Cup, but in the league, he always finished a long way behind traditional rivals PSV and Real Madrid.

– Doesn't it ever frustrate you?

'No, because I know why it happened.' But, if Cruyff had found it frustrating, we would have had the same answer. That's the way he works.

If you phone him and ask how he is, he almost always replies: 'good'. Last year, when Barcelona were playing badly, had few points and were occasionally the subject of ridicule, he'd say: 'it's going well'. He gave numerous interviews and spoke at many press conferences last season and he never gave the impression he was under pressure because of the bad results. But Johan Cruyff has a disadvantage: his appearance hides nothing. No manager's visage reveals as much as Cruyff's does. When things go badly for him, the taut lines in his thin face, his eyes deep in their sockets and the wrinkles all tell the tale of 26 years of tension.

'If things are going badly, you've got to protect the players and give them the impression everything's going to be fine soon. That's why I need to do interviews more when things are going badly than when they

go well. When things are good I don't need publicity. Internally, I need
to keep calm. I really have nothing to say when things are good.'

His eyes and cheekbones betray Cruyff's real mood this January: it's
going very well. It's now or never.

The 1990-91 season started badly. In July and August the Spanish
sports press laughed like mad about the chaos at Barcelona after two
years under Cruyff. At the pre-season press call the talk was all about
players who wanted to leave and unhappy internationals. In other words,
Cruyff started his third season at the edge of the precipice. They were
only waiting for the fatal push. Catalans who heard you were Dutch
mentioned the names 'Crooif' and 'Koyman' laughingly, gave you the
thumbs down and said: 'can't you take them back to Holland?' At the
start of the new season. Mila, the Spanish international, bought out his
Barcelona contract for two million pounds and was instantly paraded
by Real Madrid chairman, Mendoza, as the latest great acquisition
for Barca's rivals in the Spanish capital. The malicious pleasure was
considerable. As if that was not enough, another international, Roberto
also bought out his contract for 6 million guilders. He returned to Spain
from the training camp in Holland, told a press conference that no-one
at Barcelona understood a word Cruyff said any more and then signed
for Valencia.

And Cruyff himself? He remained calm and looked well-rested. He
had bought the Bulgarian striker Stoichkov, brought back Goikoexea
and Ferrer, who had been on loan, swapped the unknown Nando from
Seville for his reserve goalkeeper and said again that Ronald Koeman
really was a very good footballer. Meanwhile, by January 1991, Nando
and Goikoexea were regular members of the Spanish national team, as
Ferrer would have been if he hadn't been injured at the same time
as Koeman, and Koeman (before his injury) and Stoichkov (before
his long suspension) had become the darlings of the Catalan public.
In other words, Cruyff went on his Christmas holiday a month ago
with a big smile on his face and, as normal before a big game, he
paid no attention to the long term absence of his two playmakers,
Koeman and Stoichkov.

– Why did you let Mila go?

'He wanted too much money.'

− You don't make that decision do you?

'I do, at least partly, because I don't want one player disrupting relations. Exceptions will be considered as exceptions − not something normal. No single Spanish player earns as much in his first year as he did. Normally a player like Mila will earn 300,000 guilders in his first season. He earned double that. We have a system where you earn more every year if you play well. That's how you keep the kettle boiling. He signed for three years. The first year was over so he would have got his normal raise. Then suddenly an agent came along who said: we don't accept this raise so he'll spend the next two years under the same terms as the first year and then we'll be free. I said: OK, so he can sit on the bench for two years because I'm not going to shape a player and teach him, who wants to leave after two years. It was only a couple of games from the end of last season, and from that moment I didn't put him in the team any more. If I'd given in, then I'd have had problems with 15 other people. Unless he was going to be an exception, and he wasn't.'

− And Roberto, often the motor of your team and the Spanish side, why did you let him go?

'He could earn a lot of money, a lot more than we could pay. There was a fixed sum that would allow him to leave.'

− During pre-season you played against SVV in Rotterdam with two strikers, a system the Dutch national team later copied for the games against Italy and Portugal. Why did it look as if you were abandoning your beliefs?

'I wanted to see how it would work, because Stoichkov and Laudrup are strong from midfield. But that experiment turned out to be useless. Against PSV a couple of days later, we played 3-4-3 again: with three defenders, four in midfield and three attackers. Since then we've only played 3-4-3, sometimes with a small adjustment, but not like against SVV.'

– Why has your team done better so far than last year?

'There is more balance. Last year we had a lot of good players but in Spain you must also be able to fight. You saw that in the games between Real Madrid and Atletico Madrid. Those were real battles. And then there is the problem of the stadium. It creates enormous pressure, especially on the Spanish players in our side. It shows that players who have played here in their youth are better able to cope with the pressure of the stadium. On top of that, I have five candidates for three places up front, all of them internationals: Salinas, Beguiristain, Laudrup, Goikoexea and Stoichkov. They have to fight hard for their place.'

– Were you worried when Ronald Koeman was injured?

'Yes, because three days later, Ferrer was also seriously injured and then we also lost Stoichkov. I thought that we were losing too much quality. But I suddenly discovered that my team was mentally much stronger. And Alexanco was able to carry on much longer than I thought. I knew that I could use him occasionally, but that he could stay at this level for so long was a surprise. This team shines. The boys look good. You can see it. And it extends to the crowd. That's very strange. Against Logrones we were losing 0-1 at home. Normally they start whistling, but then something happened that I haven't seen before. The crowd got behind us as one. And partly because of that we won that game 2-1.'

Friday afternoon January 18th, after talking mainly about the Gulf War, we ask how he will play the following day against Real Madrid.

'No idea. Haven't thought about it for a second. I know how the team will look in outline but I'm not really busy with the selection. We're going to the training camp late. Tomorrow morning I'll see how the players look at breakfast, how they behave. There can always be one who'll make me think: "oh he's not acting normally".'

– Real have many problems. Last week you lost to Oviedo. Barcelona-Real Madrid is an ideal game for Real to restore their image.

'After that humiliation last week, I did taste unrest in the team. Some people started to doubt. I was worried that losing Koeman and Stoichkov could make this team uncertain, especially this week. That's why I didn't train so much this week, though I talked a lot with Laudrup, Goikoexea, Nando. Look, Alexanco is there in this kind of game. That's why I don't train on the day of a game. These games against Real are so emotional that the players will just fly straight into it. I have to try to keep them calm.'

On Saturday evening, at a minute before eight, the Barcelona players led by Alexanco yell their war cries and run up the steps onto the pitch and into the presence of one hundred thousand screaming fans.

In the morning tickets were going for 10,000 pesetas. On the black market outside the stadium they went for three times as much. Of the 120,000 available seats, 108,000 were sold before the season started to the *socios* (club members), and for the Real game the 12,000 remaining tickets are like gold. The sudden rain has kept a lot of the *socios* at home and there are numerous empty seats in the uncovered parts of the stadium. It's not going to stop the fun or the fireworks.

Barcelona score a glittering first goal through Laudrup (one to frame, according to Cruyff). Soler launches Goikoexea on the left; the Basque delivers a perfect ball and Laudrup the Dane, with a beautiful half volley, gives Jaro, after that Laudrup goal the injured goalkeeper Buyo's replacement, no chance.

Before that, Real Madrid should have had a penalty when Hugo Sanchez, suddenly alone against Alexanco, beat the Barcelona captain and was then tripped. Yes, it was inside the penalty area, but that doesn't mean much in Spain if you're playing away and your name is Hugo Sanchez. That Laudrup goal goes to Barcelona's heads and they lose their grip on the game. Butragueno's equaliser after a well-punished blunder by Soler was typical of the panic into which Barcelona can fall without Koeman.

At half time Cruyff did more than he needed to. After the break, Real weren't involved any more.

After Barcelona had gone 2-1 ahead with one of those goals made inevitable by pressure – Real's Yugoslav international Spasic unnecessarily heading the ball into his own net – we saw another great man on the side of the pitch. It must have been a historic moment: Cruyff was on one bench and Alfredo Di Stefano, once Cruyff's great hero, on the other. Di Stefano was screaming at Hagi to stop warming up and get on the pitch. The Romanian took part for a while – the former Steaua Bucharest star has been degraded to a reserve at Real – but in those last 20 minutes he showed he is the best of them all. The trainer who manages to get Hagi accepted by Real will be Johan Cruyff's most dangerous opponent.

Hagi replaces Hugo Sanchez, Madrid's fantastic Mexican striker. Before the game Cruyff had predicted Sanchez would not get a kick against Barcelona. He had just one shot and was taken off in the second half. We caught up with him in the catacombs after the game. Polite as ever, Sanchez said he didn't understand the substitution at all. We wanted to ask him if he missed Leo Beenhakker, but he wanted to run off to the changing room.

On Friday Koeman had told us to look out for Hugo Sanchez and Butragueno. 'You know they wear padded shoulders? Really, they do'. And yes, in the corridor we saw not only the stupid shirt but also his wife's shoulder pads. Only a small detail, just as it was only a detail that on Saturday evening we saw two goalkeepers who kick the ball with their left foot.

After the game all Barcelona is relieved. The second half of the league season begins with them ten points ahead of their big rivals from Madrid, Real. It's now or never. After the game, Cruyff patiently talks to dozens of television, radio and newspaper journalists from countries like Holland, Denmark, England, France and, naturally, Spain. But he also does that after a defeat. On the outside, Cruyff doesn't show his emotions.

– How is your relationship with the Spanish press, we asked him before the Real game. Do you give a press conference every day like you did last season?

'No. Last year, I thought if I gave them a press conference every day it would keep them quiet. But it was useless. Now I think it's better if the players talk. Now I only give a press conference before and after a game. But I'm sharper than I was last season. Then I had to build the players up. Now I have to make sure they keep their feet on the ground.'

– Why did you get sent off in that quite unimportant Spanish Super Cup match against Real Madrid, the game in which Stoichkov kicked the referee's foot?

'I put two young players in the team, it was their first game in the first team and it was against Real. One of them was marking Butragueno, the other was on Hugo Sanchez. It wasn't easy. So before the game I go to the referee's changing room and tell him that I'm giving a debut to two very young players – one was only 17. If they do something wrong, tell Zubi [goalkeeper Zubizaretta], or tell Alexanco and they'll take care of it, I said, because you'll understand that those boys are very tense. After five minutes he gives Zubi a yellow card. Five minutes later, one of the boys, who's done nothing wrong, also gets a yellow. So the referee doesn't want to understand. When he stood in front of the dugout for a free kick I told him what I thought of him. Look, there are things a referee can and cannot do. In a Barcelona-Real Madrid game you can't just dish out yellow cards. Something has to have happened. That referee was trying to screw us. Later I found out that the words I used were more insulting for a Spaniard than I would have thought according to a literal translation. No, I won't repeat it.'

– You talked about the pressure of Barcelona's stadium. People say the same about Feyenoord. Is that why so many players fail at Feyenoord?

'I don't know. But I have noticed – and I've said it before – that players from your own youth system cope better with the pressure of the stadium than players who come from elsewhere. You can compare Feyenoord and Barcelona a little: two harbour cities, hard workers, a love of physical football, both cities fighting against the capital, wonderful stadiums – yes there are similarities. Just like here, at Feyenoord you need a man who really doesn't give a shit who really wants to fight. The funny thing at Feyenoord is that the names change but people stay the same somehow. Now I think three people decide again. Again there are people who depend on other people. You'll never get through that.

'In Rotterdam, like here, everyone's against you. You have to be able to cope with that. You have to be able to fight. I can do that because I'm independent. At Feyenoord you had that man from Opel. He seemed to be a good man. But he didn't survive either. I've been able to cope with it here: whenever something's wrong it's over within three days.'

Sunday morning, the day after the game against Real Madrid, we call him. 'Yes, things are going well. Next week everything is going to be quiet here. Luckily, in Israel it stayed quiet as well last night.'

– Again, about your team. A midfielder with an understanding of football, maybe a player like Hagi: he wouldn't be out of place in your team.

'Yes, but you can't have everyone. Yesterday you saw how important Koeman and Stoichkov are for us. Koeman can change the game unexpectedly and Stoichkov is an aggressive striker. But yes, they can't play so you shouldn't think about them. And about Hagi. I don't understand it. You see immediately: he can play.'

– One other question. Did we leave a red scarf in the boot of your car last night?

'I don't know. I never open the boot of my car. Why? Do you want me to look?'

– Yes

(Much later) 'No there was no red scarf in my car.'

– Pity

'Only a red dishcloth.'

Nieuwe Revu
January 1991

Chapter 18

IF I WANTED YOU TO UNDERSTAND, I WOULD HAVE EXPLAINED IT BETTER – SAYING YES OR NO TO BEING NATIONAL COACH

On November 5 1992, Paul Boels, a senior KNVB official (member of the professional football selection board in charge of technical matters) said on our programme: 'Don't worry about Johan Cruyff. Everything is all right. He will become national coach if Holland qualify for the World Cup in America in 1994'. On December 3rd and 29th we spoke to Johan Cruyff on out television programme.

– Is everything all right?

'I didn't withdraw my words and they didn't either. The second thing is that a lot of other things have been discussed that I don't like. There are things that need to be discussed.'

– But there's one thing we don't understand. How can Boels say 'everything is all right'?

'Because at that moment, on the technical side, there were no problems. But that was four weeks ago.'

– Four weeks ago. Was that the beginning of October?

'In any case, a couple of things have happened that I don't want to discuss in any detail. Things I don't like.'

– What don't you like?

'It's got nothing to do with technical football things but with personal things that I think are important. But nothing has been lost yet, absolutely nothing.'

– OK, of course nothing's been lost yet, but what did you mean precisely?

'I don't want to talk about what I mean. Otherwise I would have said it. I'm saying that a couple of things have happened that I don't like.'

– Like what? We don't understand.

'Things have happened that aren't directly connected to football. That's why I said it's not a technical problem.'

– Should the dikes be higher?

'No.'

– You're insinuating that it's something to do with the appointment of Rinus Michels as technical adviser to the KNVB.

'No, it's nothing to do with that.'

– Your salary?

'Not that either.'

– Because you have a contract at home, haven't you?

'Oh, maybe, but I haven't looked at it because I don't want to sign it.'

– But you have a contract at home?

'I might have.'

– I'm sure you know. Boels says: 'He has a contract, he just doesn't have to send it back to us.'

'Yes, it's with the lawyer.'

– But you have a contract at home?

'Yes I'm sure I do.'

– What don't you like then? Will you or will you not go to America if Holland qualify?

'If they qualify! You're always running ahead aren't you? There's time for everything. There's just a couple of things I don't like.'

– We still don't understand.

'You don't have to understand. If I'd wanted you to understand I would have explained it better.'

– But we are being paid to make it easier to understand.

'Well that's your problem, but I have . . .'

– Are there still doubts?

'About what? There aren't any doubts, just a couple of things I don't like. I thought that was clear enough, wasn't it?'

– No.

'There are a couple of things I don't like.'

– Do you want Dick Advocaat with you as your assistant?

'It's got nothing to do with technical football things. There are other things.'

– But what? Preparations? Are the women not allowed to come?

'We're not even at the stage where I . . .'

– Johan, are you making something out of nothing?

'No.'

– It's not a technical problem and you have the contract. So what are we talking about?

'With me, as always, the money is not important. That's number one. It's the same thing as we talked about with the club: circumstances are very important. And outside of the technical, if we can call it that – what do you call something that isn't technical but has to do with organisation? – a couple of things have happened that I don't like. So we'll have to talk about that.'

– But what happened?

'I'm not going to tell you. It's none of your business.'

– Nothing has happened. The only thing that happened is that Mr Michels . . .

'But you don't know what happened. That's to do with technical things.'

– We're pretty well informed.

'Well you've been badly informed. But that doesn't matter. You needn't ask anything else. I'm not going to say anything.'

– You don't want to say anything?

'There's no point.'

– But is there something?

'If there was, I wouldn't say anything anyway.'

– Did Mr Nunez say that as long as you worked for Barcelona you weren't going to America?

'He can say whatever he likes. My contract ends at the end of the year and we're talking about 1994, so I'm not worrying too much.'

– Is that part of your decision?

'I will only do it if I want to.'

– And at the moment do you want to?

'At the moment I do – as long as a couple of things that I don't like can change. I can't say it any more clearly than that.'

– You said it's so difficult because no one in Holland understands anything.

'You don't have to. If I wanted them to understand it, I would explain it very clearly. I'd say "this has happened, that has happened, I don't like that".'

– Does the KNVB know that you have doubts?

'They'd be very silly if they didn't.'

– Did you make it clear?

'I don't have to make it clear because if they don't realise, then something is missing.'

– Are you just trying to make yourself interesting?

'Why would I want to be interesting?'

– No idea.

'Exactly. Do I have to be interesting for your benefit or for the people at home? I don't care at all.'

– Yes, maybe you do want to be interesting?

'Well that's your bad luck. Again, these are the kind of things that will take care of themselves. And if they don't, well it's just bad luck.'

– Recently, after the Ajax-Kaiserslautern game Louis van Gaal [Ajax coach] was reminded that Barcelona had a difficult game with Kaiserslautern and were nearly knocked out by them last year. He was asked if he was afraid of Kaiserslautern and he answered: 'Ajax aren't Barcelona'.

'I don't know what he means. If he means Ajax are much better than Barcelona, then I think he's riding for a fall. He's making a big mistake.'

– Because Ajax are not better than Barcelona?

'You see it in their qualities. Ajax has good players, but they are mostly young, so they lack experience. You can correct that by playing, especially if you have high quality technical players. When you look at Ajax at the moment, you can see the quality is declining, there is less that is special and exceptional.'

– What do you mean?

'I don't like to name names, but if someone can't get a return on extremely high qualities.

– You mean Bryan Roy?

'. . . and others who don't have that quality and you don't see a return, then something is wrong.'

– What do you mean? Explain it.

'I don't want to name names.'

– You have Bryan Roy.

'Bryan Roy is someone with exceptional qualities. The comment was that there wasn't enough return on that. That can happen. It means you're talking about a different kind of football.'

– That's not your kind of football?

'No it's not my kind of football.'

– Well, I'm getting old. I must have forgotten the reason you said there was trouble between you and the Dutch team. What was it again?

'I said, and I want to repeat it: it's none of your business. I don't want to make it clear. I will make it clear to the people who need to know.'

Barend & Van Dorp
December 1992

Chapter 19

IT'S AS LONG AS IT IS WIDE – LIFE AFTER THE EUROPEAN CUP

In 1992 Barcelona won the European Cup for the first time. A Ronald Koeman free kick in extra time decided the final against Sampdoria.

– Johan Cruyff, 1992 has been a frantic year for you. What was the highlight?

'You mean in football? Or results?'

– I asked for the highlight. What was the highlight?

'For me, the highlight was that my daughter got married.'

– Why was that the highlight?

'It's pretty logical. She's my daughter and she was the first one to get married.'

– And you're going to be a grandfather as well, aren't you?

'Yes, but that's in 1993. Don't get things mixed up. 1992 is 1992.'

– Are you looking forward to that?

'Yes.'

– Does it make you feel older or doesn't it make any difference?

'Well I like children a lot. Nothing else seems terribly important. At least that's what I think.'

– What was the football highlight?

'As a result, probably winning the European Cup. Emotionally it was winning the League. Everything about it. 100,000 people in the stadium. Waiting for the end. That was the nicest moment. I'll say it that way.'

– We've never seen you enjoying yourself so much as you did with the European Cup.

'It's something you always work for. And I think it's the nicest thing you can do with a group of players, who are in general a lovely team. And you don't often see that.'

– What's so nice about these boys?

'I don't know. They have very good characters. You could see it a couple of weeks ago when Witschge scored his first goal in the 4-0 win against Espanyol – how everyone came up to him and how they were all happy. You saw it in their eyes, their faces. It was really good to see.'

– Four months later, with the same team, to put this a little crudely, you've fallen on your ass. The European Cup has gone. Why did that happen?

'It's a consequence of how we played in the first month in the League. We played fantastic half hours, half games. Really, it was incredibly good football. Then we'd have an enormous loss of concentration. And what does that mean? That you don't have the ball enough, that you only express your own negative capacities. Every footballer has positive capacities. Our strengths are particularly in the rhythm, control and position of the ball. Even against a bad team, if we don't have the ball, then we have to start running after them. If you're playing well at a given moment and you're winning 1-0 or 2-0 or 3-0 then you don't run so fast. You're late on things. You just don't score that fourth goal. That's a normal phenomenon.'

– That's the coach's fault.

'People who don't understand football would say that, yes.'

– We don't understand. You're the coach. Don't try to blame someone else. You're there; it's the coach's fault.

'Yes, that's what people say who don't understand.'

– People who do understand say the same thing.

'Well in that case they don't understand it very well. I'm not saying it's the players' fault. It's just a human mistake. Once again, you can only avoid that with a very good team. You can't do it with a bad one.'

– Do you think you have the best team in Europe at the moment?

'I think technically we're playing very good football. Very few can play as well as us.'

– Why do the papers say almost every week that you're fighting with Nunez?

'I think it's mainly because of one correspondent reading stories in a different language.'

– No, Cruyff, we also read the Spanish press and there's always something.

'It's just journalism and the papers always have to be filled. And you know that for a long time I have refused to talk about anything that's not technical, about things that happen off the pitch. I hardly ever comment on that. Those newspapers have to be filled and that's how you get stories, you know.'

– No, but let's not make up any stories. Do you speak to the chairman regularly?

'I see him here at games.'

– No I didn't ask you that. Do you talk to him regularly?

'No.'

– Do you ever talk to him?

'A little.'

– Have you ever been to his home?

'No.'

– Have you ever eaten with him?

'Well I've eaten with him when everyone's there, but never privately.'

– Isn't it strange that you never talk to the chairman?

'No I don't think so. I want my freedom. I've been here four and a half years. So if I didn't eat with him in the first year, why would I eat with him last year? We have a working relationship. And if that gets disturbed for whatever reason, then maybe that would be a story but . . .'

– But you don't have a working relationship. You don't see him. You don't talk to him.

'I have contact with other people.'

– But isn't he your direct boss?

'If you say that the chairman is the boss. It's the vice chairman who arranges all the transfer business and I have a lot of contact with him. OK. With one I have no contact, with the other I do. I get on pretty well with the other guy.'

– What do you think when you get knocked out of the European Cup – in that very unexpected defeat against Moscow – and the chairman of Barcelona says: 'That's cost us 30 million guilders' and then he points in your direction?

'Things like that almost always go together. You can also say: he earned us 30 million guilders more last year. It's as long as it is wide. I don't think in those terms.'

– Your players have been in conflict with the chairman over bonuses. Whose side are you on in this dispute? The players' or the chairman's?

'I'll support whoever I think is right. In this case, I'm with the players. We had the same problem two years ago and then I supported the club.'

– How long do you want to be a coach?

'No idea. In the first place: as long as I enjoy it. But there are a lot of other things that are very important in life. And I love playing football. I really like joining in. It would be a pity if circumstances stopped me doing that.'

– Will the time to stop have come, for example, if you couldn't join in any more?

'Absolutely. That could be one of those moments. This morning I could join in and it was lovely. It's lovely playing football isn't it?'

– But if you can't any more, will you stop?

'Yes I guess so. But you can't know. You can't look ahead like that, but it wouldn't surprise me if I stopped then.'

– So how important is it for you to be able to join in?

'It's nice.'

– Does playing make being a trainer fun for you?

'It makes it acceptable.'

– Acceptable?

'There are obviously a thousand and one problems a day here. My only distraction is the one and a half hours I'm on the pitch.'

– And if you couldn't do that any more?

'Well, then I'd probably get sick of everything.'

– And how far off do you think that moment is?

'No idea.'

– Are you still better than the players?

'That depends. Obviously, if the pitch is big, like you saw this morning, I make it my size . . .'

– Really? You always change the size of the pitch to fit you?

'Of course, otherwise you can't join in any more.'

– And then?

'Then you can join in very well. If the pitch is bigger you can't join in any more. If I don't play on my own, if I have to play against someone, then obviously I'll lose. So you have to change the rules so you can still join in yourself. And if they train five times a week, then we train twice for them and three times for myself.'

Barend & Van Dorp
December 1992

Chapter 20

I HAVE TO WORK THERE, THEY DON'T – THE 1994 WORLD CUP

The Ajax youth system and Johan Cruyff are completely interconnected. You can't imagine one without the other. Even while at Barcelona, Cruyff keeps an eye on the talents at Ajax. By satellite, Cruyff delivers a warning to us in Hilversum and Ajax in Amsterdam about the future.

– Johan, do you hope Feyenoord will become Dutch champions on Monday?

'Yes, I hope so.'

– Why?

'Why? For many reasons.'

– Tell me one.

'A quick one – because Wim Jansen and Wim van Hanegem are there.'

– You've won everything it's possible to win with Ajax and Barcelona, both as a player and as trainer. Now with Barcelona you can become champions again this year. Are you looking forward to that? Does it make you more tense?

'Yes, very tense generally. Everything I've won is in the past tense. Everything one can win is future. And you always live for the future. For the first time in the history of Barcelona – if we win this year –

we can be champions three years in a row. In the club's 100 year existence this would of course be a record.'

– Were you nervous for the first championship in a different way than for the other?

'Well, for the first one you're nervous. For the second you're tense. I think you're tense for any game because you have so many things to think about, so many details. And it's the same now – that at the end of the season maybe you have to be sharper than normal. Each mistake now is decisive.'

– Johan, two years ago you bought Richard Witschge from Ajax. Why did you make a mistake with him?

'Mistake is a big word. In the first place there were two things. The fourth foreigner is bought to increase the pressure on the three others. These three others [Stoichkov, Koeman and Laudrup] have performed really well in the first two years. That is always at the expense of number four – in this case Witschge. They started with similar chances, but at a certain moment you see the difference in age. At the beginning, that cost him his place. The last couple of months he's given up slightly and he's been a bit lazy and that has obviously had its consequences.'

– So you'd definitely allow him to leave?

'No, it's not a question of letting him leave. There have been offers for him. Obviously that's very logical.'

– That's a weak way of putting it. You mean he can go, isn't that what you're trying to say?

'No, that's not true.'

– You mean he can't leave?

'If I say, "you're allowed to go", you think that means I want him to leave.'

– But he can still leave.

'If there's an offer and it's good for him and it's good for us, then I won't stop him. He's not allowed to go for less than we paid for him.'

– You always want it your way, don't you?

'No, but we can't let him go for half the price.'

– So you still want more than seven or eight million guilders for him?

'He has to cost what he cost us, and that's not how much it was.'

– Six and a half million?

'He cost less.'

– That's news. Good. Can we talk to you about the Dutch national team?

'Oh not that! But then again I didn't set any limits to what you could talk about, so . . .'

– No, you'd better not.

'But the advantage I have here is that I can walk away whenever I want.'

– Really?

'Yes, I can turn off the light and it's over.'

– Where are you exactly?

'At TV-3, the Catalan broadcaster here.'

– Are you there a lot?

'Well, since this is Barcelona, I have to do a lot with them. They're good people. I get on well with them.'

– The Dutch team has a new managerial selection board, did you know that?

'Yes.'

– There's a little bit of uncertainty about your potential arrival to take over the Dutch team if we qualify for the World Cup in America next year. Have you now signed a contract, yes or no, under the old selection board? And you can only answer this question yes or no.

'No.'

– You didn't sign anything?

'No.'

– But there's a verbal agreement?

'We've talked to each other, yes.'

– No, we're asking you: is there a verbal agreement?

'We talked to each other, we made agreements with people who didn't do what they said they would.'

– So, for you, that agreement doesn't count any more?

'No, that would be strange. I made certain agreements. And whether it was with the selection board or someone else doesn't interest me very much.'

– Unfortunately, the selection board decides if you get the job, not the players or anyone else.

'No. At least we do it together, because I'm there as well. I have to work there. They don't.

– Karel Jansen is in charge of technical matters. Has he seen you?

'No.'

– Will he?

'I think so. But that in itself isn't terribly important. It's much more important if Holland qualify first. Then we'll see who's going and not going.'

– What you're saying is a bit childish. The Dutch players want you. And the last selection board said : 'we made binding verbal agreements with Cruyff. He's going to be the coach if Holland qualify.' Why don't you give a clear answer?

'It's very clear, because it's not like that at all. I've said – and I'll repeat it once more – and I won't say it again . . .'

– OK, OK, calm down!

'. . . that if they qualify, at that time, if the players think and everyone thinks I should go, I am prepared to go. If there's one person who doesn't want me to go, I won't go.'

– But isn't there some agreement between you and the last selection board that you have to honour?

'Aren't you listening to me? Do you hear what I'm saying.'

– Yes, but is our interpretation right?

'Let me put it another way: I've said you can always count on me when you need me. I can't say it any clearer.'

– But if they qualify, do you want to do it?

'That depends on the situation.'

– So you could pull out?

'I've said that I won't pull out. They could pull out.'

– So you'll come if the Dutch team qualifies?

'Yes.'

– If it depends on you?

'If it depends on me.'

– Why didn't you say that to start with? That would have taken barely a minute.

'Well you have to fill up your programme. Anyway you have to go to the players and the people who work there, and they all have to agree, otherwise it doesn't make any sense. And the reason to go is to win. Otherwise you shouldn't go. At least, I don't want to go otherwise.'

– But everyone wants to win, so that's also a little bit of nothing.

'I don't think so. A lot of countries are going. Do you think they all think they're going to win?

– No, that's true. But we do. Can I ask you something else?

'Of course.'

– Did it surprise you that Ajax finished third in the league?

'Yes and no.'

– Start with no.

'That it didn't surprise me? Because too few players make it. Experience is lost because there are continuously new players.'

— Experience is lost because there are continuously new players?

'Yes. How can I say it better? You always look at one little thing. People who play for half a game. They put (Tarik) Oulida in there, who's almost 20 and he plays occasionally. It should have happened two years ago.'

— And (Clarence) Seedorf? He's 17 and he's played a couple of very important games so it can't be too bad.

'But if Seedorf is in the team, then you skip a generation and that's obviously where the hole is.'

— But those players aren't good enough, except Oulida.

'Of course they are.'

— How do you know?

'Well, because when we had Oulida and Seedorf there were also others there. I talked about it a couple of days ago.'

— What would you advise Louis van Gaal, one of our best friends, to do as trainer?

'I don't have to give any advice. It's not my problem. You only read the situation from long distance. You know nothing about the rest.'

— But what advice could you give him?

'I don't need to advise him. I think it has to do with the way they see their education.'

— Is their education wrong at the moment?

'I can't see that from a distance. I don't know. You can see the signals that Wijnhard plays in the second team, and he's also 20. And he's not going to get in the first team. As a 20 year old he's either too old for the second team or he should be in the first team. It's one or the other.'

– Have you ever said in your life: 'Damn it you're right'?

'To who?'

– Do you recognise what Willem van Hanegem has said about success?

'Yes I do, but I think he's confusing two things.'

– There he goes again. Hey, doctor what's wrong with us?

'But don't you have different qualities? One has this quality, another has a different quality. And when things don't go well for Feyenoord, Van Hanegem is to blame. And if it goes well, he gets the flowers. Everyone has their own qualities. Willem has his qualities and Geert Meijer has his qualities and, together, they make a perfect team.'

– But – and you're already saying it – Van Hanegem gets all the attention, just as you do.

'But that's his job isn't it? Don't I have the same thing? For me it's even more difficult. I have Rexach, who's also very famous. He's almost an institution here. But when something goes wrong, it's my fault. If it goes well, I've done well. But in fact he does about 60 per cent of the work.'

– When you played in the Dutch team together, Willem van Hanegem used to be your roommate. Were you so opinionated then?

'Footballers talk to each other. How can you agree with journalists? I don't understand. You can agree with other footballers.'

– Why not with journalists?

'I suspect that if journalists really understood football they wouldn't be journalists.'

– Oh, let's stop talking. You're absolutely right.

'Well that's what I think at least.'

– So what should we talk about?

'Just ask your questions and respect the answers.'

– Johan, aren't you interested in Romario any more?

'If we talk about the amount of money that I hear, then I'm not interested at all. And if Valencia are talking about more money, they're only talking about the devaluation of the peseta.'

– The question is: are you still interested in Romario?

'Like I say, not at that price.'

– What is he worth to you?

'I don't know. You'll have to think of a different story. But not the price PSV want for him.'

– You absolutely won't pay 14 or 15 million?

'No.'

– Give us an indication. Nine or 10 million? Is he worth that?

'If I want to buy something from you, I'll negotiate with you. You have nothing to say and nor do I. There are two people on the boards of the two clubs who have to talk and that's what they should do.'

– Would he fit into your team?

'Yes, of course.'

– But people say he's a very difficult individual.

'You could say the same about me.'

– There's nothing wrong with that is there?

'Absolutely not.'

– Explain why he would fit into team like Barcelona rather than PSV.

'I don't know whether he fits in at PSV any more. All I know is that he plays football very well, that he's a certain age, comes at a particular price and he can either be interested in a club or not.'

– Do you think he would have the kind of problems he's having with PSV at Barcelona?

'Maybe in that respect I'm different, but you can never ignore the facts. It's difficult to have problems with me because my rules are clear and only someone who breaks the rules has problems.'

Barend & Van Dorp
May 1993

Chapter 21

CRUYFF AND THE KNVB: EVERYTHING DESTROYED BY 75,000 GUILDERS AND A BLAZER

I t didn't happen for the World Cup in 1990 and it failed again for 1994: why didn't the Dutch players get the coach they wanted?

To become coach of the Dutch national team, Cruyff wanted the same monthly wage he gets at Barcelona. And he refused to wear a KNVB blazer. Who's being obstinate? This is a story of wilfulness and misunderstanding – a reconstruction of the 'negotiations' from the first meeting between KNVB director Jos Staatsen and Johan Cruyff on November 26 until last weekend in Las Vegas.

In August 1992, Cruyff and the KNVB professional football selection board of the day agreed that he would take charge of the Dutch national team for the World Cup finals. Chairman Martin van Rooyen and board member Paul Boels discussed the subject with him at a two hour meeting in Barcelona. Chairman Van Rooyen, never a man to shun the potential for publicity which goes with his job, was particularly keen to show off his 'oh–so–good relationship' with the illustrious Cruyff. That oh–so–good relationship seems to have seduced Van Rooyen during a brief telephone conversation with Cruyff about television rights to the Dutch league. The Spanish company Dorna, which uses Cruyff as a kind of consultant, was interested in televising the Dutch first division. Cruyff acted as matchmaker to the deal. He introduced the parties, but then heard nothing until he read in the press that Dorna's deal had not been accepted.

'So I was used to get the price up', Cruyff concluded, perhaps with some justification. And who likes being used? No-one. Especially not an international luminary like Johan Cruyff. From that moment, he wanted nothing to do with the selection board.

Cruyff has been asked if he thinks he has too many conflicting interests, not least between being coach of the national team and business adviser.

'That's not what this is about. I distinguish between those different interests. What I think is important is that Van Rooyen is not to be trusted. And I don't want anything to do with people who are not trustworthy. And there's another thing. The selection board for professional football had appointed me at that time to get to know the people at Dorna.'

In an unfortunate situation, it was a stroke of luck when the selection board under Martin van Rooyen resigned on January 16th. This is because Cruyff had received his KNVB contract but, partly because of the situation described above, had not signed and returned the document. Johan Cruyff agreed with the new board under Jos Staatsen that both sides would see if Holland qualified. For the discussion to start again, we had to wait until after the victory in Poland on November 17th, which ensured that Holland, led by Dick Advocaat, reached the finals.

Because Barcelona qualified for the Champions' League and were playing two games a week it was impossible for Cruyff to return to Holland. 'I really don't feel too good about that', he said.

That's why chairman Staatsen travelled to Barcelona on November 26th. Cruyff and Staatsen talked for two hours. More than that, they 'found' each other. Staatsen was charmed by Cruyff the man and the professional. Cruyff was convinced by Staatsen's qualities as an organiser. The funny thing about Cruyff and Staatsen is that they are both big men and didn't use their relationship to show off or appear important. They are their own men – a rare breed in professional football.

When we talked to Cruyff a day after his meeting with Staatsen in Barcelona, he sounded optimistic. 'We are both going to do our homework,' he said. Staatsen used the same words a day later during a short press conference before the PSV-Feyenoord game.

And from that moment things started to go wrong. But not because of the attitude of Cruyff or his lawyer and tax adviser professor Harry van Mens. The fax should never have been invented, because after the first meeting there never was a second and all contact was through the cold, cool fax.

What happened was exactly what Cruyff had feared: the KNVB went back to being an unprofessional prestige-seeking organisation. Why didn't Staatsen go to Barcelona again? Why did Cruyff, a day after Barcelona-Real Madrid and two days before Barcelona's match against Celta Vigo, receive only a difficult-to-read, hand-written personal fax from Jos Staatsen? If Staatsen told Cruyff by fax that he was worried things were escalating dangerously, why was there no second meeting?

But it couldn't happen because Staatsen has such a demanding job and doesn't have time. He considers the KNVB – and we don't want to sound unkind – as a hobby and on Friday he has to go to Las Vegas for the World Cup draw. This is how the KNVB functions when the lawyers don't get results. And that's why the KNVB blames the failure of the negotiations on Cruyff, while Cruyff was convinced negotiations were continuing and that he and Staatsen would work things out.

Last Friday, Cruyff was given an ultimatum. 'Why an ultimatum when we're still in the middle of negotiations?' Cruyff thought. How was he supposed to react to the combination of faxes from the KNVB lawyer Mr HP Utermark and from Staatsen, bearing in mind that it's impossible to insult Cruyff more than by giving him an ultimatum. Cruyff might not be arrogant, but he happens to be the Sinatra of football trainers and it remains very Dutch to say that Cruyff shouldn't think he is Cruyff. Think about it!

As the KNVB announced last weekend, they failed to get Cruyff for two reasons: shoes and payments. If Staatsen is to be believed, Cruyff's stubborn lawyers were responsible for the failure to reach agreement. How stubborn were those lawyers? How stubborn was Cruyff?

In the first place, Cruyff was surprised that neither Staatsen or another appropriate KNVB official (Cees Wolzack) arranged a second personal meeting and that negotiations were conducted by fax even when things looked as if they were going wrong.

Staatsen, for his part, says he tried to speak to Cruyff five times last week. Cruyff denies this, knowing of two times (and we know from experience that Cruyff was available and ready to talk until 3pm on Monday, Tuesday and Wednesday last week). Meanwhile, Cruyff's lawyers had the impression that the KNVB's lawyers, despite the meeting in Barcelona between Cruyff and Staatsen, were not willing to negotiate openly. On the contrary, Mr Utermark gave Cruyff's lawyers a list of demands from the KNVB. Cruyff just had to accept this. Last weekend in Las Vegas, it was suggested that the last selection board had a business agreement with Cruyff.

Cruyff himself said at the time of the oral agreement that he wasn't only concerned about money and that he wanted to mean something for Dutch football.

The KNVB took that offer literally. In other words, there was no business agreement. At that time there was agreement only on two points for when Cruyff became coach: 1) Cruyff would be allowed to pick his own team and, 2) he wouldn't have to wear Lotto sportswear. Lotto makes the KNVB's official kit, but Cruyff has obligations to his own sportswear company Cruyff-Sports.

Money was not discussed at this time, despite Mr Utermark's suggestion that Cruyff and the previous selection board had reached a financial agreement. Cruyff kept his distance from the previous board, and his advisers told him not to discuss a salary.

In fact, Cruyff reasoned that he and the KNVB had only been negotiating since November 26, since the meeting with Staatsen. Before then, Cruyff had only said that he wanted to be coach and that Barcelona could not and would not stop him.

Mr Utermark began his first fax to Barcelona by remarking that Cruyff had agreed to be paid the same amount as the players. Cruyff denies that. He says he was willing to talk about everything except money, because that aspect would be handled by his advisers. Cruyff is not a player: he has different responsibilities and feels he cannot just be one of the boys, financially or otherwise. So, to the surprise of Mr Utermark, his proposal was refused and there was a counter-proposal from Cruyff's lawyers.

Utermark also said Cruyff would get the same percentage as the players from advertising and possible bonuses for reaching the quarter final, semi-final and final.

During the negotiations, Cruyff reasoned that from the time of the European Cup final on May 17th until the World Cup final in America on July 17th he would be available to work for the KNVB.

Because he agreed with Barcelona that he would forfeit one month's salary when he wouldn't be working for the club, he asked for the same amount from the KNVB as he would have got at Barcelona. That is indeed not an average month's salary (about 200,000 guilders): because top people in sport and showbusiness earn a lot of money. Cruyff asked for guaranteed salary and bonuses of 350,000 guilders before tax. The KNVB didn't want to go higher than 200,000 guilders for honorarium and bonuses.

Professor Van Mens's proposal to the KNVB was to split the difference, making it 275,000 guilders, but Mr Utermark didn't want to discuss it.

So in the end, the contract between Cruyff and the KNVB broke down over 75,000 guilders before tax.

Quite apart from the basic pay, there were disagreements over bonuses. Here Cruyff wanted to start from the normal level in his world. When top players have deals with boot sponsors like Lotto, Reebok, Diadora and Nike, they can get big bonuses – 200,000 guilders for example – if they win a trophy like a league title. Cruyff's proposal came to 55 per cent of that kind of sum: and that would be for winning the World Cup.

In the latter stages of the competition – the quarter-finals, semi-finals and final – every country gets the same increasing bonuses. In relation to those figures, Cruyff wanted 50,000 guilders for reaching the quarter final, 75,000 guilders for reaching the semi final, 100,000 to get to the final and 125,000 guilders for winning the World Cup. He didn't pluck these figures from thin air, but based them on similar figures for comparable stars such as Franz Beckenbauer, Michel Platini and Arrigo Sacchi.

The second breaking-point came over clothing. As a compromise after agreeing that Cruyff didn't have to wear Lotto, the KNVB wanted him to appear at press conferences wearing their official KNVB blazer. For his part, Cruyff didn't want to be provocative. He didn't want to wear a big advert on his clothes, but just the logo of his brand on his training shirt. The KNVB insisted on their blazer. While the KNVB criticised Cruyff's 'aggressive' lawyers, his lawyers were surprised by the stubborn attitude of Mr Utermark.

It remains a pity that Mr Staatsen didn't find time to meet Cruyff a second time. On Friday afternoon, Cruyff's lawyers received a fax from the KNVB in which Mr Utermark said no agreement had been reached and he couldn't accept Cruyffs demands and that his client, the KNVB, wasn't prepared to wait any longer, and that the KNVB absolutely had to have a contract before leaving for Las Vegas and that the negotiations had therefore been stopped. That fax surprised Professor Van Mens because the KNVB wanted to sign a contract without an agreement.

In answer to the KNVB's last fax to Cruyff's lawyers, in which Cruyff was informed that the KNVB wanted to stop negotiations, Professor Mr Harry van Mens said: 'You, the KNVB, have a lot of explaining to do to the Dutch people'.

Nieuwe Revu
December 1993

Chapter 22

IF WE DON'T SEE EACH OTHER AGAIN, IT'LL BE YOUR FAULT – CRUYFF ON CRUYFF

A conversation with Cruyff about Cruyff in sunny Barcelona: on sweets, autographs, success.

– Johan, would you do me and Frits a favour?

'Do you want me to take my sunglasses off?'

– How did you know I was going to ask that?

'I saw you looking.'

– Nice eh, those eyes?

'The problem is that if it's very sunny I need sunglasses. It will only bother me if the wind changes. Do you want a sweet? I've been to the baker.'

– You went to the baker and that's all you bring us?

'I always get sweet things.'

– Can you read people's minds?

'No. But if you concentrate on something you don't get many surprises.'

– Ha ha!

'You must be happy. Sometimes you won't turn up and that would be a bad interview. You'd have to make it up yourself.'

– That would be your fault.

'It's always your fault!'

– At the press conference for the Valencia–Barcelona game, an older man came and gave you three lollipops. Is it a ritual here?

'No, but they know I don't smoke. So wherever I go, people give me sweets. It started at the baker. When I go to get bread, he gives me a sweet.'

– Do you get the bread every morning?

'Not every morning. On Sunday, because I played on Saturday, I get the bread.'

– So are you tired?

'No, but I like to have breakfast. I think it's cosy and everyone gets together . . .'

– Do the children also come . . .

'And then I get the bread. But I've done that for 25 years, every Sunday I've had free.'

– In Amsterdam as well?

'Yes.'

– Are you satisfied with yourself?

'Yes. I think that where I have to I get a hundred per cent out of fulfilling my obligations. I'm a satisfied man.'

– So when you get up in the morning and you look in the mirror do think: well, Johan . . .

'No, not like that.'

– So how do you look then?

'I never look in the mirror that way. I look in the mirror when I need to brush my hair, but not the rest. One time I thought I'd shaved and I went downstairs and they said: why haven't you shaved? And I said: have I got a beard? And I looked in the mirror and noticed I had a beard.'

– Let's move on to something else. You really concentrate for an interview don't you?

'Well I never think about it before I do it.'

– But when it starts, you're very alert. You're looking at the soundman and the cameraman . . .

'Then there isn't much I don't see.'

– Do you still remember their names?

'Not separately. But I do know they like to be called Frank when they're together.'

– That's right!

'It's also logical. This is the first interview for six months. And that was a very bad interview. [A live discussion with Piet Keizer and Marco van Basten about the reasons why Cruyff was not going to the 1994 World Cup in America as Holland's national coach – not included in this book.] I wasn't there for whatever reason, so you have to pay more attention.'

– Did you ever take it personally? Because it was quite a tense broadcast.

'That's true, but . . .'

– You didn't like the way you appeared.

'I thought it was weak.'

– What did you think was weak about yourself?

'I wasn't paying attention, which you have to do. I should have been sharper and harder.'

– You wanted to be hard and sharp?

'Yes, but . . .'

– Maybe you're just a normal human being.

'Maybe I was just tired.'

– Are you ever tense?

'Yes, positively tense, nicely tense. I don't like negative tension.'

– Have you had that?

'Not much. No tension because of fear, but positive tension, yes, like before you leave the dressing room and you say things like: "if he does this or that, then I need to do this or that" – those little things.'

– Do you ever wake up at night?

'No.'

– Another nice detail. At half time in the Monaco–Barcelona game the referee stood waiting for you, didn't he?

'Yes.'

– And at that time, psychologically it's already 1-0.

'Yes, but I have that with nearly all foreign referees. In that case it was because there was a lot of press there. But almost all foreign referees ask for my autograph. It's always been like that. For their friends, their sons, themselves, I don't know. A man like that comes from Greece, Romania or wherever. And his friends hear he's taking charge of a Barcelona game and they say: "maybe you can ask so and so for his autograph?"'

– And you do that for them?

'Yes, why not.'

– But this referee was waiting for you. He wasn't going to go onto the pitch before you arrived. What did you say to him?

'We were joking before that anyway. Barcelona were warming up and I said something like: "shouldn't you warm up your whistle?" It was something like that.'

– And the Dutch referee John Blankenstein will be in charge of the European Cup final, if you get there. Is that something in your favour or against you?

'Normally speaking, I think it's a disadvantage. Dutch people especially want to be more Catholic than the Pope. But on the other hand you know that he's so experienced that he'll be able to keep his distance a little bit from those sort of things. And if you want to help, you must always help a Dutchman.'

– Johan, will we see you next year again?

'In Spain we have a nice saying: If we don't see each other again, it'll be your fault.'

Barend & Van Dorp
April 1994

Chapter 23

EVERYTHING YOU KNOW ABOUT IS NOT A PROBLEM – ANOTHER CRISIS

Once again things seem to be going badly at Barcelona. So Cruyff said yes when we invited him to do an interview about Barcelona, Bergkamp and Romario.

Things are not going well, but Johan Cruyff doesn't look worried as approximately 50 journalists interrogate him at the weekly press conference before the derby game with Espanyol. That Friday morning, Barcelona had again trained behind closed doors.

– 'What did you work on in training?' asks a Catalan journalist.

Steely eyed, the little face behind 15 or so brightly coloured microphones answers: 'We tried to play in a circle inside a square.'

– 'What was the objective?'

'I'm not saying. That's why we trained without the press and public.'

– 'Johan, aren't you jealous of Real Madrid – they're six points ahead of you?"

'I thought that Real and Barcelona were both knocked out of the Spanish Cup last week, the league has not been decided yet and we are still in the European Cup while Real lost to Odense. Do you understand why I'm happy to be here?'

There is nothing to suggest that last week Barcelona lost 0-5 to Racing Santander and were knocked out of the Spanish Cup three days later. Almost everyone knows the reasons for the mediocre performance. Firstly, Cruyff should never have allowed Real Madrid to buy the Dane Michael Laudrup. He should never have let his Spanish international goalkeeper Zubizarreta leave for Valencia, and he should never even have talked about swapping his international winger Goikoexea for Eskurza.

A couple of hours after the press conference, Cruyff makes this comment: 'I've been thinking about it. We also did badly in the first half of last season. We even had one point less than this season. Laudrup was a regular at that time. In the second half of the season, we got 28 points out of 30 and, in principle, Laudrup was then our fourth foreigner. He was a reserve. Koeman and Romario always played. The other place was between Stoichkov and Laudrup.

'I will not denigrate Laudrup. He is and remains a very good player. I myself brought him from Italy when everyone had written him off. Everyone called me crazy because at Milan – or was it Juventus? – he was always on the bench. When he came to us, he played very well, but at a certain moment, we noticed he was playing less well than in his early years. I can't prove it, but I don't think we'd have had better results if Laudrup had been with us this season, which doesn't take away from the fact that I think Laudrup is still a very good player. I always want to win, and I'm not going to get rid of someone if I think he's still the best! Stoichkov hasn't scored enough this year. Yes, they say, that's because Laudrup has gone. Do you know how many assists Laudrup gave Stoichkov last season? None. You obviously have to pay attention.'

– Yes, last season was worse. In mid February, Barcelona had 28 points from 23 games, and this season you have 29 points from 22 games. But how do we check what you say about those assists?

'You don't need to. You just needed to stay sharp when I said "none". Your answer should have been: logically, you are right, because they hardly ever play together, because last year it was either Laudrup or Stoichkov. And again, of course I've also wondered if I made a mistake, if I got it wrong. But if you exchange Laudrup for Hagi, then you have to assume you're not trading down.'

– We've watched Barcelona play a couple of times with the Romanian Hagi. He was one of the superstars of the World Cup and recently he was chosen as the fourth best player in the world but, in a manner of speaking, he doesn't give the ball to anyone else.

'Nonsense. I want to bet you that Hagi scores at least double the number of goals Laudrup managed and provides at least as many assists. I really don't know how many he's scored and how many Laudrup scored last season, but I still know I'm going to win the bet. Unfortunately, Hagi is injured again. Everyone in the squad who played in the World Cup – I think there's about 13 of them – has been injured for a short or a long time. It can't be a coincidence.'

– So you understand the point of view of the Ajax players who this week refused to play for the Dutch team against Portugal because the KNVB ignored their club's interests?

Cruyff suddenly sits up straight in his chair and beams: 'Fantastic! I think it's fantastic! We had the same experience 20 years ago when Piet Keizer was sent home by Ajax after he'd been sent off in an international. We didn't accept it then either. I think Danny Blind's action is excellent. What those international boards do is incredible, it's terrible. Look at what Koeman experienced under Michels. He was wanted for a friendly against France when we had to play the championship game against Bilbao. Koeman had to miss that game. He couldn't play in the championship game and he can never get that back. Recently, Laudrup was taken out of the league because Denmark was playing in some kind of FIFA-tournament in Saudi Arabia. I won't take any player now who won't sign that he puts the club before his country's interests.'

– Are you allowed to do that?

'I don't care. But if you pay a lot of money for a foreigner, I don't want other people to be able to take him away whenever they want to.

These days we also arrange that a player who plays in an international comes back to Barcelona as soon as possible. If it was up to those football associations, I'd lose players for 10 games a season. That's a quarter of all our league games. Then there'd be no point in getting foreign players.

'I think those Ajax players have class. It's typical that the Dutch are the first to do something like that. We've all been waiting for it. When FIFA think they can get away with anything they want. They organise a junior world championship in Nigeria in the middle of the season, when it doesn't only affect Ajax and Twente but also Real Madrid and our sister team so we have to lose a couple of important players. Those people at FIFA think they can do whatever they want. I like this sort of action.'

– We have incredible appreciation for the Ajax captain Danny Blind, who has to bear the pressure of this action on his own. Isn't the pressure too heavy, more than if he actually played in the friendly international match? Would you as a trainer have done the same as the coach and board of Ajax did, which was to make Danny Blind the only spokesman to the outside world?

'No, I would always have taken the initiative myself and would have kept Danny out of the spotlight. Of course such an action would have happened after discussions between the players, the technical staff and the board: who had the idea is not important.

'The players are the ones who have to do it, and that's difficult enough. As a board, you can never hide behind your players and say it was their initiative because if the board and the technical staff don't want it to happen, it's really not going to happen. I agree with you that you have to have a lot of respect for Blind. What he's doing is absolute class.'

Cruyff not only looks relaxed, he is relaxed. During the first interview, we drink a glass of wine and eat a delicious oil and tomato spread on Spanish bread. Johan wants garlic on his. 'Tonight we go to the training camp so I'll be sleeping on my own, so I want a lot of garlic'. The team goes to a training camp the day before Barcelona play their home games. The game starts here when we announce the 16 players (team and five substitutes). If players stay at home, they'll eat at around 10.30, go to bed late, they'll talk to everyone. Players aren't allowed to leave the hotel either. We don't accept that from each other, so I don't have to play policeman.

'I wouldn't mind stopping the training camp – I also prefer to sleep at home – but if you lose once, then everyone starts to complain. Most players don't mind going to bed on time. They can sleep in, don't have to get up at night if their kids cry or because their pregnant wife isn't well. On the other hand, if they ask me after dinner if they can sleep at home because their wife of child is ill, I'm not the type who says no.'

In the morning in the hotel where the team stay for their training camp, as guests of Cruyff and Bruins Slot it is no problem to speak to the players too. No one directly involved with the team is panicking. 'Where's Cruyff?' we ask assistant Carles Rexach. 'Oh he's out in the sun doing a puzzle.' Indeed, in a grassy corner by the swimming pool, we find the puzzling coach. 'You look well,' we say. 'I feel well', he answers. 'Bad, eh, the death of Ischa Meijer?' we say, knowing Cruyff has been interviewed by him. 'Yes, terrible,' he says with typical Cruyff logic, 'but he had a heart problem.'

In the evening we're lucky: we see Barcelona play probably their best first half of the season. Espanyol are played off the field. Ronald Koeman shows once again how indispensable he is for Barcelona. Cruyff on Koeman: 'I am a great Koeman fan. His future depends on whether he can keep it going physically and mentally. The pressure in countries like Spain and Italy is much more than in Holland. Koeman has his best years behind him. He has to decide about next year himself. I will only make that decision if he has doubts. It will depend on why he has doubts. Does his family still support him? That's a big influence and I understand that. These aren't small decisions and they're more complicated than a lot of people think. In itself it sounds simple. If he's like he is now, it's no problem and I'd love to keep him. But, again, can he do it for another year? Because a player of his stature should at all costs avoid playing on when he can't do it any more. He's got such a big name here, he should never lose it. Only he can determine this. I don't have to do that work. He knows what he wants. We'll have a nice little dinner, have a nice glass of wine and we'll decide.'

– Is Rijkaard right to retire at the end of the season at Ajax?

(decisively) 'No, because physically he can do much more.'

– But maybe mentally he can't do it any more?

'Oh stop it. We're talking about Holland, where all you have to do is train and play games. No long journeys, no four sports newspapers and microphones under your nose every day. I think it's a pity he's going to stop, and stupid as well. No, I wouldn't try to bring him here, because I can understand he doesn't want to. In principle, Frank is someone who loves nice and good football. He likes it at Ajax, he's got good players around him, he plays in an ideal climate, and that's why he can do well at that level. What's Frank going to do otherwise? He can go to the office and have meetings but he absolutely cannot play nice football. Think about it. In the morning, you say to your son: "You're going to school" and he says to you: "Daddy, what are you going to do?". And Daddy says: "I'm going to play nice football". Can't be better than that can it? I played myself this morning for 15 minutes. What a delight is still is! If God gives you the gift of being able to play the beautiful game at a high level, then you have to keep playing every year you can. So says an old player/coach who, if you look at the results at the moment, should be having some problems. I speak from experience. I stopped as well. I had the experience of my body. But Frank's body is much heavier, so if he regrets it after a couple of months, he's going to have it a lot tougher than I did at the time. I've seen it all. If there's ever been a copy of Heintje Davids, then it's me.'

– But if Rijkaard can't do it any more?

'That's all nonsense. How can you not do it any more? Getting out of bed in the morning, having a nice breakfast, a bit of training six days a week? And on the seventh day you do the most wonderful thing that exists: play a game. Listen, if Frank was nervous before a game, or was getting more nervous, then he should stop. I do advise him urgently to think again about this. Someone who loves football like Frank does should not retire.'

– Why did you say some time ago that you couldn't use a single Ajax player at Barcelona?

'Because it's true.'

– Johan, that's nonsense! Let's start at the back. Take Edwin van Der Sar. Isn't he a much better goalkeeper than your Busquets?

'You don't understand. I've never said I don't think the Ajax players are good. If I mention an Ajax player that I'd want, he has to be better than the three foreigners I have now. So he has to be better than Koeman, Stoichkov and Hagi. Van Der Sar is a very good goalkeeper, but he's a foreigner. If Van Der Sar was Spanish, he would have been a candidate.

   'I saw the Ajax-Feyenoord game. After Van Der Sar comes Reiziger. I know him inside out from the time Tonnie Bruins Slot and I worked at Ajax. We found him, like we found all of them: Seedorf, Davids, Kluivert. I know them all really well. Frank and Ronald de Boer made their debuts under me. We had a fight about it at the time, because we were not allowed to pay their father's travelling expenses. We couldn't do that until they were in the Junior B team. And we said: in that case AZ Alkmaar is going to sign them instead, so then we did a trick with them and put them in the B juniors immediately. From the Ajax-bred players, Wooter and Musampa are the only ones I don't know. We found the rest ourselves, so I know what I'm talking about. Again: a player like that needs to understand the place of a foreigner.'

– Were you interested in Frank de Boer?

'Frank would have been a candidate. He has good vision, a good kick, he can head well. He's a very good footballer.'

– So if they were Spanish?

'They're not. Let's say Koeman doesn't stay. I have the whole world to choose from. Firstly, his replacement must have something exceptional, as Koeman does. But he also has to be able to cope with the pressure, he has to have something. Here you not only have to play football well, you have to be hard and mean. Playing in Spain is different from playing a couple of times with a Dutch club against a Spanish club. Look at Richard Witschge: being a good player is not enough.'

– One of Ajax's best players, the Finn Jari Litmanen . . .

'We had him here for a trial. Again, a very good player. But he had to fight for a place with Laudrup and Stoichkov. Should I ever have done that to such a nice, modest Finnish boy? A foreigner who comes here has to have something extra, like Rijkaard, Gullit, Van Basten and Koeman all have.'

– And Bergkamp has?

'Yes, he also has it.'

– Is he coming to Barcelona?

'No.'

– No?

'No, definitely not. There are too many things I don't like. But that's all I want to say about it. Only that at this moment, if we're talking about next season, I won't buy him.'

– Sometimes you're so obstinate.

'And that's the reason for what?'

– Bergkamp fits with you.

'Not at this moment, not the way he presents himself. I know Bergkamp as well. I picked him myself from the youth team when he didn't have to go, just because he was such a pleasant boy. So . . .'

– So, going back to your own team, everyone thought you could have handled Romario, that he wouldn't have done whatever he wanted. You must have been enormously irritated when he failed to turn up to the training camp without even calling.

'Of course he could have called, but that's not the way he is. The clever people can get away with anything. And of course you can see his attitude as an insult. Privately I can be angry and feel insulted, but professionally, you can never be guided by such feelings.'

– Would you want him to come back?

'He is making a comeback. He is not playing well, and he'll never again be like he was. The teeth of time have also gnawed on him. He had a fantastic quality. Without doing any work, he could still produce an act of genius. But when that goes, you can't use him any more because it's like playing with 10 players. So you have to put your private feelings aside and make sure you sell him as soon as possible, which is what happened.'

– Was he as good as you were?

'No, of course not. He couldn't work hard like I did. I made others play better, he can only score goals.'

– When Romario left, you bought the Russian Korneyev. We saw him do good things against Espanyol. Does he have many extra qualities?

– Firstly, he has not been bought. At the start of the season, he was redundant at Espanyol and we put him under contract for our feeder team. He's a Russian international. He played in the World Cup against Cameroon and this week was called up again for his national team. So he's not bad. Like I said, I saw Ajax-Feyenoord last week.

Now really, he could play for Feyenoord with one hand in his pocket. When Romario left, we only got him for our A-team because in the second half of the season he was available for all our games.'

– You weren't a bad player yourself, especially at Ajax. Wouldn't it be nice to name the new Ajax stadium after you, to call it the Johan Cruyff Stadium?

'I would really like that, I must admit.'

– We hope we're wrong, but we get the impression that's not going to happen. Do you have any idea why the stadium will not bear your name?

'No. It would be an honour, but it's not something I'm concerned with. Because you asked me about it, I answered honestly.'

– Is it because the Ajax board thinks you're negative about Ajax?

'I'm not negative. I'm realistic and honest. I know that I've never had a fantastic relationship with board members, so that's not new. I'm not a friend of the chairman here, either. There's one thing no board can ever take away from me, and that's my experience which gives me the right to think. If I give my opinion it's usually because I'm worried that something's going to go wrong. Unfortunately, I have to say a lot of things are going wrong at Ajax.'

– Don't you think you're taking things a little out of context? Ajax are playing fantastically. They're top of their group in the Champions League. They get huge crowds, have no debts. They may be stronger than Barcelona.

'Why don't you stop talking shit? We've both got through two rounds of the European Cup. I'm looking further ahead than today. And is Ajax stronger? It would be wonderful if we could fight it out because that would mean we were both in the European Cup final. And am I not allowed to talk about Ajax because at the moment Barcelona aren't playing as well?

'People always see me in black and white. When everyone said everything was going wrong in Dutch football, that we never won anything in Holland any more, I said: "Give me the chance to prove the opposite without a diploma". I showed them it wasn't that bad. I wanted to do the same with the Dutch team, but in my own way. They wanted to do it their way. OK, fine.

'Let someone give me a normal human argument why I should be negative about Ajax. I live like a god, I don't want to come back ever, I've been through this so-called bad period and they just extended my contract until 1997. You think I'm going to be kicked out here because it's going slightly less well at the moment? Really not, even for the amounts involved.'

– Van Gaal is doing well at Ajax.

'I hope he's doing well. I can't judge that.'

– But aren't they playing very well?

'Yes, Ajax have a traditional way of playing, their own style that no-one can ever change. It's been like that for 20 years and luckily Van Gaal is not trying to change it. And if the left back or the right back plays a little more inside or outside, if you play with three or four men in midfield, those are details.'

– They almost humiliated AC Milan twice.

'When Milan was something like sixth from bottom. You must have a little bit of quality. I don't want to denigrate them, because Ajax are playing well, but at the moment all the clubs that belong there are in the quarter finals of the European Cup, except Manchester United. And of course, give me two wingers who are better than Overmars. I really hope from the bottom of my heart that Ajax will do well until the end of days, that everything is not going to collapse in three years. It's just that so often you see people getting light-headed from a bit of temporary success. So let them think about it for a moment and ask themselves: why does Cruyff say this? I'm not saying it because it's not true. I've been champions four times with Barcelona. Barcelona is having its best period this century. History repeats itself, so I say learn from it. That's what I always say.

'Everyone says Ajax is now so much better, looking better than ever. But, in the youth system is there a Vanenburg, a Rijkaard, a Van Basten, a Witschge, a Roy coming through? I hope so. And again I have the right to an opinion. I always say: "in the land of the blind, the one-eyed man is king, but he still only has one eye." I miss the extra quality that Ajax was always identified with. I hope it will come back again.

'And if you don't agree with something, you have to say so. That goes for me, it goes for journalists, and it goes for you as well.'

Nieuwe Revu
February 1995

Chapter 24

I THINK HE'LL ALWAYS KNOW WHERE HE HAS A FRIEND – THE DEPARTURE OF RONALD KOEMAN

On March 23 1995 Ronald Koeman announced he was definitely leaving Barcelona. During our interview with Ronald and Bartina Koeman we showed a short film of his coach Johan Cruyff's reaction to the decision. Here is that interview with Cruyff:

– When did Ronald Koeman tell you he was going to leave Barcelona?

'We had a conversation last week and that's when he said it.'

– Are you disappointed?

'Yes. In one way, of course, you can understand it because at this level, in this climate, it takes so much out of you. But of course it's disappointing because he's always been a regular player. I think he's been the most valuable foreigner, at least in the period that I've been here.'

– Do you think he's been the best foreigner out of all the foreigners you've had – Romario, Stoichkov, Laudrup, Witschge . . . ?

'Well, I think so. When you talk about a top player at that level then you're talking about different things. Firstly, on the field itself: being there at important moments, scoring decisive goals in the European

Cup, giving passes. Secondly, his behaviour off the pitch. You just have to look at the past year to see there's a gigantic difference from the rest. Then you see that from my side – from someone who's always been on the technical side of things. Of course there is admiration and I've counted on him. They go together. It's always been there 100 per cent.'

– Are you going to miss him as a person?

'Of course, that's another story, the off-the-field story. However you talk about it, we've lived together very closely for six years. And not in a distant way, but through all the emotional things involved, like them having a baby, the parties, the attacks on us, the blows you've suffered together. Of course it makes a strong bond, a very strong bond.'

– Would you have been so successful without him?

'You never know, but if I classify him as our most important foreigner, it shows how much I appreciate him.'

– What advice would you give him for the future?

'Don't stop, don't stop. That's what I said immediately. That would be a terrible shame! It's one thing to put up with the crazy atmosphere at Barcelona. It's quite another to say: hey guys I just want to play football. Because that's what he does, and he should keep doing it. If you say: I don't want to do *that* any more, I want a bit of peace in my life, I can understand that. But to retire? He definitely shouldn't do that. I said the same thing to Rijkaard as well. I don't think he should stop.'

– You think Rijkaard shouldn't stop. But if Ronald Koeman goes to Groningen, isn't that too big a step down for such a great footballer?

'He loves football and that's the most important thing. For the rest, you have to decide yourself as you see it.'

– Does it make a difference whether he plays for Groningen, PSV, Ajax or Feyenoord?

'Oh yes, of course. After Barcelona it has to be Ajax or Feyenoord. It's a lot more quiet with the press and people around him. But there is and still will be pressure. At Groningen there will be pressure also, but that's something else. You can do it with more smiling, let's put it that way.'

– How long can Koeman go on playing football?

'Another couple of years for sure.'

– And finally, there was an interview in *El Pais* today in which you said you are 95 per cent certain to leave Barcelona. Is that true?

'I said a lot of things have to change, otherwise it's almost impossible to have success.'

– But has anything happened since last week?

'No, it's the same.'

– Are you really going to leave? Is it 95 per cent certain you're leaving? I can't believe that.

'If things don't change, and it's not in my hands, then you have to say: "guys it's all nice and fine but there's no honour to be had here".'

– Have they said they're going to change things?

'I haven't had a conversation with them.'

– Aren't you at all worried?

'No.'

– To really finish, what do you want to say to Ronald Koeman who you worked with for six years?

'Health and pleasure. And I think he'll always know where he has a friend. That's the most important thing.'

Barend & Van Dorp
March 1995

Chapter 25

DETALLES, DETALLES, SIEMPRE DETALLES – CRUYFF IS ENJOYING IT AGAIN!

I n August 1995, Barcelona prepared for the new season as usual in Drenthe, in the Netherlands, with several new players. During training, Cruyff enjoyed himself like a 10–year-old kid on holiday. It was to be his last season.

The two best Dutch footballers of the seventies, Johan Cruyff and Wim van Hanegem, are both looking back at poor seasons as coach and trainer. Both have changed their teams to make them title candidates this year, Cruyff at Barcelona against traditional rivals Real Madrid, and Van Hanegem as Feyenoord coach against the eternal opposition of Ajax and PSV. It only makes life more fun. In contrast to Van Hanegem, who remains incredibly popular with Feyenoord supporters, Cruyff was booed by the 40,000 Barca fans who showed up to see him present his new squad.

The Romanian Gica Popescu, one of Barcelona's many new faces, who played for PSV and Tottenham Hotspur last season, said: 'That wasn't nice. It was terrible for Cruyff but it was also painful for us as players'.

Cruyff himself isn't bothered. In fact, he's laughing about it. He won't walk away from any conflict, so long as he thinks that conflict is in the interest of his club and his team. Sometimes, perhaps, he appears to look for trouble. The words 'cowardice' and 'excuse' are not in his vocabulary.

'The new boys may have been scared, but I don't care any more. It's an inherent part of the club. I've said it before: Barcelona has had the best trainers and the best players have played there. And what did they win in all those years? Nothing. They were always in Real Madrid's shadow. Do you know why? Because no-one was ever prepared to take decisions people might not like because they didn't want to be unpopular. Nine out of every ten decisions they did take were the wrong decisions. So they have to take decisions and if no-one else dares do it, I will.

'I've been doing this for too long to start doing things just to be popular. So I will take responsibility for unpleasant decisions. Then the public gets the impression it was just me who wanted Stoichkov to leave. Believe me, everyone wanted it, but you know how it goes. There's always someone who says: "I don't think it should have happened".'

− Because you did let Stoichkov go and, according to the Bulgarian himself, you killed the championship team of 1993.

'I know. If things go well, I'm responsible, and if they go badly, I'm also responsible. The book on Stoichkov is closed. When we asked ourselves the question "are we going to continue with Stoichkov?" we started to analyse him. We looked at three criteria: personal, sporting and economic.

'On the personal aspect, he got on either badly or not at all with more than a third of the other players. I'm not even talking about myself. He had no respect for the club, his fellow players, the board or the trainers. So on the personal side, it was an easy decision.'

− He said in a Spanish paper that you treated him without respect when you wouldn't let him leave on Thursday to prepare for a big party on Friday where lots of awards were being presented. You made him come in and train and after 10 minutes you told him he could go after all.

'When you've lost 0-5 to Real Madrid the Sunday before, you don't go to a party. You should be modest. I'm the one who decides whether or not he should train, not him. I'm not interested in what he thinks or says. I was invited myself but I thought after the Real Madrid defeat we should stay away from parties and things like that.

'But OK. Let's look at the sporting aspect. He wanted to show who's right on the pitch. It's logical: that was the only place where he could have taken his sporting revenge on me. And I wish he had. But if you only scored three goals in the second half of the season, then on the sporting side, you have nothing to say. Listen, Stoichkov was and is a very good footballer, but he wasn't functioning with us any more. It can't be that he was a very good player two years ago and now he can't play any more. That's impossible. So what happened? It has to do with his stamina, his mentality. With a player like that, everything has to be 100 per cent. He's 95 per cent and he'll go downhill very fast. With Prosinecki it was really the same story: he was very famous when he was very young. Everyone wrote great things about him, everyone in Europe wanted him. Real Madrid, the great Real Madrid, paid 15 million for him, maybe more. They think they're Lord Jesus, and then they fall very hard. Prosinecki went down a long way. I think and hope we got Prosinecki at the right moment, because he's a very good player. Oh yes, I compare him absolutely to Roberto Baggio. Maybe he can be even better. Now he can show us what he can do. I would have liked to have had him last season, but at the time Real Madrid was still asking money for him, and that's always a little bit sensitive between Real and Barcelona. This year he cost nothing. I expect a lot from him. He trains with so much effort and pleasure that I have the feeling we got him at the right moment. Stoichkov was up in the air. I can understand that, but it shouldn't last too long and unfortunately he didn't come down to earth. So aspect number two was not in his favour.

'Then you come back to the economic aspect. If we hadn't sold him, we would have paid at least 1,650 million pesetas to him over three years. That's about 6 million guilders a year. I think that's too much anyway, especially for a player who doesn't achieve anything and is completely confused as a footballer. The other side of it was that we could ask 1400 million pesetas, more than 15 million guilders for him, which covered half the other investments.

'So when you add up those three aspects, you don't have to think for one moment. Also, it was not a topic of discussion within the club. I announced the decision. Everyone agreed, but I'll bear the consequences. I wasn't impressed by the whistling and booing because we didn't take the decision to get a sympathetic reaction from the public but because it was in the interests of the club. The supporters don't want another year like last season do they?'

Cruyff saw the entire Spanish press last Monday. On Tuesday, he talked to the Dutch media, which also arrived en masse. Anything could be asked and everyone got an answer. Despite the pressure of journalists who watch him every second, Cruyff enjoyed the press conference, especially because this year he's enormously pleased with the building of a new team. The Spanish press, with 30 journalists, was present during the whole two weeks of the training camp. Catalan television showed pictures of every training session.

After the Monday press conference, the Spanish journalists were invited for a long lunch with Barcelona's press officer Ricardo Maciens. At the end of the meal, Maciens explained what the club expects from the journalists and what the rules are for in-depth interviews with players. At the end of the lunch, Maciens asks if we know where 'Mister' is. 'He's gone for a little sleep'. Maciens rings Cruyff and asks if he wants to come downstairs.

Drowsily, he comes down – 'I wasn't sleeping deeply' – and joins the journalists in a toast and sings 'happy birthday' for a woman present. Then he repeats what Maciens said about long interviews having to be cleared with the club using his well-known motto: everything you know about is not too bad. After that a joker in the company sits at the piano and does a parody of the trainer/coach and everyone joins in:

'Detall-all-all-all-alles, siempre detalles
Details, details, always details, it's about the details
One and one make two details
Prosinecki, Hagi, Figo, Kodro, Popescu
Who they're playing
It's about the details
Always those details
But we love 'cojones'
We love fooling around
And going crazy with the details'

Cruyff sits there and smiles. The singer, Bernat Bafatuy, says: 'It was classy of Cruyff to be there because we're not big friends. He doesn't like talking to me. I work on the weekly satirical programme on TV-3. On the programme we have someone who does a fantastic impression of Cruyff, with dolls like a sort of 'Spitting Image'. And he doesn't always like that'.

After the singing, coffee and cognac everyone leaves.

Cruyff says: 'I hear the same jokes every week, but I have no problem about joining in. It's all part of it'.

– Have you got too many players?

'Yes, we need to get rid of a couple. Just before I went to sleep, I heard Thomas Christiansen is going to get some experience with the French champions, Nantes.'

Christiansen is a similar player to Cruyff's son Jordi, a young, talented Danish player with dual nationality, who's played a couple of times for the Spanish national team, who was on loan to Sporting Gijon last season and is, once again, not going to be good enough for the elite of Barca.

– Since Ronald Koeman left you haven't attracted a single Dutch player.

'There wasn't one that I liked – and don't misunderstand me again, because they're masters at misunderstanding me or misinterpreting what I say. Let me not say it negatively. Either I didn't like them or they were asking too high a price.'

– Like Frank de Boer. You would have liked to sign him.

'He could have been the next Koeman. But when his contract expired they were asking such an idiotic price, at least I understood he would cost way too much. So in the end I preferred to take Popescu. He cost me only a quarter of what I would have had to pay for Frank de Boer.'

– Ajax wanted Popescu as the replacement for Frank Rijkaard. Just before the European Cup final, they hoped Popescu would agree not to come to Barcelona.

'I don't know anything about that. That's the first I've heard about it.'

Cruyff has always been charmed by Dennis Bergkamp.

– You did ask about him, didn't you?

'Yes, but he had to believe in it 100 per cent and it had to be done at an achievable price. I didn't need him, but in principle I was very interested in Dennis. I've said sharp things about him, but Dennis remains a footballer with those extra qualities.'

– The past year must have been tough on you?

'It wasn't nice. I've obviously felt it a lot. But I haven't been so upset that it's eaten me up. I saw things getting out of control without being able to change it. I've seen people change. That's sad, especially as it concerns people who have that little bit extra that I love. I realise such people are always difficult, but I like working with difficult people. I like emotional people. At a certain point they really have to understand what top football is about. And yes, that was lost. That's a pity because these days, there are very few phenomenal players who are head and shoulders above the rest.'

According to the Spanish press, Cruyff paid a total of 25 million guilders for his new arrivals. Bosnian striker Meho Kodro cost eight and a half million. Barcelona paid seven million for the huge talent of Cuellar. Popescu came from Tottenham Hotspur for just six and a half million and the Portugese Luis Figo cost four and a half million.

– What kind of centre forward is Kodro, two times a Yugoslav international?

'A real one: a good head, an English type. You'll see. He's up there for every ball at the near post. Headstrong and someone who wants to work hard as a centre forward. Because of him, later, when we've got used to each other, we'll be able to play a more pressing game. And then we'll use the Portugese Figo, who's a very strong technical player, only 22 years old. From Betis Seville we've got Cuellar: as small as Maradona, very strong in one-on-one situations, two-footed with a very strong left foot.'

– Your son has stayed.

'He could have gone anywhere, could have played in the Champions League. But he stayed with Barcelona. Why? Because I like him to stay with me. There are more bad than good people in football. He's a good player, so I thought it might be better for him to stay with us.'

Despite the heat, Barcelona train in the morning, starting at 7.30 with a run through the forest. At 11 o'clock there's some gymnastics with the ball and at 6 o'clock, on the wonderful pitches of the Drenthe Reds, we see old-fashioned Barcelona training. There are eight-a-side games, with four players continuously on the bench, and four-a-side position games in the penalty area. Sometimes Cruyff stops the game, gathers the players around him and, in a controlled manner, explains what he wants and doesn't want. In the four-a-sides, using real goals not imaginary ones, we see the return of the old street football rule that after three corners it's a penalty. The penalties are taken at the end. Kodro hits the crossbar, repeating his miss in the first real test game – against local side FC Zwolle. In the final friendly, against FC Utrecht, his penalty hit the post. Gica Popescu seems to be blossoming after his disappointments with PSV and Spurs.

After the Utrecht-Barcelona game, the players and trainers have another surprise at their hotel in Amsterdam: Ronald Koeman and his wife Bartina. Players, trainers and everyone else in the party are all very happy to see the return of the lost children.

– Koeman is missed isn't he?

Johan Cruyff: 'Yes, and it's well known that I wanted Koeman to play for another year. But now we have Popescu, a player with other qualities – let's see how it goes. Yes, I'm really looking forward to this season.

'Whatever you've won doesn't count any more when you start a new season. It's nice when I see how many illusions all the players started with, how good and intensively everyone has trained And if you find out that you can be a pillar of strength for young players, and also for experienced players, then try to be what they expect and try to help the players.'

– Why do you like to prepare for the season in Holland?

'Where else can you find such wonderful pitches, such peace, such good opposition to practice against in the lower levels of paid professionals? You want to play without being scared when we have three attackers against us. I think it's ideal here and of course it's easy because I speak the language when I need to arrange something quickly.'

– Is playing with the group still the trainer's greatest pleasure?

'Yes.'

– And you make the pitch as small as possible so you don't have to run too much?

'Or I train the players so hard they're dead tired.'

Nieuwe Revu
August 1995

Chapter 26

OFTEN A RESULT IS CONFUSED WITH THE SITUATION – THREE MONTHS BEFORE THE SACK

Three months before he was sacked, we had a satellite link to the studios of TV-3 in Barcelona where Cruyff sat with his son Jordi. It was a question and answer game in the typical Johan Cruyff style. We've always enjoyed the way Cruyff – and Gullit too – despite his long life in different countries abroad still talks like a man who's lived his whole life in Amsterdam.

– Johan Cruyff, this season you've had a fairly new team and it hasn't gone too well. There's a lot of criticism of you in Spain from people who say you should be at the top of the league. Are you comfortable at a time like this?

'In the first place, problems are obviously there to be solved. But often a result is confused with the situation. It's not that we're playing badly, but in principle we don't score enough goals. And if you don't score enough goals, everything becomes a bit more insecure because normally we do score a lot of goals. When you let one in, it doesn't normally matter. But if you're not scoring, then every goal we concede is one too many or can cause problems with the result. So you can see how you lose 1-0 or it's 0-0 or 1-1. If you scored three or four you'd solve the problem. And if you take it back a stage, you see that of our six forwards, each week three or four are injured.'

– You are eleven points behind Atletico Madrid. Since October, that's four months, you haven't won an away game. That doesn't fit either with Barcelona or with you.

'We always play attacking football, but it's just not going well. The first thing you have to do with attacking football is score goals. If you look at all the goals we've scored in all our games, it's just not enough. And that shows what the problem might be.

'If you have six forwards of whom three are foreigners and you have three Spaniards injured, then you can't play those Spanish players and you try different things but there's nothing you can do about that.'

– This year you bought a striker, Kodro, who was a top scorer last year and this year he's only scored six goals. Why did he score a lot last year but not now?

'When you play for a big team, there's a lot of pressure, especially if the results are a little disappointing. If someone like that can play in a more relaxed way and the rest can join in, then you'll win your games and he'll score goals. He'll take those half chances. At the moment, he misses good chances. That's part of being a striker and the problem of pressure and getting the chances you need as a striker. And there are just fewer of them because you miss individual attackers.'

– Have you missed Jordi?

'Of course. As I said, we have five or six forwards . . .'

– Yes, but have you missed him?

'Jordi is someone with outstanding qualities, especially offensively. Then you have Cuellar, who also has a lot of quality. Neither of them has played all year. Then there's Hagi and Prosinecki: one of them has always been injured. Of course you still have Figo and one other, but they have to do everything. Jordi is someone who can beat someone when it's one-against-one. If you play that correctly, you automatically create chances because that's what attacking football is.'

– There's been a lot of criticism of you. Would that have been different if your son had been fit?

'You never know, but I think so. And you have to look past that criticism a little. When you see how journalists in Holland translate everything, you see how they've made that into an easy story.'

– Well, we've read a number of Spanish papers and *Sport* magazine which says . . .

'Well, it's well known what's in there.'

– Is it a paper that is by definition hostile to you?

'I have little or no contact with them. But they carry on writing. I stopped reading that magazine months ago.'

– It must get to you. Eleven points behind, a great trainer, a great club. I don't think you're having a good time at the moment.

'No, but I think you shouldn't exaggerate these things. In the first place . . .'

– But we're not exaggerating are we?

'For 80 per cent of the time, yes. But listen. When you have a 75 per cent new team, then it's going to take time. That's logical. If there's a lot of injuries in that team, it's going to cost more time. Then you say: OK, we're second, eleven points behind. With the game coming up on Wednesday, we're in the last eight of the Spanish Cup. We're in the last eight of the European Cup. Then you say: are things really so terrible? Take it easy. Easy. Little by little, the injured players are coming back. The prizes haven't been handed out yet. We're still in everything. We can still win everything. So being calm is the only thing that can help you.'

– But in one of the daily sports papers it says the players don't trust you any more. Do you feel that? Or is that all nonsense?

'The players? As a matter of fact, I have very good contact with them. I've always had that with almost all players, though there are obviously exceptions. I don't think there's a single problem between me and the players. There are a few – and it's logical – who are unhappy because they're not playing so well. I think that's pretty normal. If it wasn't like that, you'd have doubts about their mentality. But in general there isn't a single problem.'

– Your contract expires at the end of the season, doesn't it?

'Some time ago I said it was one of those things I wouldn't talk about. In principle, a contract makes sense until there's a problem.'

– But there is a problem now!

'No, that's not true. If there are problems at the end of the season, then we'll get the contract out.'

– We read in the press that you're going to stay until June 30th, whatever happens. They won't fire you. Do you get the impression things are over or would like to keep that honour to yourself?

'Of course everything is being said and written in a particular way. Little hints are given to see how people react, how they see the situation. To see whether or not the situation solves itself, and so on. That's why I call them "test balloons". You have to just leave them alone. Anyway, I'll see what happens.'

– No, wait a moment, Johan. If it doesn't go well, are you going to leave at the end of the season?

'Listen, the problem with these broadcasts is that there's a couple of guys here who speak Dutch. Those are exactly the kind of stories you get in Holland all the time.'

– Say it in English then.

'No, it means you always have to be careful what you say because it depends on how it's translated. There is an impression of uncertainty about what's going to happen here because of all the stories and nonsense. There was a story about the contract at the time. And I said: boys, don't talk about it any more.'

– But will you stay until the end of the season or not?

'Normally speaking, we'd wait until the end of the season. And if there are problems, we'd take the contract out of the cupboard.'

– But be concrete: you had an offer to sign for another year and you didn't sign. Why didn't you?

'At the point where there's a proposal and you have an oral agreement, there's nothing to sign, is there?'

– So are you saying you have a contract for the next season?

'I'm not going to talk about this subject any more. I've said I'll take the contract out and look at it in May.'

– Do you actually know what's in the contract?

'To be honest, no. I signed it in 1992, and if no one objects, it just continues.'

– Do you want to carry on after June 30th?

'You sit and laugh, but that's really how it is. I'm sick of all the moaning about carrying on and money. In that respect, I've always had a good name: "money wolf", and it continues. I said: you know what we'll do? We'll sign the contract once and each year I stay, we'll add ten per cent. So you only have to do it once, and the moment you say "here's three months notice", it's over.'

– But if it goes up by 10 per cent each year, are you going to stay another couple of years?

'Well, I might.'

– What advice would you give Jordi regarding the Dutch national team?

'It's a personal decision. If you play in the Spanish team, you have to change your nationality. It's not just a simple football decision. It's a decision that affects your whole life. There are no easy choices. That's why he says that when he gets a hint that he's going to be invited to play [for Holland or Spain] and he's fit, he'll take a decision. That's the moment to take a decision. Everything else is just hot air.'

– What do you do in your spare time?

'I have family, grandchildren and a son who has a few problems, although they're nearly behind him. And I like to play a little golf.'

– What worries you more: the current situation at Barcelona or your son's knee?

'Both. Of course I'm worried about Jordi's knee because I'm not a doctor. So I have to listen and take the good things. As things stand at the moment – reasonably optimistic or not optimistic – it's a question of time and then the problem will be over.'

– We want one more thing from you. When the board meets and is unhappy – because they meet and are unhappy every week – how does that affect you? Does it make you nervous? Or do you say: it doesn't interest me?

'In principle, of course you have to deal with it, because you have to deal with results. But I think you have to keep your mind where it should be: on the team, on the situation, on one confrontation after another. We play almost every three days so you don't have a lot of time for things that are a bit outside of that. If those are things that are to do directly with the sporting part, then you say: well maybe it can solve something. But it's nearly always arguments outside of sport and you think: I have almost nothing or nothing to do with it. It depends what it's about. In any case, it's logical that you have worries as a coach: the players, the situation, scoring or not scoring goals; that kind of problem.'

– But does it keep you awake?

'No, definitely not.'

– You don't do that anymore do you?

'No, that's long gone. I think that's a negative influence and it doesn't make any sense.'

– Would you like Edgar Davids and Michael Reiziger in your team next year?

'I think these are two guys I know pretty well, Reiziger maybe a little better than Davids. No, that wasn't the question: I think they're two good young footballers.'

– No, we asked: do you want to have them in your team? You did understand that didn't you?

'Yes, but that's the problem. I could answer those kind of questions with all the love in the world, but then it creates some other kind of game. It doesn't help me at all.'

– We're only asking: would you like them in your team next season?

'I think they're great footballers.'

– Do you think they'll go to Spain or Italy?

'I think the new transfer rules will definitely make a difference anyway. It's just a question of how big a difference. I think it will have to do with the interests people have in their own national teams. Because

Uefa can't make the rules any more, teams will have to make their own rules. You won't have anything to do with anyone else when you make up your own rules.'

– Yesterday we read in the paper, in nearly all the papers, that your vice-chairman, Mr Gaspart said in an informal conversation: 'Johan has admitted a couple of mistakes to me'.

'A lot of things are being said.'

– But have you admitted making mistakes?

'There will always be mistakes. You can't avoid it. The only thing is that if you point out your problems they go on about it even longer.'

– But have you admitted mistakes?

'You don't have to admit anything. And if it doesn't go well, it doesn't go well. And they'll blame you anyway, whether or not you admit making mistakes. What's the difference?'

– We would really like to hear from you whether you admitted your mistakes.

'Everyone makes mistakes. It's logical.'

– Did you admit it to the board? You've had an informal conversation and then Mr Gaspart said: he admitted such and such mistakes.

'It didn't go that far.'

– Would you like to become national coach of the English team?

'The England team? I don't want to be national coach at all because I'm not suited to it.'

– Why not?

'Because I need a daily relationship with the players. And you can't do that if it's once every three or four week, whenever it's suitable. I'd have to follow players, invite them, that sort of thing. I'm just not suited to that.'

– And do you think you'll still be at Barcelona?

'No idea. I've been here eight years and no-one expected that.'

– Johan, do you have one more thing to tell us?

'I can say a lot of things but . . .'

– No, just one!

'I thought it was very cosy and I hope things go well for everyone.'

Barend & Van Dorp
February 1996

P.S. The next day two newspapers wrote that Cruyff would stay at Barcelona on one condition: Davids and Reiziger must come. That's what Cruyff had told us privately, the evening before this interview. Judge for yourself.

Chapter 27

UNCLE HENK –
MEMORIES OF DE MEER

T he demolition of Ajaxs old De Meer stadium takes Cruyff back to his memories of his second father and his debut in the stadium.

'I don't remember anything about my first match in De Meer, except the date: 22nd November 1964. I dont know who it was against. Was it PSV? If it was, it must have been when we won 5-0. There are books you can look those things up in. Yes, I have scrapbooks, but I don't know where they are.

'Before I made my debut for the first team at De Meer, I'd played many matches there for the youth team. We became champions of Holland in the stadium, against Volendam, I believe. There were between ten and twelve thousand people in the stands. Who did I play with in that youth team? Strijks, Van Dijk, Splinter, Schipper, I believe, Tonnie Fens, Driessen – but you can find all that in the books.

'The season of that game against PSV was a terrible season. I know I scored in that game. But if you want to know details, you'll really have to look in the scrapbooks because I don't have such a good memory. I definitely know my first game in the first team was against GVAV and we lost 3-1. The last time Barcelona played PSV in Eindhoven, I bumped into Fons Van Wissen. Maybe he played for PSV against me at the time.

'When I made my first team debut, I already had a whole football life behind me at De Meer. I have nothing but beautiful memories of De Meer. I knew every inch of the place. I was 17 when I made my debut, but I'd been running around here for 10 years. I'd put up corner flags, cleaned boots, scraped nap off shirts, painted corridors, put sand in the goal mouths. I helped Uncle Henk with everything for as long as I was a child.

'Uncle Henk, my second father, was the Ajax groundsman. We cleared snow together, rode the tractor, put up nets, marked the lines, hung flags on the roof of the stand. I did it all: I was there day and night. I arrived when I was six years old, became a member of Ajax at ten and left when I was 26. De Meer is 20 years of my life. When I see the old photos now . . . the uncovered stands . . . magnificent memories. Now the paths around the ground are asphalt, but it wasn't like that then. Before a first team game, we had to lay gravel on the paths and approach roads.

'Helping Uncle Henk, all those things we did together: that means much more to me than that one first match.'

Nieuwe Revu
March 1996

Chapter 28

I THINK MANKIND IS DEGENERATING – CRUYFF'S HEALTH CARE

S eldom has he looked so healthy. It's a nice opening sentence for a story about Johan Cruyff and health care. No, he's not performing operations yet, but his ideas about people and their bodies have the same kind of logic that once made him the best player in the world and, later, the best coach in the world.

'At one point when I was coach of Barcelona, I was wondering why it was that so many players had torn muscles, as well as all sorts of real injuries that never seemed to happen in my time. I think I only had my first torn muscle when I was 34. At Barcelona there were 20-year old players who had torn muscles several times. In my time you only saw someone with damaged knee ligaments once a year, and that was usually someone at the end of his career. But it didn't happen very often. These days, a player tears his knee ligaments every weekend. I asked myself: how is it possible that healthy players around the age of 20 get injured so often?

'We never used to do a warm-up. We knew nothing about stretching and we ate whatever was on the table, but we were hardly ever injured. And then you wonder how it comes about. For example there's less sport played in schools and people don't play in the streets any more. And people eat differently. So maybe these players have a physical disadvantage compared to the young players of my time. We used to go everywhere by bicycle. Who comes to training by bike nowadays? When I was young we used to play all day in the street, on stone. These days youngsters only play on grass, if they play at all. I think mankind is degenerating.

'And now I'm coming to it: what I thought, what my experience as a player and a trainer told me, they've now done research about. Where I always said: "that doesn't seem right, it's not good" they had it on computer. And that's how we found each other.'

By "they", Cruyff means Arboservice Preventive Physiotherapy (AFP), a young organisation which, alongside the many existing sports groups and physiotherapy centres, studies the highs and lows of how the human body functions. Cruyff is a kind of ambassador for the new centre.

'I understand that the current stresses in top football – the pressure and too many fixtures – increases the chance of injuries and decreases the time available to recover. At the same time, I realised that stress, pressure and a very busy schedule not only affects top-level sport. A lot more people have to deal with this. A lot more people have to avoid getting injured. Because being ill for a day costs money. Ten days off costs a lot of money. So you have to look for methods of prevention, training and care so you avoid getting ill or injured.

'That's what AFP wants to do. You know that I was always interested in medical things. No, I never wanted to be a doctor, because then you only deal with sick people, and I don't like that, but I did want to understand what was happening with my own body. Call it self-preservation. I was always looking for possible ways to avoid surgery. I always felt that surgery, cutting the body, can't really be good. Prevent that for as long as possible – that's what I thought.'

– When we were busy reading all the interviews we've done with you for different media over the last 25 years, we noticed you were always at war with the doctors at your clubs.

'I had to be. In top level sport, because of the egos and personal PR of the doctors, you don't only have to deal with the medical aspect. The doctor didn't like it if you interfered. A club doctor is very important if he knows what he's doing. The ideal team doctor is a police officer who knows what's going on. When someone has a knee problem, the doctor shouldn't interfere himself, he should send the player to the best knee specialist around. In 20 per cent of cases, he shouldn't act as the doctor, and he shouldn't be the friend of the knee specialist. He should be keeping his eye on him. In those 20 per cent of cases, he should always try to get a second opinion.'

– Are there any clubs where things happen in this ideal way?

'Nowhere.'

– Does that make you feel powerless?

'No, just the opposite. It makes me more interested. I like to try things out. I remember about 10 years ago I asked Reinier van Dantzig (physiotherapist to Marco van Basten, among others) if he'd like to treat my daughter's horse. I'll never forget it. When he was in the horse box, he was scared to death because he thought that he was going to be kicked. He used his machine on the horse's muscle.'

– Did it help?

'Yes of course, because blood also flows through a horse's muscles. So I'm always looking for things like that.

'One time at Barcelona, we had someone who looked after people's feet. What do you call that? Pedo . . . something. So, let's say we had a pedophile in the dressing room. He couldn't do any harm because we were all grown men. And that man looked at your feet, the posture of your feet, the consequences of that for the rest of your body. Later, we also had an acupuncturist. I was looking for all kinds of medical experts who could avoid us having to have operations, who could make sure you didn't get injured, or, otherwise, make sure you got fit as soon as possible. At one point last season, as you might say, all I had were injured players. And if someone is injured for three weeks, that costs you the six games he's out. Once I met the director of AFP, Geert-Jan van der Sangen, it turned out there were many more common interests between the way AFP works and my practical thoughts about health care. It's as much about a cab driver as an athlete who wants to get injured as little as possible.'

– What is your role in the so-called prevention centre?

'It's not the technical part.'

– Are you sure?

'Yes. You're surprised, aren't you? Listen, I'm behind the concept. Otherwise, I wouldn't do it. I've had a double bypass myself, but I still play football in my spare time. A lot of people are so scared after an operation like that they don't dare do anything and they're scared to walk down the street. It's a question of mentality. I think of it like this: I haven't had an operation on my heart in order to be scared for the rest of my life. In a manner of speaking, if I hadn't needed to play football, I wouldn't have needed an operation. Do you understand what I'm saying?'

– Not exactly.

'People should dare to do more, dare to play sport. If I go to a sports school and see a guy with a ponytail lifting 100 kilo weights, I'm not going to join him. Of course I'll be careful. Perhaps I'll lift 15 kilos, but I have no interest in looking foolish. There are many people in that position. There are fantastic spaces that a lot of people are afraid to enter. You have to get rid of that aversion.'

– But our experience at the good sport schools in Holland is that there are programmes, say, for both the unfit couch potato and the muscleman with the ponytail.

'Most visitors to a sports school are sports mad. We don't think you have to be sports mad to be fit. But, fine you may be right. What we do is offer opportunities to people who aren't used to physical exercise or to being fit. With us, people who have neck and back problems get physiotherapy not only when they have a problem but to stop them having a problem in future.

'Look around and you see the authorities can't afford health care any more. You have to pay for medicine yourself. You see a reduction in the amount of money available for physiotherapy. You see the movement of responsibility to employers, and employees who look to insurance to cover the costs. So it's in everyone's interests that as few people as possible are ill. So you have to pay much more attention to prevention after recovery.'

– Sorry, but how did you get all this wisdom?

'I read the papers too. It really is crazy that our employees don't want to play sport because they might get injured. How many people don't feel wonderful after running for an hour? That's why we want to set up inside businesses. And if, after a while, we see that it's successful, then I'll go further. But at the moment, the main thing is that I'm working with AFP because it's something I believe in.'

Nieuwe Revu
January 1997

Chapter 29

I ALWAYS TAKE MY NAME AND MY FACE WITH ME – CRUYFF AT 50

O ur last interview so far took place in an Amsterdam coffee house.

– Do you like turning 50? Or do you mind?

'I like it.'

– Why?

'Because I have no problem about getting older. I think you have a lot more pleasure now. When you're young, you had the players you played with, maybe your wife, maybe your kids. Now you're busy with grandchildren, with sons-in-law. The tree gets bigger, as I like to say.'

– But don't you feel you'd like to be 25 again, playing beautiful football?

'I do play beautiful football. For myself though.'

– You think so?

'For myself. It's not to watch. I do it for myself and I get a lot of pleasure. Then you really feel you're 25 again. I really feel it when I come home in the evening.'

– Are you knackered?

'Yes. Or the next day, when I have to stretch, or can't walk down the stairs.'

– There are people who think it's terrible to turn 50. You don't think that way at all?

'No. Maybe because I haven't done anything this year. So you have more peace and you have a lot of pleasures that you haven't had for the last 30 years. That's why I've really enjoyed myself terrifically.'

– You're still very thin. Do you do that on purpose or do you eat everything you can?

'No. The only person who makes sure I keep an eye on things is the doctor who I go back to see occasionally to make sure that everything is still working properly.'

– To see how well your heart is beating?

'He looks at everything and then he says: cholesterol. And if you start complaining about cholesterol, then you have to be careful about what you eat. And then, automatically, you have fewer problems.'

– You're not worried that your hair is thinning and you're getting greyer? That really doesn't interest you at all?

'Well, if its a hot day, because when you comb your hair in the morning, you think: oh that hurts, because it can burn now. You have to pay a little more attention to those things.'

– So you have little bald spots on your head?

'Yes, but it doesn't matter too much.'

– You've always said to us: I have two personalities. The first is Cruyff at home. The second is Cruyff outside. What's the difference?

'Well, I think its the difference in behaviour you have to have. At home you're the way you are. Usually very quiet, very peaceful. It seems very nice. Very happy with my children.'

— Are you a sweet father?

'I think so, yes. But what is "sweet"? Giving in to everyone is not being sweet. You don't have to be sweet for that. I think you try to bring up your children so they can go their own way in life. So these days your task is more of an adviser.'

— Are you still a caring father? Do you still have the feeling that they're your children?

'Oh yes. Because they're at home a lot, if something comes up, you're there. And you can do that because you have more time. And the other personality of course is the one who had to be really sharp, who had to make sure that everything had to go the way it should. And that means you really were a bit of a strange footballer if you look at idealism in professional football.'

— What do you mean 'idealism in professional football'?

'Professional football means money. It means achievement. Idealism, of course, means loving beautiful football. And it means never in your life making concessions about one or the other. They are equally important.'

— Results and idealism are really opposites, aren't they?

'I don't think so. They turn out not to be.'

— Not with you, but for most people.

'Yes, but it means you have to be really alert to those two things.'

— In your work as player and coach you had a kind of defence mechanism around you, didn't you?

'Yes, but of course you need it because you're constantly under attack.'

– But didn't you want to show people how you really were?

'No, because that's nothing to do with it. When you look at all those other players you've played and worked with – and also the people you've coached – that was really soft and sugary, a nice football atmosphere. When at some time, you've taught someone something, or made him achieve things, well, yes, then you have to be a little tougher sometimes. But in general, with all those guys, those people I worked with as coach, I really have enjoyed myself fantastically. In the footballing sphere. Like I say, there's also another side and that means, you should score beautifully. Or rather, a goal should be beautiful if you can do that. But when it's 0-0, you can't say: I'm not going to score this goal because I only want to score beautifully. You have to teach that kind of thing.'

'Take Michael Laudrup for example. In Italy, he was a beautiful footballer, but with no return. But once he understood the difference and made it his own – and that's what its all about – you saw a fantastic player who everyone has enjoyed for years.'

– It's good you mentioned Laudrup's name. He had fantastic years with you and then, at a certain moment, you split up over a small problem.

'No, it wasn't a small problem, and not a big one either. You have to keep the return in mind. For a great footballer the return lies between the 20 metres and the goal. It's never between 30 and 20 metres. Goals make the difference.'

– So you think he played too deep?

'Yes, and that didn't help me at all.'

– Did he accept it from you when you put him on the bench a lot?

'It's not a question of accepting. Why didn't he do it like he did in the first three years? For the first three years he was a fantastic player for us, decisive at almost all moments, with every action, and always inside the penalty area. He either scored himself or gave the ball to someone else, it didn't matter, but he was never outside the penalty area.'

— You were just talking about the beauty of football. Have you ever scored a goal you didn't like?

'Yes, of course, but they count too. I don't say why don't you disallow this goal because I didn't like it. Not at all.'

— Did you ever think: 'I should have scored a nicer goal?'

'No. I remember [the 1972 European Cup Final] against Inter Milan when the goalkeeper and the defenders jumped into each other and fell down and the ball fell at my feet. I put the ball into the empty net. That was fantastic. On the other hand, you say: yes, football should be played beautifully, you should play in an attacking way, it must be a spectacle. When you are 4-0 ahead with 10 minutes to go, it's better to hit the post a couple of times so the crowd can go "oooh" and "aaaah" because if it's 5-0 nil, it's only for the score, it doesn't affect the result.'

— Have you ever tried to hit the post at 4-0?

Yes. And then you get angry as if you hadn't meant to. Those were obviously good moments.

— But did you really plan to do that?

'No, not consciously. It just happens. Everything happens so fast. You don't say: I will do this or that. But I must admit I was never sad when the ball came back off the post or the goalkeeper saved it. I just always loved that sound when the ball hits the post hard. That sound . . .'

– So you could enjoy a good save by the opposition goalkeeper at 5-0?

'Yes of course.'

– Even if it was 5-0?

'Yes, but obviously not when it was 0-0. If the keeper makes a save when it's 0-0, you have to try and still get to the ball. That's the essential difference.'

– You talk about beauty. What is the most beautiful goal you've ever scored?

'Luckily I've had a lot of beautiful goals, like the lob against ADO. It's often about the moment. When I returned to Ajax – against Haarlem – everyone was really ready with the trumpets in the stands. Everyone was saying: that old guy shouldn't be out there any more. And when it happened, especially the way it happened, then of course it was killing two birds with one stone. It's not only scoring a goal, it's the way you do it. That makes it really special when you score a goal like that.'

– And the goal against Brazil in the 1974 World Cup?

'Yes, there was that one against Brazil. And I scored a similar one at Barcelona with the outside of my foot, and that goal, against Belgium.'

– You have a bad memory for bad things, don't you?

'You have to forget those.'

– A selective memory. What were the bad goals you scored?

'One I always remember, probably because I've seen it replayed so often, was for Feyenoord against Volendam. I wanted to pass with my left foot, but I miss-hit it. The ball hit the underside of the crossbar and went in off the goalkeeper. It looked like a fantastic goal.'

– What was your nicest club?

'Nicest? I've really enjoyed it with all my clubs.'

– You have to choose just one.

'I can't choose. Well, yes, the nicest time was at Ajax between the ages of 12 and 17. That was obviously the most beautiful time.'

– Why?

'Maybe because there was nothing at stake. Maybe because everyone was still helping. Maybe because I was still to achieve something. That's a lot of maybes, but I think that's what it was. That illusion. Maybe.'

– There were a lot of talented players at that time. Can you remember any players who you thought were going to make it, but didn't?

'Yes, because the difference between making it and not making it is so small. You find there are certain rules. Splinter was one, Strijks was one. Van Dijk, Hennie Schipper, and a couple of others. They were ahead of me. They were two or three years older than me. They were super footballers. But then again you go back to what is professional football and what is beautiful football. And then you understand that footballers who have a little less don't succeed because their speed of action is too slow, or their technique is a little less, even though when they stand still maybe they're very good technically. Then it's about vision and other things.'

– What kind of players have you known whose speed of action wasn't good enough?

'Van Dijk. That guy had a nose for goal. And Fens. Very good players. But at a certain moment, it has to be done quicker, where instead of having two metres to control the ball you have half a metre, and if the ball moves half a metre you've lost it.'

– Why didn't Louis van Gaal make it as a top player?

'Rhythm. I think his vision was good. The technical quality was very good. But, yes, when there was pressure, it was all over. It had to be faster.'

– The speed of action?

'Yes. Much faster. But again, it doesn't make you a lesser player. It's just one detail.'

– But you're not going to reach the top?

'No, not good enough for the top. Especially the position he played. If he'd been a libero, he could probably have played very well, but it would have to have been as a real libero. And you can't be a libero at Ajax because they play in the opposition's half, so you need to have speed to deal with that. It's always one thing plus the other. That's why so many people don't make it.'

– You said your nicest time was between the ages of 12 and 17. Were you someone who said: I want to be like him, or him?

'Yes. Faas Wilkes was always an example to me.'

– That's what I mean. As a child you wanted to be Wilkes?

'And Di Stefano. Probably because of the elegant way he played and the way he oversaw the whole game and could do anything.'

– Did you pretend to be Wilkes or Di Stefano when you played with the other boys?

'Yes. Maybe a little more Wilkes than Di Stefano, because at that time, of course, we didn't see too many foreign players. We didn't have television.'

– That Wilkes had fabulous technique . . .

'Yes.'

– Who are the talented young players of today who we should look out for over the next couple of years?

'Unfortunately, there aren't too many. You can see the technical qualities are declining sharply.'

– Why is that?

'I think it's mainly because of the way they train.'

– Do you think they're breaking through at Ajax?

'No.'

– How come?

'One of Ajax's biggest weaknesses, of course, is it's education.'

– But Co Adriaanse, the head of education at Ajax, says, for example, that 15 players have come through his system into the first team and 10 of them are internationals.

'Yes, he's right, they came through. But how good are they? What's the quality? When I talk about quality, I'm not talking about the last few years, I'm talking about a period of 30 years. Then you see a Keizer, or myself, or Rep, or Swart, to mention one great period.'

– Van Basten, Van't Schip, Roy, Winter . . .

'Van Basten, Van't Schip, Roy, Winter. And then you have Bergkamp. And then you're talking about special, specific quality.'

– Kluivert, Seedorf, Davids, or do you think that's already a little . . .

'. . . but Davids and Seedorf and so on were not scouted by Ajax. If they really had been discovered by Ajax, then I would agree with you slightly. But they were not discovered by Ajax.'

– So who discovered them?

'It doesn't matter.'

– But we want to know.

'I don't scout any more, but what matters is the philosophy coming down from above.'

– But Kluivert, Seedorf and Davids were discovered by you, and then comes . . .

'And then you see what came through has a lower quality. And again it may sound a bit strange, a bit . . .'

– Obstinate? Pedantic?

'Especially because I'm saying it, of course.'

– But you've always said it.

'Yes, you should read my interviews from three years ago. Then everyone said I was jealous. But even then I was saying: "look out guys, things are going wrong".'

– But specifically, what do you think is wrong with this very highly-regarded education system at Ajax?

'What's missing is the exceptional. It's all average.'

– Why is it average? Is there no place for the exceptional?

'Of course there is space for the exceptional. But you have to see it first. That's one thing. So you have to see it, and then you have to give it room to develop. And then let a player develop so that he discovers himself. Because people like Roy, Van Basten or Witschge, have to develop through shame and getting things wrong. We used to have those boys play two teams higher than their age level and we put them ahead of other players on purpose. At the higher level, they got kicked so hard that they really understood. I believe in a very hard school.

'Then you get to the next stage: turning playing football into the mentality of winning. Then you see that a lot of players fall by the wayside. Why? Because few people have taught them how they could bring higher returns on their qualities. Quality football is one thing, but how do you get the maximum return on that quality? Because that's what it's all about in football. If someone has a lower return than he should, it can only be for two reasons. Either he's not good enough or he's not looking for the position where his return can be maximised.'

– And that means that, since 1988 – when you left – the players they have educated are not good enough in your view?

'Not good enough is not the right expression. Ajax has become famous because of a mixture: extremely rare talents together with players who have been well-taught. Take them together and they make a whole. Take me. I'm an idealist, maybe chaotic. So you always have to make sure you have a counterbalance – that was Tonnie – who always made sure things happened when they needed to. But the genius, of course, had to come from someone else. You need someone who has it in him to be both a genius and all the other things. But you can't find such a person on earth. So you need to look for two people.'

– Do you think Van Gaal and Adriaanse, Ajax's head of education, are too similar?

'Yes, neither of them quite reached the top, and they both came from educational backgrounds.'

– They are both leaving at the end of the season. Is that a loss for Ajax?

'Ajax will always be Ajax. I don't think Ajax needs to despair about Adriaanse leaving. Just the opposite.'

– Do you think talented people should be put on a short lead if they behave a bit strangely or try to be a bit different?

'Do you mean there aren't enough of the bastards? That it was fine for 30 years but in the 32nd year it suddenly fails? I don't think so.'

– So how would you change it? Is that one of the reasons you never get into talks with Ajax? That you would have wanted to change the education system if you came back?

'It's got nothing to do with me coming back. It has to do with understanding the subject and acting on that whatever the circumstances. So if you are at Ajax and you let the De Boer twins make their debut at the age of 17, or Vink when he was 16, just to mention a couple, you're talking about people who are going to reach the top. So the way it's going now is nonsense. Bergkamp was 17 years old and still at school when he made his debut. And at Barcelona, where it's even more busy and chaotic, five good players came through last year.'

– Yes, but talk more practically.

'Then you're talking about why it's not happening now. It's a question of education.'

– If you'd been at Ajax, would you have changed things?

'It's got nothing to do with what I would have done at Ajax if I'd been there. I just think Ajax has made an enormous mistake.'

– And can it be put right?

'It will take time.'

– How?

'You need people who are opposites. There always needs to be someone there who's a genius.

– Do you need more chaotic genius? People who don't think the same way as Van Gaal and Adriaanse?

'You need a genius and the other kind. Never two people who are the same.'

– Have you ever had an opponent where you thought: 'this guy drives me nuts'?

'Well, there you're talking about types and I'm really bad at that. But, for example, you could take a Vogts type.'

– Berti Vogts of Germany?

'He's the type where you think you can beat him on either side and make him do whatever you want. But when you go past him and turn around to see what to do next, there he is again. That's the big problem.'

– So you mean people who have no vision in football, but do have a good pair of lungs . . .

'. . . and keep coming back at you, relentlessly.'

– Was Suurbier also that type, a defender you wouldn't have wanted to play against?

'Suurbier was also the type you had to be careful with. A good defender but, yes, when it had to be less orthodox, he'd do that too. So, not only did you have to make sure to beat him the first time, even when you'd got past him, you still had to pay attention.'

– Do you think it's a pity that those kind of players – people like Suurbier, Keizer, Swart and Rep – have no role at Ajax now? If you were at Ajax, would you get them involved?

'I would have involved almost everybody. Not because they need to have influence, but because everyone has something to offer, and they should use that. I don't want to say that one or the other has super insight, because you don't need that. It's more about the team. If you take youth scouting, no one made any decisions without everyone being there.'

– What do you mean?

'Everyone. Lets say there were 100 boys at the end of one of the selection gatherings and all the leaders were there. With me, leaders had an enormous influence where youth were concerned. Because they are around those little guys for the entire week, the whole year. And they always know what the quality is and what's there. Because they see them every week. They're our automatic quality control meters. I think they should have a lot of influence.

'Imagine that at a certain moment you had one of those gatherings where the boys show how good they are. One of the trainers – it doesn't matter which one – says: "why don't we have that kid back?". And I say: "Have the kid back? He hasn't touched the ball." And he says: "That's why! Has he not touched the ball because he can't play? Or because he's so good at finding space?" Yes, they could both be true. So why send the kid away? Yes, let him come back. If it turns out later he's no good, well OK. But that's not proven yet. It only shows that everything is possible. I think at the moment that there aren't enough people who would dare to say that.'

– You also used to go to those sessions, and you'd be standing, watching with five or six men and a couple of old grumblers.

'No. I'd stand with a group of footballers because everyone has come to give leadership to everyone else. You can't have a leader or a youth trainer being in charge of all first team players. You can't do that. So you have to split up the groups and when they have something to say, it has to be intelligent.'

– And when it was obvious to you who the first 11 would be, you also needed a 12 and a 13 because you needed someone on the bench. Did you look to see who had the best-looking mother?

'No. Ajax was too serious for that. Of course you always had fun, but the only thing that was really important was when you had four or five or six really good players in that age group, the rest had to serve those five or six.'

'I've never been involved in discussions about numbers 14, 15 or 16, because it's pointless. But you do discuss numbers 6 and 7, because they're the people about whom you're thinking: can he do it, or can't he?

'At Ajax, the opposite happened. Bergkamp was rejected every year because, as a right winger, he was in the second team. He really would have been kept there. No-one knows why. It's really inexplicable that two or three people said: "why don't you let him go? He's such a shy boy". Because if he gets through and lets say he becomes really fanatical, the chances are that he'll become a very good footballer.

'Another example who was kept because of the system – or really was taken on because of it – is Aron Winter. I think he was also turned away four times. And one leader, one trainer disagreed with that and said: "I want to take him to an international tournament because I'm convinced he can do it." And I said: "If you're convinced, you must take him with you, and if you think he should stay at Ajax, then he should stay. I'll give him a year. We'll see. If you're convinced, of course, I'm 1,000 per cent against sending someone away".'

– We're making a book out of all the radio, television and written interviews. What's especially important here is your eye for talent. Two years before you bought him, you were talking about Jan Wouters. You said he should be an international. When Rijkaard was 17 you said: 'He'll reach the top'; Winter: 'He'll reach the top'; Witschge: 'I don't know'. Do you still have that? Do you still see more than we do?

'Yes, but that's obviously nothing more than logic. If you're a good footballer, it doesn't mean you're a good coach. But on the other hand, one of the best things I can do as a coach is to analyse. You know what someone can do, see what they can do and then choose the best position for them so it can come out in them. And if it doesn't come out, that's what you see nowadays.

'One of the reasons there are hardly any wingers coming through is that these days our positioning is so bad. When a winger has the ball, he's facing two or three men. It's just a question of positioning. It's a pity that people who move well, have a good eye for goal, and are very good when it's one-against-one – offensively, I mean – are always in the wrong place when problems come.'

– Have you ever been wrong?

'Probably. Well, no, I've always taken a lot of risks. Of course there are dozens that you've tried, and, again, until you say it, it's not going to happen.'

– Can you give us an example of a player you expected more from, where you thought: I've made a mistake.

'It's not a question of expecting more. It's more a question of "can he do it?" We give him a chance and either he takes it or he doesn't. It's in his hands. Either you can or you can't cope with the pressure. You don't know till you try it. Nine out of ten players you buy are big players in a small club. But will they be big players at a big club? If it's someone from the youth system, there isn't really a problem because if there's a problem, your education is wrong, so you must have made a mistake along the way. That's how you always keep a check on the education system.'

– You gave a chance to a player like Rijnink, but he didn't make it?

'Rijnink, and in Spain I had Luis. If you look at the current Espanyol team, there are five of my old players in it. Then you say: OK, you try, you give someone a chance, and then you try again and give them another chance. But at a certain point it's not going to work. Then you say: guys look out for yourselves and make sure earn your bread somewhere else in football.'

– We're sitting here in an Amsterdam coffee house, right in the middle of Amsterdam. Did you miss this sort of thing?

'Yes, of course. The atmosphere of Amsterdam is wonderful.'

– And a nice little egg sandwich.

'Yes, everything a shop like this has to offer. It's the kind of thing you don't find anywhere abroad.'

– So this is 'back to your roots'. Do you feel like that when you walk along the canals?

'Yes, I walk along with my hands in my pockets, whistling. Then I have no worries at all.'

– Do your children miss this? Do they know it?

'They don't know it, so they don't miss it. Sometimes you find out things like that. But those are the disadvantages. There are not only advantages to the life we've led, but disadvantages too.'

– Are you proud, when you look back, at the way you put your children on this earth?

'Yes. Although I give more of the credit to my wife. If you take all the time I've been away, it would certainly add up that she's done one or two years more than me. I think we've done well. If you have three children and they turn out reasonably well, and they've had a reasonably good education, they haven't got drugs problems or other problems, then I think these days you should be very happy.'

– How important is it to you that they've studied? You didn't study yourself. Nor did your wife . . .

'Study and sport. Both things. I think sport is very undervalued, it's not appreciated. I think clarity of spirit almost always comes from sport. And you also need to study. I say that because, in my day, sports teachers at school were withdrawn because they cost too much. I don't know how it is now, but I do see a lot of weak people. Normally speaking, I think that sport should be an ideal guide – and I mean sport simply as sport, not top level sport, as I did, because that's obviously less healthy.'

– Do your children get you angry if they say: 'Dad you're wrong'?

'Not angry. But we once got hung up on something Michels said: Rule One: the coach is always right. Rule Two: if the coach is wrong, Rule One applies automatically. I hung that up at home too. I found it quite convenient.'

– Still, it's never been the strongest part of your character. You've said: 'if I'm not right, I'd prefer not to talk about it any more. I'll put it away quickly'.

'Yes of course that's a way of talking. But when you talk about children and you teach them as we taught them, or really what experience has taught them, then you know that at a certain moment, you don't know so much in certain areas. You can compare it to skiing. If you're a reasonable skier, and you take a boy of five with you, you say: follow me. But three weeks later he'll say to you: hey, come on follow me.

'I've always been reasonably good with languages – in a clumsy way. Don't ask me how I speak in Dutch, English and Spanish, but it's good enough. But when you look at the children who've been to international schools, of course they speak much better French, much better Spanish and much better Catalan.'

– Do they laugh at you? Because you speak Spanish like a real Amsterdammer, don't you? Like a real boy from the Jordaan.

'I speak Spanish better than any Dutchman, but worse than any Spaniard.'

– From the team that made you a star, the Ajax of 1970–71, one player died: Nico Rijnders. How did you experience that? Someone dying so young, someone you'd played with?

'I think at that age it's a shock, but you don't realise it. You only think: that's really bad, a fault at the factory, you say it like that. It's not normal when someone dies at that age. If someone dies now – an older player – you get scared, and then you think: you're now about that age, it's coming closer. And what is closer? You don't know. Because if someone dies at the age of 48, you think I'm already past that. That's the problem. But I think that those two impacts, if you can say that in good Dutch, are totally different.'

– Are you scared of death?

'I don't think about it.'

– Why don't you think about it?

'Why would I think about it?'

– People sometimes think about it. We think about it for example. We don't think it's very pleasurable.

'No, I'm enjoying myself.'

– So are we.

'Yes, but you will go one day. In the first place, does thinking about it help you? Can you avoid it? No. Do you know when it's going to happen? Also no. So you say: does it make any sense? If someone has a problem with it, then maybe they should think about it. That might be true. It's something I don't have under my control. It's not something you can make a difference to. Of course you can take precautions. For example, I've undergone an operation and once in a while I go to the doctor.'

– You don't smoke any more . . .

'But it shouldn't be a great obsession, because that comes at a cost to your life.'

– Isn't your heart an obsession?

'No, because otherwise it would cost you your life anyway.'

– And were you scared when you went into hospital for your heart?

'When I went hospital, I said: I don't feel well. Then they gave me a little pill. So I wasn't there that long. Or maybe only at a very low level. Then you don't think about it.'

– But in March 1991, you had a heart operation.

'A bypass, really.'

– Didn't you think afterwards – that was a close call?

'I think it's always a close call, and it's always good for something. The other thing that's a close call is to have an operation and you're going to die the day after tomorrow anyway. I don't think that's the purpose of an operation. I think an operation makes sense if you do something with it and then you say: OK then, I can live at home in a reasonable way, though obviously with some restrictions.'

– You're explaining it very rationally. There's no emotion there.

'No, you should keep emotions out of it. If I say: I had a bypass, and if I walk just a little bit too quickly over that bridge, then . . . then I'll never get over that bridge, will I? So I say let's turn it around. I say I now have very good veins, I've got more oxygen, so, in principle, I can do more.'

– There are people who say that the heart operation changed your life. Is that true?

'Well, I don't think about it consciously.'

– I'd say you were enjoying things more.

'Yes. Of course, you go and enjoy different and other things, but I also think it's because of circumstances. As you get older, you think about other things. For example, you can't do the things you did when you were young, so what do you do? You get grandchildren and you learn to play golf. You find other interests. Then you walk in the fields, with the trees and you pay a little more attention to the trees, in a manner of speaking. Not because you think: hey, I'm going to get mad about trees. No. You walk in the field and say: that's nice, or that's ugly. You pay more attention to that because you've got more time for it.'

– Something different. Of the 1971–72 team, Nico Rijnders died. Other players have got divorced. You're still with your first wife. You've been married a long time. Is it because of all the pressures and all the things around that it's almost impossible to stay married?

'No, I don't think so. I don't think it's impossible because the opposite has been proved. Probably the biggest credit for that lies with her, if you really look back honestly and ask: could you really have functioned at such a level for so long? I don't mean just being there, but doing it for so long. I think that's also to her credit rather than mine. The peace has been there and that's because of her.

'When you look back, of course the qualities were mine, but the rest, which meant I could get the most out of it, came from her. Because you see – and it used to be exactly the same – how people write about boys now, how they write about their money and talk about the temptations, the possibilities. When you don't have an anchor, the chance that you'll fail is obviously many times greater.'

– You never went out much did you?

'No, but that was also because I had someone there who . . .'

– And the outside world always explained it negatively, eh? They said your wife stopped you going to the World Cup [in 1978]. Now NOS [Dutch broadcaster] wants to organise a gala evening for you, they say your wife doesn't want it. Does it disturb you that your wife always gets blamed for those sort of things?

'It used to be very easy for me, because it took the problem away from me. And she didn't care about those sort of things. And I gratefully made use of that for a long time. Imagine if she had decided differently, and I hadn't agreed with it: we wouldn't have been together for so long. So really the answer is clear.'

– People who know you know that if you want to do something, it'll happen.

'Yes, that's true.'

– When you wanted to resign as trainer of Ajax, your wife couldn't stop you either . . .

'No, it was my decision.'

– You were very happy here. Your children were happy in Vinkeveen yet still you resigned and had a lot more misery.

'Yes, but it couldn't have been any other way.'

– Why not?

'Because I was with people who I think knew nothing or hardly anything about the subject. And really 99 per cent of board members know nothing about it. That's point one. Point two is the scandalous underestimation of the sport and the profession of football. What does Ajax have? 30 million guilders?'

– No. 70 million.

'70 million guilders. Then you think: these are people who can be lazy in their spare time. What company do you know of here in the city with a turnover of 70 million guilders where the two of us can go along in the evening and take care of things? You can't do that, can you?'

– The two of us could do it.

'Yes, you two, but that's an exception. No, it really is too crazy to talk about. And if you're a professional who knows how and why, you think: people, what are you doing?'

– But it still happens.

'Yes, but that's inherent in the phenomenon of sport.'

– A month ago, at the beginning of March, Fabio Capello said: 'I really want to leave Real Madrid'. What do you think when you read a comment like that. Do you think: hey, maybe that would be something for me? Would they call you?

'Everyone calls me.'

– Real Madrid too?

'Everybody. There's no-one who hasn't called.'

– Do they ask you to come and be their coach?

'There's no-one who doesn't call. I want to say that in general terms rather than include or exclude anyone. If there have been 100 calls, 92 have been for that.'

– And top of that list has been Inter, AC Milan and Ajax? They've all been interested?

'Yes, but it's not about names. All those people have coaches in position. So it doesn't make sense to talk to one or the other.'

– You don't do that? You won't talk to a club if they have a coach?

'No, there's a coach there, so why say they wanted me and I said no? What good does that do?'

– But do you ever want to do it?

'At the moment I don't want to do anything.'

– Does that include next season?

'It includes next season too.'

– What if Ajax waited till your birthday and said: we've got Wim Jansen and Wim Rijsbergen coming as trainers, Piet Keizer is going to be involved in youth education and Co Adriaanse is leaving as head of education? Would you say: 'well, maybe I'd like to'?

'No. I always see Piet Keizer anyway. I don't see the departure of Adriaanse as a big loss for Ajax. Maybe it will be their salvation. And for the rest of it, I don't want to do anything next year.'

– Don't you regret that you've never done the Dutch team? Don't you think that's a pity?

'Yes, but that's how it went. There must have been a reason. If it was meant to be it would have happened. Those are the things you don't look back at as much as other people do. So it didn't happen.'

– Do you think it's a pity? You've won everything, but you never won the World Cup. Not as a player nor as a coach. That's the only thing you're missing. When we compare you with Beckenbauer, you were club champions, world champions with your club, but never with the national team.

'Not with the national team, no.'

– Beckenbauer, Pele, Maradona – the people we compare you with – all won the World Cup.

'It doesn't matter that much to me. It would have been nice if it had happened, but I can never win the World Cup as a player now. So you have to forget about that. It's over. As a coach, I've had a wonderful time. I've worked with two very important teams and I really did it the same way I played football. In whatever way, I did something different. I like that.'

— Would you like to work with any club other than Ajax or Barcelona? Because those are the clubs of your heart.

'Maybe not. Maybe that's why I don't do it. I don't know.'

— And is that why you said goodbye with pain in your heart on both occasions when you left as coach?

'It's because my standards are a little different to those of other people. My idea when I was a player was that when the team was good, it couldn't go badly for me. Training too. When the team played good football, you enjoy the people. And you never know in advance if you're going to become champions. All you can do is play good football. Above all, we've always chosen for good football. That's why, when you see 50 matches, you watch with pleasure 40 times. 40 good days: that's what you work for. It's difficult if you get irritated at 40 or 50 matches a year, and on top of that, not even be champions. It's not the way I think. That's why I have such an attitude.'

— You left Ajax three times with pain in your heart. And once the same way from Barcelona as coach.

'Yes. No one took those decisions for me. The first time I said: I always take decisions myself. So at Ajax they said to me: "You're too old". So I said: "That's not your decision. It's my decision." "Yes, but we think you should stay here". "Oh good, that's your right, but I'll go whenever I want to".'

— But at Barcelona, they said: 'Johan, I'm sorry, but you have to leave.' Didn't that hurt you a lot?

'That's as a trainer, so the frame of reference is completely different. That's that man's obsession. The club doesn't matter at all to him.'

— You're talking about Nunez now.

'Yes. How long has that man been chairman? Is it one year or 20? It's not so important to that man if things go well for a year or not. The important thing for him is that he remains as chairman.'

– So the club is unimportant.

'At this moment the club is completely unimportant. Perhaps "unimportant" isn't the right word. Less important.'

– The club is less important than his interests?

'His interest is to remain as chairman, because there are elections now. Everything has to make way for that. And, if, via a different route, his team could have been a little better this year, or not have been champions, it's usually just a question of good thinking. I was there for eight years and the last two years I didn't win anything. So before the public starts to complain, get rid of the coach. It's not as if he said: I know it takes two years to build a team. He's probably never heard of that. I have to talk statistics which I don't know much about, but, if I remember correctly, after 27 games this season, the team had as many points as we had last year . . .'

– But with Ronaldo.

'They have, I think, 15 more goals against them than I had last year. And we had a keeper who, according to you, only played with his feet.'

– You didn't think so?

'No. That's not what it's about. That [new goalkeeper Vitor] Baia is 20 times better, I agree with you. But they've let in 15 more goals. Then you say: where's the wisdom in that? And this is someone who spent how much? 70 or 80 million.'

– But you go so far that you were hurt in your heart by a man like that. We've seen you making a speech in Majorca where you were very emotional. People there were impressed. They said it had hurt you.

'Of course.'

– Why, as a professional, do you let it go that far?

'At a certain moment you have to say: why don't you all drown. I don't think I've ever had a problem about myself. There have been enough fights. I think 80 per cent of the fights have been for other people. If they talk about bonuses, then you're talking more about other people, because if you want to get some extra money for yourself, it's never been a problem. If it's about insurance, then I was really well insured myself, but the other people weren't. You know how board members are: "For you, yes, but don't say anything about the others". We all know that.'

– Really?

'It's always been like that.'

– Is that how boards are?

'Yes, in general.'

– You really hated that.

'There are things I don't like. Because I always say: if I do something for others, then they are there to help me. That's how I win in the end.'

– But at that moment you were hit in your heart.

'Let's put it this way: I did everything in my power to make the club take care of us a little bit. There was a nice development. Because if you take the basis of last year's team . . .'

– You've just explained that.

'. . . and you had all new players, then you had a fantastic team.'

– Johan, be honest. That last game, when you weren't allowed to sit on the bench – Rexach, who you'd taken out of the gutter, remained there while he'd always been with you . . .

'That's all in the past.'

– You don't have to cry, but couldn't you admit it?

'I don't. And I also don't admit that it's not like that. I say only that I'm emotionally involved. And the question was: why did I let it get that far. I tried to postpone it for as long as possible. Because I thought: "how can I convince those people"?'

– That's the nice thing about you. You're so professional but you still have an Achilles heel.

'I've said that from the start. I'm a bit strange. An idealistic professional. That's how you have to see it.'

– We have to talk about money. You were a player at Barcelona and soon after you retired you could say you went broke. You lost a very large part of your money.

'I lost three quarters of it.'

– How could someone as smart as you lose three quarters of all his money?

'By making mistakes you shouldn't make. By being opinionated and doing at a certain moment what you shouldn't do. You shouldn't be bigger than you are. I could tell you a lot of other things. It just means that you think you can do something . . .'

– You thought you could do business?

'You can do business. But you have to do your own business. Like I say: in football I'm a good businessman. And why? Because you know what something costs, you know what you can do and what the return will be. So it's easy. Well I don't understand other things, and that's how you fail. They told me 20,000 times at the time. For example my father-in-law said: Don't do what you can't do. And what happened? It turns out that it happens to 99 per cent of players. So you always warn players, under all circumstances, players who worked with me, you say: do this or do that. And all the players came to me saying: can you read my contract? That's obviously the most beautiful compliment you can get, when you've made a mistake like that yourself.'

– Maybe it's a very Dutch thing to say, but if you had so many millions, you could have put two or three million in the bank, at such and such per cent interest, and speculated with the rest. Why didn't you do that?

'Well, you only find out at a certain moment. You talk now as someone of about 50 and you talk about other people. We're talking about the time I was 30. The big problem at the time, and maybe still, was that players stop playing football, with the huge income and the enormous adoration. And then what do you do? Then someone happens to walk past who says: "I've got something for you!" And that's the moment you walk into it, the moment you go and make your mistakes. I think I have one very nice compliment from my side, and that's that I've only made one mistake. That means you've learned a lot from that one mistake. But it was very expensive for one mistake. A big mistake, that's for sure.'

– Do you lose sleep over it?

'No, never.'

– Did it keep you awake at the time?

'No, also never.'

– It's a shame, though!

'Yes, it's a shame, but on the other hand, maybe that was the reason I started again with double power.'

– Has it made you suspicious?

'I don't know about that. Often something in life is probably for a reason.'

– And then you went back to playing football.

'Not because of that. That was a year later. I went to America in another way and through all kinds of strange thinking on my part – not to the New York Cosmos but to the Washington Diplomats. Or first to Los Angeles and then to Washington. In Washington I could go to the biggest sports organisation in the world, the Madison Square Garden group. That was almost like having a university level education. Those people are so far ahead of us Europeans. A couple of years later, you really needed everything that you happened to learn there.'

– Give us an example.

'When you become a trainer, you obviously have very different work. You come into a football where changes have come so fast over the last 10 years. Take public relations, take television rights, take buying players. It's a whole organisation. It doesn't just depend on people coming and sitting in the stands. I was one of the first who had to deal with that. And of course that's part of professional football, the merchandising, the marketing.'

– If we say to you now: Johan, were going to do something for the three of us, for 10 million guilders. We'll bring half a million and you provide nine and a half million, would you not get into that immediately?

'The time that I put money in myself is long gone. I always contribute my name and my face.'

– You keep saying during our conversation: it must be good for something, there must be a higher power. What is that?

'There's something circling around us somewhere and which takes care of us a little. And like I've said before: every disadvantage has it's advantage. I've lost two fathers. That's a very big disadvantage, but I've got two who watch over me. And I think that if something is wrong, they'll warn me.'

— Do you believe that? When did it start, your feeling there was a higher power?

'Years ago. I lost my father when I was very young. I was 12. He was 45.'

— That's really the same age as you were when you had your heart attack.

'He probably had the same as me. Or, it would be better to say, I had the same as him. Only they didn't know what a bypass was, or about blood vessels or cholesterol.'

— Have you passed it on to Jordi, so does he get checked out more often?

'Yes, because it's a question of genes and you just have to keep an eye on it.'

— How old were you when your second father died?

'33 or 34. I was playing at Ajax. It really made a huge impression on me.'

— How?

'I think that when you get older, when you have children yourself, it really hits you terribly hard.'

— What were the biggest blows of your life?

'Emotional blows, obviously.'

– The death of your two fathers. And what have been the biggest blows in football?

'If you can call them blows, though compared to that I think they are small things. It has to do with work, but nothing else. Not winning the World Cup when we had the chance to.'

– Do you mean in 1974?

'Yes. That was a pity.'

– In hindsight, do you understand why you didn't become world champions?

'I think it's a question of Dutch mentality. I think we just have to accept that. At the time we always won so easily because we were so much better. But we lacked that one little bit.'

– Lets talk about religion then. You say there might be something around us. When you were 12, when your first father died, did you have that feeling? Or did it come later?

'I can't remember it very well because I was very young.'

– And that influence of God, or whatever it is, was that strengthened by being in Spain for so long?

'No. In the first place, when I was 12 or 13, I was at a bible school. In our village, there were two schools. One was a public open school, the other was Christian. I was in the Groen van Printererschool my whole junior school career from 6 to 12.'

– Did you learn to pray?

'Yes. My father used to say to me: you don't need to go to church. We had a greengrocer's shop and we delivered to the church. That wasn't strange. Sometimes I had to run errands, delivering fruit

and vegetables to the church in a little basket on the back of my
bicycle.'

– And what about all those players in Spain who cross themselves 20
times before they start?

'You have to see that as the way they've been brought up. If you
think about it, it doesn't make sense, because if all 22 of them do
the same thing, who's going to win? You're all going to draw and
obviously that's impossible. You have to see it as a given.'

– You see that's your typical simple thinking: if all 22 of them . . .

'Well you can't can you.'

– When you didn't want to do an interview, but had to do it anyway,
you've always been a master of speaking in incomprehensible sentences
so that no-one could understand anything. I think you did it on purpose.
You thought: they'll forget the question.

'Sometimes you have to. You obviously get a little experience in
those things. You know what's coming. I often did a lot of live
interviews. And if they're live interviews, you can't cut anything.
They can't take you for a ride, and that's the big advantage. There's
a time limit.'

– But you also thought: I don't want a second question. I'll give
such an answer that . . .

'That's what I mean. The time has to be used up.'

– Can I read to you your own words? 'Well, in the first place,
problems are obviously there to be solved. But often a result is
confused with the situation. It's not that we're playing badly, but in
principle we don't score enough goals. And if you don't score enough
goals, everything becomes a bit more insecure because normally we
do score a lot of goals. When you let one in, it doesn't normally
matter. But if you're not scoring enough, then every goal we concede

is one too many or can cause problems with the result. So you can see how you lose 1-0 or it's 0-0 or 1-1. If you scored three or four you'd solve the problem ...' Do you have any idea what you're talking about?

'Well, it sounds nice.'

– Do you know when you said that? Precisely a year ago, when you were thinking about a lot of things with Barcelona and you lost everything in the end. That's what you said.

'But, for example, that's something where you think: well now I'm really going to make a big speech.'

– You remember that?

'Yes, it's right. When you analyse it, it's not nonsense.'

– Good: 'well, in the first place, problems are obviously there to be solved.'

'Well that's true. Otherwise there's nothing to be solved.'

– '. . . but often a result is confused with the situation.'

'That's right. You can play well or you can play badly, and you can play well and still lose.'

– '. . . It's not that we're playing badly, but in principle we don't score enough goals.'

'That means: you're playing reasonably good football, but you don't win and everyone complains when you don't win. So you have to score goals.'

– '. . . And if you don't score enough goals, everything becomes a bit more insecure because normally we do score a lot of goals and when you let one in, it doesn't normally matter . . .'

'No. When you're 4–0 ahead and you concede a goal it doesn't matter. But if it's 0–0 and you let one in . . .'

– '. . . But if you're not scoring enough, then every goal we concede is one too many.'

'That's right. It's as true as it can be.'

– '. . . or it can cause problems with the result. So you can see how you lose 1–0 or it's 0–0 or 1–1. If you scored three or four you'd solve the problem.'

'It's a beautiful story. There isn't a single lie in there. And it fills up the time.'

– But when you come out with sentences like that, we think: what is he talking about!

'That's the problem. When I get home, my wife says: "what did you say?" And I say: "even if you beat me to death, I don't know. I really don't know".'

– We've listened to a lot of tapes of you. There's a lot of verbal battles, because you always want to talk rubbish and then we say: Johan, be clear. And then you say: Let me talk, let me explain. As seen through our interviews, your life is one big war. You've been active for about 35 years in professional football, and for almost 35 years it's been a war. Why is that?

'War? Arguments!'

– With board members, with coaches, with organisations, with officials – never with other players.

'At a certain moment, those people have a different way of looking at things. They have a different goal than we do. The goal of a professional footballer is very simple: play good football, enjoy yourself and win. Nothing else. The coach is already further away because he's not on the pitch and he has to lead. But does he lead for himself or not for himself? There are a lot of different coaches, but there are very few who lead for the football itself.

'And – I don't know who used to say this, it might have been Piet Keizer – there are more coaches who break people than there are coaches who make footballers play better football. That means: there is also a question mark over the coach.

'Board members are a further step away. They have a completely different point of view, a point of view that is often wrong, though I don't want to say it's always wrong. Because they are normally chosen because of circumstances that have nothing to do with football but with social status. You see it in Spain, where nearly all club presidents these days are – what would you call them – builders. Business people or builders. I mean, you can separate business people easily. But builders are different kinds of people . . . There's a certain influence. Lets put it that way. It's got nothing to do with sport or with football. And then of course you get into a fight.'

– If it's with Harmsen, or in the past with Jaap van Praag, or with Nunez, there's always a fight.

'Of course there's always a fight, I don't remember it, but from different perspectives. The detail is different. With Van Praag it was very different than with Harmsen or like now with Nunez.'

– Take one of the small differences.

'Well, big differences. Harmsen, for instance, said when I left as a player: "you're too old". I think. Me, who's so important in football. I've always played well, always trained well. Does someone like that have to tell me I'm too old? Isn't that crazy? I haven't the words to describe it! Then you say: "hey, what are you talking about! If you don't want me, I'll show you something".'

– So you went to Feyenoord.

'That's right. That's one. The second is that he was going to make a whole different plan for football. He was going to pay people less and that's why they could leave for less. Paying someone always costs less than getting rid of an investment cheaply.

'For example: Marco van Basten wasn't allowed to earn a hundred thousand guilders more, but he was allowed to leave for 2 million guilders less. Then I say: what are you talking about? Are you a businessman or not? How can you bring the transfer money down in order to pay less? The scale was one to ten: if you earn earned a hundred thousand guilders, you could bring in a million. So if someone earns three hundred thousand, he can bring in three million, right? That was one of the fights. I said: what's the philosophy here? In one year I lost Rijkaard and Van Basten and someone else, I don't know why. And for an amount that I could only buy Meijer with.'

– What was your biggest conflict with Harmsen?

'That was the biggest. I said: I want a different sort of contract, because otherwise I don't want to stay here. It's a mad situation when three people have left before I've even started.'

– And the conflict, when you were a player, with Ajax chairman Jaap van Praag, who's dead now.

'Van Praag was a different chairman. He was really a chairman for the club and he picked on the player – in this case me – in the interests of the team. Then you say: OK, he can't do that, he's not allowed to, but . . . For example, he said: "you can leave for so much". And then, when the moment really came, he said: "No. it has to be double". He didn't put it in his own pocket, but in the club's pocket. So someone lied, but in the interests of the team. Then you say: you can't do that, but yes, it's reasonable.'

– You had big conflicts with him, but when he died, you carried the coffin.

'Of course, because that is a different kind of conflict. That's why I say: you have to classify those conflicts accurately.'

– But there's always been the conflict you just talked about . . .

'. . . that keeps you sharp. And to play good football, you have to be sharp.'

– Has there never been a moment in your life – apart perhaps from the last year – when for example you sat under a big tree for a week to read a book? Don't you do that?

'No, though on holiday I'm always very relaxed. But in general I think I'm a reasonable example of a Dutchman. Someone who functions best when the knife is at his throat. We all function best when there's tension.'

– Where did you get that piece of wisdom?

'I don't know. I'm about to turn 50. You always pick up a bit of wisdom from life.'

– By the knife at your throat, you also mean Ajax. Chairman Harmsen thought you were too old. So you went to Feyenoord.

'As revenge.'

– And out of revenge, you must have thought, there's one thing that's going to happen: Feyenoord, not Ajax, are going to become champions.

'Yes: I'm going to become champion. That's why you do it. Because if you say: I'm just going to go training at Feyenoord, of course you can't do that. Especially because the situation was that Jordi was playing for Ajax. Obviously that was a very sorry situation – which had been provoked – and for which I also blamed Harmsen. I don't blame him for the situation itself, but the pain they inflicted on him.'

– Have you ever used doping?

'I don't know what that is.'

– Have you ever used anything to get fitter? You said: 'I had too many injections at the beginning of my career'.

'One obviously has injuries and injuries. Sometimes you needed an anaesthetic, or you got an injection to help it. Sometimes it happened before an important game. Now I ask: was that responsible or not.'

– We ask because we once interviewed Barry Hulshoff in his time at Ajax. Before European Cup games, he used to get a couple of white pills from Dr Rolink, who has since died. And he'd think: I'm running like a horse, I'm playing fantastically. And then he'd realise: I haven't even kicked the ball.

'I know you can blame Rolink – in that Michels era – and also Michels. Concerning that, they played a reasonable game. Rolink was at that time famous from cycling. You'd read the word doping, but you didn't know what it meant. We're talking about a long time ago. Rolink had the name from the cycling profession, so he said: take this, and don't say anything to anyone. Probably it was nothing – ninety nine times out of a hundred. But, yes, even then you know that suggestion does a lot.'

– But did they ever ask you straight: would you take this please?

'No.'

– And did you ever take anything where you didn't know what it was?

'No.'

– Are you sure?

'One hundred per cent certain.'

– But you've had too many injections?

'You can't say too many. I don't have much cause for complaint. I always had a very good doctor at Barcelona, who went right up to the line but never crossed it. Up to here, and it's responsible – beyond, it's not. I must say I once had a problem at Ajax. It was a groin problem which took a long time, a couple of months. Apart from that – knee, knee ligaments, ankle ligaments – I never had operations.'

– And as a coach? We've read back about you and Marco van Basten when you won the European Cup Winners' Cup. That year when you were coach, Marco got six weeks off from you – as long as he played in the European Cup Winners' Cup Final. At the end, Marco van Basten wondered: was my ankle perhaps ruined at that time? Did you realise that or were you really obsessed with the result?

'I've never been so obsessed with a result. There were two things that played at the time. One was that he was going to Milan. I said: I played abroad myself. I know what that is, and you're a bit younger than I was. You always have to arrive with a little bit of "luggage". If you don't have that luggage, things are a lot harder: you're young and you're in Italy. Make sure you win that trophy.

'I can also understand that you don't want to take too much risk, so we're going to forget about the league. So at least you're going to win this European Cup. It was the best thing for me as well, because when we took that decision, I think we were five or six points behind PSV. You're not going to pull that back anyway. But then PSV lost two games in a row and we were almost equal. Then you just have to stick to your word or you backslide. And at that time I chose to keep my word and didn't play him in the league. But that has nothing to do with his injuries.'

– Who were the most beautiful players you worked with as a trainer?

'That depends on what you like of course. OK. Van Basten was beautiful. Rijkaard was beautiful. Wouters was beautiful, in a different way . . . and Laudrup was very beautiful.'

– Why?

'Wouters was seen by everyone as a certain type, and to show him that he was much better than he thought himself was a challenge. Van Basten: to make a very beautiful footballer a professional player. It didn't cost him terribly much, because he had a mentality that was in that respect perfect – hard as nails. Rijkaard: to make Rijkaard conscious of his own qualities and to let him take the steps he needed to take – which he did later.'

– But only after conflict with you.

'Yes, but it doesn't just happen. Often you have the conflict first, and then they do it. There's nothing you can do about that.'

– He was mad at you at one time.

'Because I always talked about his responsibilities, and when he doesn't take them, you keep on about it. Later he took on his responsibilities and no-one ever spoke about it again. And of course he showed how very good he was.

'Laudrup was obviously the example of a super talent who never won anything. You could really say the same about Bergkamp. It's obviously very disappointing when you have so many qualities and you don't win anything. And that's how it was with Laudrup. He went to Italy when he was 17 or 18, and never won anything until he was 25. Until, at a certain moment, the mixture was made . . .'

– We missed Ronald Koeman in your little list.

'Koeman? You can talk about a lot of people. Koeman too. Koeman especially, probably. I worked with him for a long time, I won't say for the longest time, but very long. He's a good example of the right mentality, someone who could go far for a very long time.'

– Are you surprised Gullit is doing so well as a coach at Chelsea?

'No, not really. He's Dutch. He played football in Italy, he played football in Holland, he played football in England. If you pick up something from everywhere, you should do pretty well. And we'll have to see if it goes really well. He's at a good level now, and we'll have to wait to see if he gets to the next one.'

– Now we're on the subject, which player did you think was fantastic to play with?

'The nicest was always Piet Keizer, of course. I think we were always on a different wavelength to everyone else. When Keizer had the ball and was going to do something, I knew what was going to happen and where the ball would come. That's where you ran to and the ball would be there. It was just a different atmosphere. Keizer was someone who could do a little bit more than everyone else.'

– Is Piet Keizer the Einstein of the people you played with?

'Yes I think so.'

– Isn't it a terrible, terrible pity that these days Piet Keizer only writes the occasional column and is no longer active in football?

'Well, there are a couple of others where it's also a pity.'

– Who?

'It's a great pity about Wim Suurbier. Wim Suurbier is a much better coach than anyone thinks, even gets close to thinking. He's much more serious than anyone realises. There are a lot of people who just don't do it. And then you ask me: why?'

– Is it because Suurbier has the image of a waster?

'But where has he coached that anyone could say: he can't do it? It hasn't happened. It's never happened in 10 or 15 years. Even clubs in the middle of the first division have never asked him. And are they world-class teams? No. That's a terrible lack of vision. And if we consider all those chairmen. OK, lets say the top three or four think: our name, should we take a risk? Yes or no? That you can understand a little, but the rest of those 30 chairmen who never dare to do it, you can dismiss them immediately. No one would have a problem with that.'

– But, in a manner of speaking, if you go to a team, would you want Suurbier . . .

'I look at other trainers who walk around and I think of who's done what. This one has a story, that one has a story, and they all put something together, and I think: Jesus!'

– Get Suurbier?

'Yes.'

– Who was your nicest chairman?

'My nicest chairman? I haven't had too many of those.'

– But which did you like the best?

'Like? Well, I had Harmsen and Van Praag, so, not really, eh?'

– Montal and Nunez . . .

'Montal and Nunez? Well, really the nicest was Montal. If he'd been a little bit cleverer, it would have been a different story.'

– In what way?

'That was the great Barcelona. Everything was possible. Very impressive, a lot of things. Really very impressive. Always very neat, always very nice, always flowers at home at Christmas, always little things, little presents, a ring with the club emblem . . . That was fantastic, really fantastic.'

– What about a chairman you had doubts about.

'Almost all chairmen are, and maybe it's justified, a necessary evil. Maybe it has to be like that. For the rest, I'm busy and happy with football, and those guys have their meetings in the evening and, luckily, I'm not with them. And he never travels, so he didn't bother me then. When it was in the papers, then it bothered me. For the rest, I lived my own life with the players, which I enjoyed.'

– You're still very popular around the world. When you played a European Cup match in Israel with Barcelona against Maccabi Beersheva, the president came to see you.

'Yes, those are lovely things. We were waiting for the game to start and at a certain moment – probably because he loved football – he said he wanted to come. The great Barcelona. So then he came in: lots of police around, we were just warming up. I was on one side, as usual. Then he came up to me and shook my hand. He said: "Good football, eh? I saw a lovely game last week".'

– And then you won 7-0.

'Yes, but of course I have to show a man like that why I'm there.'

– What happens to you now?

'I don't know. I'm really enjoying myself. Maybe I won't coach again. But again, maybe it's too soon to say things like that. Lets put it this way: I don't want to do anything next year.

'And the other thing I'm considering is: why don't I start a consultancy for club chairmen? But with a couple of good people. I think there would be interest in that. No, I'm not joking. I'm deadly serious.'

– Chairmen Plc?

'No, I'd tell them how those sorts of things should be arranged. For example – and we're talking about Holland now – television rights. Sport 7 are talking about Football Plc. But who are they talking to? Those chairmen again. Who among them understands television rights? None of them. They just talk and talk.'

'If I started a Chairmen Plc, I'd have a specialist in television rights, an expert in I-don't-know-what, and I'd talk about football myself. It would be a very good consultancy for those chairmen.'

– Would you ever want to be chairman of Barcelona?

'No, definitely not.'

– Of Ajax?

'No.'

– Do you see yourself going back to Barcelona? Because at the beginning of the year the cry was: Bring Back Cruyff.

'Well, that chance is obviously growing. That's the only way it can go, when everything they said you were wasn't true. That's what I said at the beginning: 40 per cent more goals against.'

– Does that make you feel better?

'Well, let's say I've had 20,000 conversations with you such as: "that goalkeeper is blind; it's suicide to play that way." All those texts – just read them yourself – after all you've asked me. And then I'm like this: "It's not like that because . . ." And then you say: "you're just bullshitting, because you thought I was just wasting time".'

'And how has it turned out now? It turns out they have conceded more than 40 per cent more goals. That's a lot, you know. 40 per cent! After 27 games this season, they've scored two goals less against than I did last year with all season with all the youth teams put together.'

– You're so bad at statistics!

'That's not what it's about.'

– Well, Methuselah, at midnight, you're going to be 50. Last season, you were sacked by Barcelona. Do you think the chairman should go? He's also responsible for what's going on.

'Of course, the chairman is always responsible for what happens, good or bad. When a coach is employed, they always say: if it's not good, he should leave. In this case, the chairman took decisions that were very dramatic: he got rid of the coach, kicked out all the youth, invested 70 million. And now it turns out that they've lost more games than I did last year. Even though that was almost a youth team. Same number of points. So nothing has improved. If you sack the coach, you should be big enough to leave as well. Barcelona is one of the few clubs where the members can vote. So you can also vote against a chairman. If I was him, I'd say: OK. But he doesn't do that. That's why he's the chairman.'

– I read a couple of months ago that health care is very important for your heart.

'No, not the heart.'

– You mean health care, you're getting involved with that.

'Some time ago I me a couple of guys who were creating an initiative in the area of health care. And there was the new European law that everyone has to take care of themselves a bit more because governments aren't going to do it anymore. We were talking about investments. You said: "you bring nine and a half million; we'll put in half a million". But here we're talking about a good programme. You do something good with it and I'll take care of the PR. I think everyone's interested in it because people don't play enough sport.'

– You also have a foundation. What exactly is the Johan Cruyff Foundation?

'Yes, I have a foundation. Because in the last 10 years I was involved in everything. And after the operation, a lot of other things have come in as well. I used to be asked by the Asthma charities, and this charity and that charity. And then you've got the heart, and circulatory diseases, and then you got . . . well, it just never stopped.

'And you've seen for the last four or five years that governments pay less to handicapped people, at whatever level, whether they're physically or mentally handicapped. Then we said: let's start a foundation, because I'm always being asked to do things. And that's what we did. The only thing we really try to do is raise money, through a golf tournament, dinners or whatever. To make sure all handicapped people, whether physically or mentally are able to play sports.'

'The fact remains that handicapped people are just like us. Perhaps somethings happened to them in the street in car and bike accidents and so on. People are often mental wrecks and – it turns out – the only way out of that is through *sport*. The moment you give those people a little bit of help, you can do a tremendous amount.'

– And the Foundation helps people to . . .

'. . . to do sport.'

– How much money is involved? How much do you raise each year?

'We've just started. We haven't even started in Holland. But in Spain, were talking about a couple of hundred thousand a year.'

– Is there a giro number you want to give out?

'No, we're not that far yet. When we get there I'll tell you and you can write it.'

– You lend your name to that?

'I give my name for that and it's checked by the people there. I'm the light, they say, that gets switched on. And when I play golf, a lot of famous people come along.'

– Would you like to be a sort of ambassador for Holland?

'It already happens. Because of my work, there was never a lot of structure, but I think that will come soon. I've asked them for that.'

– One more question about sport: who was your best coach?

'I think it must have been Michels. He's the one I learned most from. Kovacs was maybe the nicest. But I got the most from Michels.'

– What did he teach you?

'That the beautiful is very important. But at the same time, the end result is also very important. That's what I took with me.'

– And who's meant the most to you in your life so far?

'Without a doubt, that's my wife.'

– Why?

'I've told you: we've been married for 28 years. Three fifths, as they say.'

– Three fifths?

'50 divided by five, times three is 30. Said simply: three fifths of my life. Being held back when we had to, being supportive when we had to, because otherwise it would never have been possible.'

– Who are you going to celebrate your birthday with?

'In a small circle, as always. So with the family and everything that belongs to that. Like I say: the tree is getting bigger, but that's only nicer. It's a little bit more expensive.'

– You have grandchildren. Do you play football with them?

'In the hall. You know that. Until their mother or grandmother starts complaining, because sometimes the ball goes in the air.'

– Do you like that? Do you hope they'll become footballers?

'Yes, why not? It's fantastic. I've had a fantastic time. Despite all the blows and whatever, I think Jordi really enjoys playing football. And the rest, all those people who complain . . .'

– Have your grandchildren changed your life?

'They've added a lot. Those little children come in and those children go out. That's how it goes.'

– Does grandpa take them to the zoo?

'Of course! To the zoo, football, skiing, whatever. No problem.'

– Do you phone them as well? You're very clumsy. You can barely deal with a video, a fax, a phone.

'With anything modern: credit cards, mobile phones. I can't cope with the video. I can't cope with a camera. I can't send a fax.'

– Can't you turn on the video?

'Well, I know how to do that. But I can't record.'

– Johan, thank you very much for coming into Amsterdam. We hope you have a wonderful day tomorrow. And as they say at our place: another 120 years! Amen.

Barend and Van Dorp
24th April 1997, 10pm

Curriculum Vitae: a football life

Player

November 15th 1964 – Ajax debut. GVAV 3 Ajax 1 (first league goal)

September 7th 1966 – Dutch international debut. Holland 2 Hungary 2 (first international goal)

November 6th 1966 – international against Czechoslovakia. First Dutchman to be sent off.

August 19th 1973 – last match of his first period at Ajax. Ajax 6 FC Amsterdam 1 (one goal).

October 28th 1973 – debut for Barcelona. Barcelona 4 Granada 0 (two goals)

May 1978 – last game in Spain. Spanish Cup Final. Barcelona 3 Las Palmas 1.

October 26th 1977 – last game for Dutch national side. Holland 1 Belgium 0.

November 7th 1978 – 'official' farewell game in Amsterdam. Ajax 0 Bayern Munich 8.

May 23rd 1979 – debut for Los Angeles Aztecs (one season); then moved to Washington Diplomats.

March 2nd 1981 – debut for Levante (10 games).

December 6th 1981 – return to Ajax. Ajax 4 Haarlem 1 (one goal).

May 14th 1983 – last league game for Ajax. De Meer stadium. Ajax 6 Fortuna Sittard 5.

May 17th 1983 – last game for Ajax. Dutch Cup Final. NEC 1 Ajax 3 (one goal).

August 21st 1983 – debut for Feyenoord. Volendam 1 Feyenoord 4.

May 13th 1984 – last game for Feyenoord. Feyenoord 2 PEC Zwolle 1 (one goal).

Coach

July 1st 1985 to January 4th 1988 – Ajax. Technical director, trainer, coach.

1988 to 1996 – Barcelona. Coach.

Main honours as player

League champion
Ajax – 1966, 1967, 1968, 1970, 1972, 1973, 1982, 1983.
Barcelona – 1974.
Feyenoord – 1984.

Cup winner
Ajax – 1967, 1970, 1971, 1972, 1983.
Barcelona – 1978.
Feyenoord – 1984.

European Cup
Ajax – 1971, 1972, 1973.

European Supercup
Ajax – 1973

World Club Champions
Ajax – 1972

European Footballer of the Year
1971 – 1. Cruyff (Ajax) 116 points
2. Mazzola (Inter Milan) 57 points

1973 – 1. Cruyff (Ajax/Barcelona) 96 points
      2. Zoff (Juventus) 47 points

1974 – 1. Cruyff (Barcelona) 116 points
      2. Beckenbauer (Bayern Munich)
         105 points.

Main honours as coach

League championship
Barcelona – 1991, 1992, 1993, 1994.

Cup
Ajax – 1986, 1987
Barcelona – 1990.

European Cup
Barcelona – 1992

European Cup Winners' Cup
Ajax – 1987
Barcelona – 1989

European Supercup
Barcelona – 1993

Spanish Supercup
Barcelona – 1991, 1992,
1993, 1994

. . .

Johan Cruyff was several times voted
Footballer of the Year in Holland and
America. In 1974, he was Sportsman of the
Netherlands.

. . .

(With thanks to John Fredrikstadt)